Encyclopedia of Bi...

Nancy Ann
Storybook Dolls
1936 – 1947

IDENTIFICATION
& VALUES

Elaine M. Pardee
Jackie Robertson

COLLECTOR BOOKS
A Division of Schroeder Publishing Co., Inc.

On the front cover:
Top left: Hand-painted face of bisque Nancy Ann Storybook Doll
Middle left: #17 Hansel and Grethel
Middle right: #83 Mammy
Bottom left: #126 Pussy Cat, Pussy Cat
Bottom middle: #510 Margie Ann in Playsuit
Bottom right: #33 Chinese

On the back cover:
Top left: #17 Goldylocks and the Baby Bear
Top right: #191 A Flower Girl for May
Bottom left: #127 One, Two, Three, Four
Bottom right: #116 Little Red Riding Hood

Cover design by Beth Summers
Book design by Karen Smith

COLLECTOR BOOKS
P.O. Box 3009
Paducah, Kentucky 42002-3009

www.collectorbooks.com

Copyright © 2003 Elaine M. Pardee & Jackie Robertson

The current values in this book should be used only as a guide. They are not
intended to set prices, which vary from one section of the country to another.
Auction prices as well as dealer prices vary greatly and are affected by condition as well as demand. Neither the authors nor the publisher assumes responsibility for any losses that might be incurred as a result of consulting this guide.

Searching For A Publisher?

We are always looking for people knowledgeable within their fields. If you
feel that there is a real need for a book on your collectible subject and have a
large comprehensive collection, contact Collector Books.

•●● Contents ●●•

●●● Dedication ●●●

Dedicated to Nancy Roeder in grateful appreciation for her inspiration and her many years of devoted research on the bisque doll molds and costumes by the Nancy Ann Storybook Doll Company.

●●● Acknowledgments ●●●

Our appreciation to Mary Ann Watkins and Lillian Roth, who were always there to boost our morale, and Judi and Ray Radley who never let us give up on our vision for this research book. We are especially beholden to Joan Mitchell for her expertise and generous hours devoted to editing this book.

We are also indebted to the following collectors for their unselfish contributions of photographs, research, and support: Sandra Arnold, Shirley Barstow, Elsie Beaver, Beth Bender, Carrie Bush, Doris Cermak, Joyce Christensen, Marion Clouser, Colleen Conn, Anne Walker Cragg, Marsha Cumpton, Terri Jean Davila, Judy Day, Le Day, Marie Day, Candy Denman, Sally Doyle, Susan Dunham, Arlene Eidemiller, Jim Fernando, Marianne Gardner, Susan Group, Bonnie Hagan, Carol Jackson, Liz Kennedy, Sara Kessing, Debra Klein, Ruth Klockow, Lu Lane, Ruth Laursen, Anne Lien, Nelrose Mahoney, Jane Mann, Debbie Markowitz, Joan Mitchell, Carol Nation, Lynn Neagle, Kathy Nilsson, Johanna Park, Hilda Pitman, Kay Polli, Judi Radley, Ray Radley, Nancy Roeder, Kathy Rossi, Lillian Roth, Lisa Romo, Marge Smith, Candy Summers, Carol Sumpter, Ann Tester, Mary Lu Trowbridge, Sari Van Otegham, George Uribe, Carolyn Vack, and Mary Ann Watkins.

We offer sincere gratitude to Patsy Moyer for her inspiration and her faith in this project.

Judy Ann mold Bride, Groom, and Bridesmaids. See Family Series, page 92.

●●● About the Authors ●●●

Elaine Pardee was born in Detroit, Michigan, in 1936, and moved to northern California in 1958. Having had Nancy Ann Storybook dolls in her childhood, she discovered her love for them once again in 1974 at a local doll show, where she met co-author, Jackie Robertson. Bonded by their appreciation of these dolls, the two of them have remained friends ever since. Now living in the Sacramento, California area, Elaine has added to her original dolls from childhood, expanding her collection to fill two rooms devoted to these costumed dolls.

She is a past president of Pollyanna Doll Club, and now belongs to the Sierra Doll Discovery Doll Club and the Pioneer Doll Club in the Sacramento/Auburn, California area. She is a judge for the modern competition for United Federation of Doll Clubs and the Nancy Ann Gathering. She also presents seminars, workshops, and slide programs on the various dolls by the Nancy Ann Storybook Doll Company, paper dolls, and other doll-related topics at UFDC national conventions and regional conferences, Nancy Ann Storybook Conventions, and UFDC Doll Clubs.

Jackie Robertson was born in Idaho, in 1934. While growing up, she played with Nancy Ann Storybook dolls and enjoyed designing and making dresses for them. She attended college in Berkeley, California, where she met and married her husband. While their children were growing up in the San Francisco Bay area, she discovered that the dolls she had played with during her childhood had become quite collectible. She joined a local doll club, Doll Keepers of California, and has served as treasurer for eight years and is currently serving a second term as vice president.

Today her collection of original factory dressed bisque Nancy Ann Storybook dolls numbers over a thousand dolls. She also collects the 18" Style Show dolls, along with Muffie and Debbie, Miss Nancy Ann, Little Miss, vinyl Sue Sue, and a few of the sleep eye/painted eye plastic Nancy Ann dolls. Jackie's interest has always been in the variety of fabrics used by the factory in costuming these little dolls. Her need to identify each doll with photographs that could then be shared with various other collectors can now be appreciated by all who will read and enjoy this book.

• • • Preface • • •

On my bedroom bookshelf when I was a child stood my cherished possessions, Little Red Riding Hood, Saturday's Child, Roses Are Red, Little Miss Muffet, and Cinderella, small 5" bisque dolls by the Nancy Ann Storybook Doll Company. These toddler-like bisque dolls were by far the prettiest things I owned, and I knew instinctively that the dolls deserved respect and gentle care. They were poles apart from the typical large composition baby dolls so popular with little girls at the time, and definitely not play dolls to be casually tossed in the toy box when boredom set in. They were charismatic little treasures dressed in a multitude of fine fabrics, delicate laces, and imported ribbons. Wearing enchanting costumes from the make-believe land of storybooks, these dolls were designed purely for a little girl's dreams.

After being stored for years by their owners, dolls like these are gradually surfacing from attics and basements. The adults who once knew, as a child some sixty years ago, the names of these Nancy Ann Storybook Dolls have long ago forgotten what costume each doll represents. Because so many children destroyed the identification tags and boxes for these dolls, the need to identify these costumes has become a challenge. The factory left no illustrated catalogs of the dolls they dressed, only a few pamphlets listing the character names.

In 1980 Marjorie A. Miller published her pioneering book, *Nancy Ann Storybook Dolls,* but showed only a sampling of dolls. With the devoted help of numerous collectors, we have complied a reference book to be used as both a research tool for identification and a picture book for pleasure. It is written for you, yes *you,* the one with the question on your lips and the wistful look in your eyes. For all those grownups that have come up to us and excitedly said, "I used to own one of those dolls," followed quickly by the most often asked question, "What character does my doll represent?" this book is for you. We hope it will be the resource tool needed for those searching for answers to the countless questions raised about these precious Nancy Ann Storybook Dolls.

Although this book is an encyclopedia of the bisque Nancy Ann Storybook Dolls, we have not included the bisque Hush-a-Bye Baby Series, and Little Miss Pattycake Series, the delightful babies also dressed by the company. However, we plan to illustrate the bisque baby series of the late 1930s and early 1940s in our next book now in progress, including the various plastic dolls of the late 1940s and 1950s that also were dressed by the Nancy Ann Storybook Company.

Most importantly, we would like to give credit to the important part that Nancy Ann Abbott played in the history of doll collecting today. Never having children of her own, we are thankful for Nancy Ann Abbott's precious gift to the children of her era. An innovative concept for children in the 1930s and 1940s, Nancy Ann Storybook Dolls were a

child's introduction to the hobby of doll collecting. Each doll came with a list of dolls that the child could collect. Cabinets for proudly displaying the child's collection were offered by the company. Although these were great marketing tools, they also instilled in children the appreciation for quality dolls and the fun of collecting them. Who can say how many doll collectors of today innocently started their hobby with Nancy Ann Storybook Dolls as a child. It is the hope of the authors that you truly enjoy this book. It is for us a long-awaited triumph!

Elaine M. Pardee

Rare black bisque Topsy marked Judy Ann. See page 230.

•••A Bona Fide••• Storybook Fairytale

Once upon a time… as this story was told to me, there was a girl child born on February 22 in Lake County, California, United States of America, the land of opportunity. It was the year 1901. The blue-eyed baby was named Rowena Haskin, and her life would become a veritable fairytale. As a shy young lady, after reading an article in the *Youth's Companion* about a "know-how" girl, she was resolute in her new conviction that she, too, could accomplish anything, she could become a "know-how" gal. So she attended California School of Fine Arts, changed her name to Nancy Ann Abbott, moved to Hollywood, danced and acted in Universal Studios silent western movies, was reportedly in love with Merv Griffin's uncle, became a Hollywood studio designer, and, when not working at the studio, relaxed by spending eight to ten hours a day on horseback. In 1936 she left Hollywood and moved to San Francisco to take care of her ailing mother. Over the preceding years she owned three houses, living mostly in the Georgian-Colonial three story, 22 room magnificent estate with a poodle, two Pekingese dogs, Fat-so and Butch, and a parrot named Owen. She wrote children's jingles, wore Adrian suits of blue or beige, often gave San Francisco society parties, drove a Buick convertible to work, built a brick fence around her estate with her own hands, grew 3,000 orchids, and founded the San Francisco Orchid Society. Miss Abbott was, it seems, a cross between a San Francisco socialite and a western movie star/cowgirl.

Interestingly enough, however, her fondness for costume design would end up overshadowing all else. First costuming dolls for amusement, she reportedly gave her first dressed doll as a present to the movie star, Dolores Costello, a doll dressed in a costume she wore in the movie, *The Sea Beast.* Her zeal for costume design became a consuming passion. By 1936 she was continuously designing costumes for small bisque baby dolls, and soon was operating a business. With the assistance of Allan Leslie Rowland, she ultimately opened a 400-square foot shop with four employees and incorporated The Nancy Ann Dressed Dolls Corporation on February 23, 1937.

One of the first dolls she dressed, called Hush-a-Bye, became so popular that she finally discontinued the doll, as it stood in the way of her plans to expand her line of dolls. And expand she did! Eventually 10,000 to 20,000 of her costumed dolls a day, depending on which newspaper one reads, were produced from her Nancy Ann Storybook Company based in San Francisco. Her dolls were sold, not only in the Philippines, England, and Canada, but as far away as Egypt and South Africa, and also to our Armed Forces in Hawaii. Until the war, Harrod of London Department Store was one of the company's regular customers, and the dolls were even collected by England's Princess Margaret Rose and Princess Elizabeth. Nancy Ann Abbott's company unquestionably flourished, even during the crisis of World War II, thriving when it was rare then for a woman to succeed in business. By the late 1940s, in terms of volume, she was running the largest doll company in the United States. By 1950 the company was turning out two million dolls and had to move four times to larger quarters. She effortlessly had made the transition from a designer of clothes for motion picture actresses to a designer of dolls and doll clothes. Nancy Ann Abbott died of cancer on August 10, 1964. Sadly, Miss Abbott's fairytale life had ended, and the company she started with her "know-how" attitude finally closed its doors in 1965.

Following Miss Abbott's death, the tragic postscript to this doll story began. A handwritten one-line will awarded Miss Abbott's entire estate to Allan Rowland, her business partner. A heartbreaking lawsuit developed over this will that would have shocked and embarrassed the shy Miss Abbott. The widely publicized battle for Miss Abbott's fortune could almost be straight out of a movie script. The San Francisco and San Mateo newspapers relished in printing articles about the sensational bitter court drama played out in a San Mateo, California courtroom. The lawsuit brought by Miss Abbott's mother challenged the will and was crammed with titillating love letters and accusations of fraud and undue influence. The famous attorney Vincent Hallinan, representing Nancy Ann's mother, fought to get Miss Abbott's handwritten will ruled invalid. In the end, the jury ruled that when this will was written Nancy Ann Abbott was not of sound and disposing mind due to illness. The handwritten will was ruled invalid. What Miss Abbott's real intentions were regarding her estate we will never know, but as a result of the lawsuit the estate reverted to Miss Abbott's mother, Edna Mae Haskin.

To this day, Nancy Ann Abbott's little dressed dolls are still treasured by those who once owned them as children. Now joining this dedicated group are new enthusiasts who are discovering Miss Abbott's creative costume designs. The finale to the captivating bona fide fairytale life of Nancy Ann Abbott ends with her legacy, her enchanting Nancy Ann Storybook Dolls, that now live happily ever after in doll cabinets all across the United States.

Abbreviations
•••and Terms•••

AMERICA – A 5" doll with a mold mark on the back of doll incised "AMERICA."

Beading – Lace-like edging made of loops, see Picot.

CM – Crude Mark, refers to the mold mark on the back of a 5" bisque doll incised with large crude letters "Story Book USA."

Corded Ribbed – Ribbed cotton fabric woven of light to medium weight pure cotton.

Dunce Cap – Conical hat.

Dust Cap – Cap made of circle gathered to head, narrow hem at edge.

FAN8 – A 4⅞" bisque doll imported from Japan marked on the back with a fan design, the number eight below, and the words "MADE IN JAPAN."

Felt – Thick, firm-packed smoothly matted fabric.

Frozen leg – A bisque doll with head, body and legs together in one mold, and separate molds for arms strung to body, often abbreviated as FR or Fr.

JA – A 5" child-body bisque doll with "JUDY ANN" mold mark, a gold sticker marked "JUDY ANN" on clothing, or the character name Judy Ann.

Japan – A 4⅞" bisque doll imported from Japan marked on the back with the single word "JAPAN."

Jointed leg – A bisque doll with "STORY BOOK DOLL USA" mold mark and strung arms and legs, often abbreviated as JT or Jt.

MIB – Mint in box.

MIJ – A 4⅞" bisque doll imported from Japan marked on the back "MADE IN JAPAN 1146" or "MADE IN JAPAN 1148."

Mold – A hollow form for giving a certain shape to a doll in bisque or plastic.

MS – Molded socks, a doll with incised molded socks.

MS/MB – Molded socks, molded bangs, a doll with incised molded socks and molded bangs.

NADD – Nancy Ann Dressed Dolls, refers to the company itself, or to the foil sticker marked "NANCY ANN DRESSED DOLLS."

NA – Refers to the mold mark on a 5½" frozen leg bisque doll by the Nancy Ann Storybook Company that has the words "NANCY ANN" added to the mold mark.

Nancy Ann – Miss Nancy Ann Abbott or the doll made by the Nancy Ann Storybook Company.

NASB – Nancy Ann Storybook Doll.

Net – Generic in this book for square, hexagonal, or octagonal mesh fabric, also tulle.

Pantalets – Long loose drawers, showing beneath the skirt, often lace trimmed at the ankle.

Picot – Finished edge having tiny points, produced by cutting machine hemstitching in half. Also often referred to as openwork through which ribbon may be run — or as beading.

Pinch face – A smaller scale face and body, 5½", no mold mark.

PI – Plastic

PT – Pudgy tummy bisque 5" doll with "STORY BOOK DOLL USA" mold mark having jointed arms and legs and a pudgy tummy body, as opposed to the later slim tummy body.

Ruche – Strip of fabric pleated or gathered used as trimming on clothing.

SBD – Mainly used in reference to the foil sticker on the clothes that reads "STORYBOOK DOLLS."

Teen JT – Teen jointed, a 5½" bisque doll mold with a teen figure and jointed arms and legs.

WT – The gold foil wrist tag that shows stock number and name of character.

⚫⚫⚫ Identifying Bisque ⚫⚫⚫
Nancy Ann Storybook Dolls

Molds

5" Molds

One can sort the various 5" bisque Nancy Storybook Dolls into three major mold eras, the imported dolls from Japan; the California-produced jointed-leg era; and the California-produced frozen-leg era, the most common mold used. As the company expanded, several additional mold marks, sizes, and variations of the California-made dolls occurred. We would like to stress that the company left no known records at this time as to the precise dates these doll mold changes took place. Listed below is the approximate sequence we believe these changes transpired.

Doll Molds Imported from Japan

When Nancy Ann Abbott started costuming dolls in 1936, she purchased small bisque dolls that were imported from Japan. These nude bisque dolls were widely available and bought by many other companies as well as the Nancy Ann Storybook Company. At first she just dressed bisque baby dolls, but soon

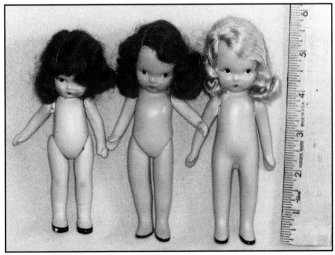

Japanese import dressed in costume.

progressed to also dressing 5" dolls as storybook characters. By 1937 the Nancy Ann Dressed Dolls Company was incorporated, and a little gold sticker with the company's name was placed on each dress that read "Nancy Ann Dressed Dolls."

To help identify these early dressed dolls by Nancy Ann Abbott, recognize the molds marks on the dolls she purchased from Japan and the construction and style of her dress designs. These small bisque dolls, so exquisitely dressed in quality fabrics, were a new concept on the market at the end of the 1930s. Wearing pantalets and slips under their ribbon and lace trimmed dresses, each doll was obviously labor intensive, and responsible for the company's success. The molded-bang hair was sometimes painted and had a ribbon running though the topknot on the head, and quite often a hat or bonnet was added. The first wig used was made of wool. However, soon the mohair wig replaced this wool wig. When wigged, the hair was usually left unpainted.

The face had bright red puckered lips, rosy checks, and long black eyelashes. The paint on these Japanese dolls is now unstable and flakes off easily to reveal the white china underneath, so we advise one handle the dolls with caution.

Three different doll molds were imported from Japan, and all three are marked on the back. They have indentations of bangs and socks incised into the bisque. Their arms and legs are strung with elastic. We believe the company used the mold mark "Made in Japan 1146" dolls first, as some of these dolls have the painted hair or early wool wig, and have been found in the earliest marble design box. The second two molds, "Fan8" and "Japan," have the

Japanese doll with wig.

Left to right. Imported doll from Japan; California-produced jointed-leg doll; California-produced frozen-leg doll.

The painted face of a "Made in Japan 1146" mold.

An example of the instability of the paint on Japanese imported dolls. Handle with care.

The "Made in Japan 1146" mold has a toddler appearance and measures approximately 4⅞". It may have either a wool wig as shown here, or the later mohair wig, and a few have painted hair with no wig at all. Silver safety pin closure was used on clothes. Of the three imported Japanese molds, this mold was used most often. This mold doll first came in a pink or blue marble design box followed by the sunburst design box. The doll had a gold foil sticker "Nancy Ann Dressed Dolls" on the costume.

FAN8 Made in Japan. Circa 1936 – 1937. A similar imported bisque doll from Japan, this mold measures approximately 4⅞". The top line of this mold mark has a fan shape incised with the figure 8 below the fan. This mold mark was used briefly, and was certainly in the minority, in terms of the quantity of imported Japan dolls used by Nancy Ann Abbott. Silver safety pin closure was used on clothes. This mold doll came in a sunburst design box with gold foil sticker "Nancy Ann Dressed Dolls" on the costume.

Japan. Circa 1936 – 1937. This mold also measures approximately 4⅞". Imported bisque doll from Japan.

Made in Japan 1146/1148. Circa 1936 – 1937. Imported bisque doll from Japan. (Often it is difficult to distinguish whether the number reads 1146 or 1148.)

The "Japan" mold was probably the last Japanese doll mold imported, as the construction and designs of the costumes and the fabrics used were beginning to change, resembling the clothes on the dolls we find the following year using molds from their newly acquired pottery plant in Berkeley, California. A silver safety pin closure was used on clothes. This mold doll came in a sunburst design box with gold foil sticker "Nancy Ann Dressed Dolls."

later mohair wigs and clothing construction that indicates use toward the end of 1937. The Japanese-mold sequence is only an educated guess, as no data is available as to when these imported dolls were used and in which order. Possibly the company just used whatever they could find available as world tension was escalating and receiving imports was becoming difficult. However, the exact sequence is not crucial, since all three were only used for approximately a year or two, until the company opened their own pottery plant in 1938.

Molds Made in the United States of America
Early Jointed Leg Molds

Not satisfied with the dolls imported from Japan, the company began making their own bisque dolls in 1938 at their newly acquired pottery plant in Berkeley, California. Because bisque is china fired in kilns at an intense heat, the process of its complicated manufacture required tremendous skill. Wanting a high-quality doll, Miss Abbott, working from old German formulas, made improvements, making her dolls many times more durable than the fragile

imported dolls from Japan. The new Storybook Doll kilns were fired twice a month and then the molds were sent to the company's San Francisco factory. There they were placed in a tumbler and given a sand bath so that they came out smooth and white. The next step was tinting the dolls. Workers sprayed the dolls with either flesh or occasionally a brown lacquer. Assembly of the parts then followed and defective pieces were eliminated in the first of many inspections. Once assembled, the dolls made their way to the artists' tables, where the faces were hand painted with carmine-tipped paintbrushes. Most eyes were painted blue, but a few were painted brown for certain characters. All received the sweet red rosebud mouth.

The following three bisque doll molds, now made at this new pottery plant, are marked on the upper back of doll, and have strung arms and legs with molded socks and bangs and a child body. Shoes were dipped in different colored paint, depending on the character to be represented. These doll molds have a slightly shorter left arm than the right arm. They do not have the topknot found on the Japanese mold dolls.

Shows the front and back of the "Judy Ann" mold. Both the "America" and the "Judy Ann" molds still retained the toddler body look of the imported Japanese molds.

America. Circa 1938. Obviously proud that this doll was made in their own plant and not Japan, the company marked this first mold "America." This doll measures 5¼". However, very few dolls with this mold mark are found, as the company quickly decided to give the mold and doll an actual name, "Judy Ann," and quickly discontinued the "America" mark. A silver safety pin closure was used on the clothes. This mold doll came in a sunburst design box with gold foil sticker "Judy Ann."

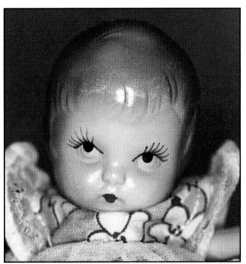

The face has the cute bright red mouth, hand-painted eyelashes, the chin is tucked under, and the hair has the molded indentations of curls, known as molded bangs. Although most dolls using this mold have mohair wigs over the molded bangs, a few are still found with painted hair, particularly the character, "Miss Muffet," as shown here. Unable to trademark the name, "Judy Ann," the company briefly used this mold and quickly discontinued it. The brass safety pin closure was used on clothing. This mold doll came in a sunburst design box with a gold sticker "Storybook Dolls."

Judy Ann USA. Circa 1938. Incised with bold letters "Judy Ann USA," on three lines, this 5¼" mold is not as heavy or chunky as the "America" mold.

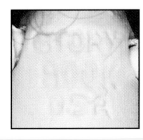

Crude mark. Circa 1938. Incised with bold letters "Story Book USA" on three lines. The company trademarked this name, using it on the same 5¼" mold with the toddler body with molded socks and molded bangs. To differentiate between this larger mold lettering and the smaller mold lettering that came next, collectors use the term "crude mark" for this mold mark, as the letters are larger and not as stylized as the lettering on the mold that follows. This mold doll came in a sunburst design box with a gold sticker "Storybook Dolls."

Storybook Doll USA Molds

The following dolls are all marked Story Book Doll USA. Notice, the word "Doll" has now been added, and the mold mark is in smaller, more precise letters.

#11. Circa 1940. The number 11 was now added below the "U.S.A." on the mold.

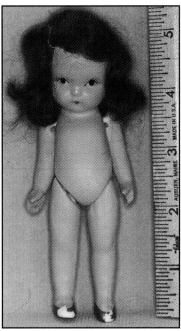

Molded socks/molded bangs. Circa 1939. The mold still has the molded socks and molded bangs, but has the new smaller mold mark that will now be used for several years. This mold came in a colored box with small silver dots with a gold foil sticker "Storybook Dolls."

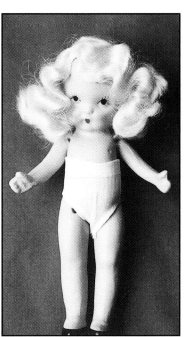

Molded socks. Circa 1940. The molded bangs that were incised in the mold were eliminated and the doll now has a smooth forehead. The strung legs with the molded socks are still used. This doll still has a pudgy tummy and came in a colored box with large white dots with a gold foil sticker "Storybook Dolls" on the clothing.

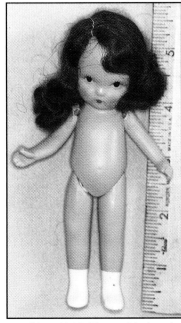

Pudgy tummy. Circa 1941. The molded socks were eliminated from the mold and the leg is now smooth. The mold, however, still had the pudgy body of a child and the one shorter arm, and the same mold mark. The gold foil wrist tag is introduced, replacing the sticker on the clothes. These dolls came in a white box with various large colored polka dots. Both the wrist tag and white box now remained throughout the bisque period.

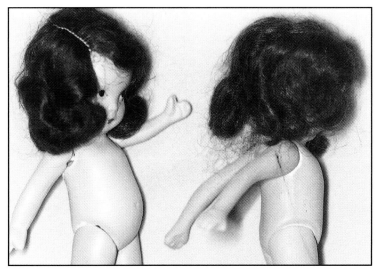

Jointed leg. Circa late 1941 – 1942. (Often referred to as the slim jointed leg mold.) During the end of 1941 and throughout 1942, the mold mark remained the same, but the body mold changed from the pudgy tummy mold to a slimmer child body shape. Shown here, for comparison, are the pudgy tummy mold on the left and the new slim body on the right. Although a few dolls may still be found with the shorter arm from the earlier mold, as the company used the remaining shorter-arm stock from the pudgy tummy era, eventually this slim-body mold converted to the new thinner, longer arms.

Frozen Leg Molds

Story Book Doll USA PAT.APP.FOR. Circa 1946 – 1947. The "PAT.APP.FOR" line was added to the mark below the USA, and used very briefly. The doll still had bisque arms at this point. Common floris ribbon was used on the costume.

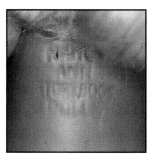

Nancy Ann Storybook Doll. Circa 1946 – 1947. The words "Nancy Ann" on separate lines were added to the frozen leg mold. This mold mark often appears on dolls that have the plastic arms. Common florist ribbon was used on the costume.

Story Book Doll U.S.A. Circa 1943 – 1945. This was a noticeable change in the bisque doll mold. Although using the same mold mark as the jointed leg doll, this new 5½" mold has a one-piece body and legs with only the arms strung.

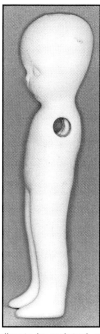

Still needing to be painted, of course, the frozen-leg mold did, however, eliminate the labor and expense of stringing the legs, as only the arms needed this handwork. It is the most abundant mold we find today. The white box with large colored dots was used throughout this frozen-leg period for all the various sizes.

Teen Storybook Body – Jointed Legs

Teen JT. This teen-shaped mold is marked "Story Book Doll USA PAT.APP.FOR," a mold mark identical to top left that is on a frozen-leg child body. It is a 5½" bisque mold with a teen-shaped body, jointed legs, and plastic arms. From head to end of torso it measures 3½". The legs from side of the hip to foot measure 2½" long. When strung, the doll measures 5½" long.

Left, the child body frozen-leg mold; Right, teen jointed-leg mold both marked with the same "Story Book Doll USA PAT.APP.FOR" mold mark. Although wearing different style capes, both these Little Red Riding Hoods are wearing the same dress with gold snap closures and florist ribbon. These two molds are close in sequence, but we cannot verify dates of production. Since a number of different characters using this teen jointed-leg mold have been observed, we feel they are authentic, as they have been found in original bisque boxes, mint with their wrist tags. We theorize that the factory was experimenting with a change to their 5½" frozen leg storybook child mold. This Teen JT mold does not have a child body, but most importantly, it now has a bisque teen-shaped figure with indented waist and slight bust, a mold shape similar to the taller molds already used for the Months, In Powder and Crinoline, and the newly introduced Operetta, and All-Time Hit Parade series. This Teen JT mold's body and legs are identical in size and shape to the painted-eye plastic mold that would soon follow.

Teen Pinch Face Body — Jointed Legs

Pinch Face. It seems to be the age-old question of which came first, the chicken or the egg; which came first, the experimental bisque teen mold on the left or this pinch face bisque teen mold on the right? The mold on the left is heavy, so perhaps that was the reason they also experimented with this lighter-weight scaled down pinch face style mold, as illustrated on the right. The pinch face mold is more petite in scale, measures 5½", and has no mold mark at all. The mold has a shapely body style with a slight bust and tiny waist. Collectors, because of its pinched-in cheek appearance, refer to it as pinch face. Although a few costumes are found with a safety pin closure, the majority of the costumes have a small gold snap closure, placing it at the brink of the company's change-over to plastic. Eventually, after testing the market with these two molds for their storybook line, both bisque molds were discontinued. The experimentation continued, however, with both molds made next in a painted-plastic mold.

Left: pinch face bisque jointed leg mold; right: pinch face jointed painted-eye plastic mold with swivel neck.

Left: teen jointed leg bisque mold; right: teen jointed leg painted-eye plastic mold with swivel neck.

Brown Bisque Molds

The painted brown 5" bisque doll has been in the Nancy Ann Storybook line as early as the Japanese molds. It was used for Mammy through the jointed leg period and for Topsy, even longer, continuing through the frozen-leg era. The mold-mark modifications follow the same sequence as the flesh-painted molds. The only difference is that brown-painted dolls for the Topsy and Mammy characters had a black fuzzy wig. (A brown 3½" baby mold was also made.)

Japan mold face.

MS/MB mold face.

MS body.

6" Molds

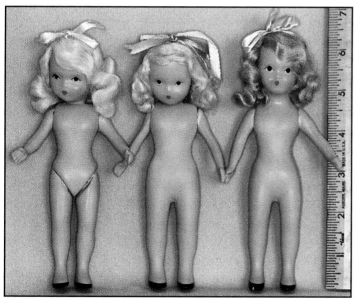

There are three different 6" molds. Left: the 6" socket-head jointed leg mold; center: the 6" socket-head, frozen leg mold; and right: the 6¼" frozen leg mold. The mold marks on the back all read "Story Book Doll U.S.A." These molds have more mature figures with a definite waistline and bust, unlike the toddler appearance of the early 5" storybook molds.

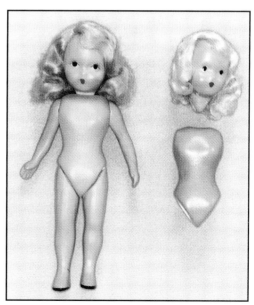

Socket-head jointed-leg mold. Circa 1941. The head is a separate mold and is strung with elastic into an opening at the top of the body, allowing it to "wobble" in this socket. The arms and legs are also separate molds and are strung to body with elastic. This mold is used only for the Months of the Year Series. There are, on the average, two costume changes for this mold, so judging from this, the mold probably was used about two years.

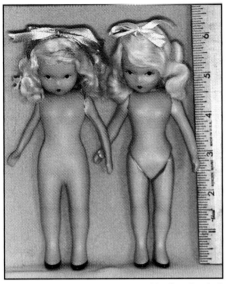

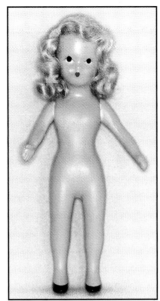

Frozen leg 6¼" mold. Again, the exact time these changes occurred in this mold is not verified, but by 1946 the one-piece body and head had replaced the socket-head frozen leg mold. This frozen leg mold was used for the Months of the Year Series, the introduction of the Operetta Series, and the Hit Parade Series. In fact, it was used so often that sometimes the mold mark has completely worn off and the doll may appear unmarked.

Socket-head frozen leg mold. On the left the socket-head is positioned on a frozen leg body, replacing the earlier jointed-leg body shown on the right. The time period this mold was actually used is unclear. However, the mold most liked was used from approximately 1942 through 1945 based on at least two to four costume changes for the Months of the Year Series found on this mold.

There is a slight difference in the appearance of the faces of the socket-head. On the left, the earlier, narrower face; on the right, the later, more rounded face.

7" Molds

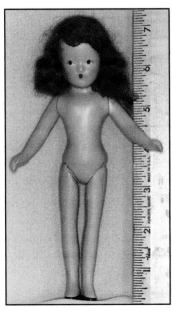

In Powder and Crinoline 7" mold, marked "Story Book Doll U.S.A." Circa 1942. The company began a series, In Powder and Crinoline, on a new 7" jointed leg mold created especially to wear the more elaborate costumes of this series. The first version of the 7" mold has jointed legs. Quickly, the jointed legs were discontinued and the 7" frozen leg mold was used until this series was discontinued.

4½" Molds

Story Book Doll U.S.A 10. The small 4½" child-body doll with strung arms and legs was used for Flower Girl and Ring Bearer.

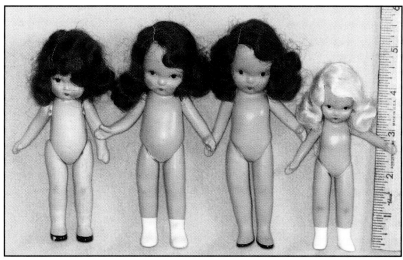

Left to right: the 5" jointed leg Storybook molds, Japan, pudgy tummy, and jointed leg, compared to this smaller 4½" mold.

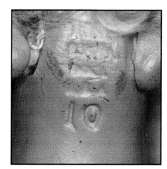

Mold mark on the 4½" doll.

Audrey Ann Molds

Story Book Doll U.S.A. 12. This rare bisque mold is a chunky, taller, heavier doll. The 5¾" doll has molded socks with white boots, strung arms and legs, and has the number 12 added to the mold mark. This mold came in a colored box with large white dots with a gold foil sticker "Storybook Dolls." Left: the 5¾" mold dressed as Audrey Ann; right: the 5¼" jointed leg mold dressed as Margie Ann.

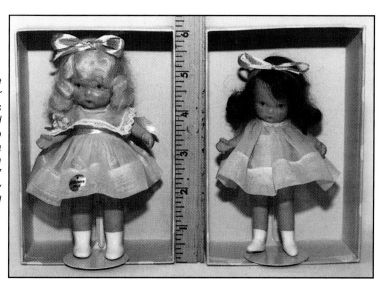

Plastic Molds

Starting at the end of 1947 and moving into 1948, the company slowly was converting to hard plastic for dolls. To keep pace with the doll market that was excitedly using this new material for dolls, the Nancy Ann Storybook Company also started introducing hard plastic dolls. This book does not cover the plastic-mold era of the company and the many costumes from that era. However, we do feel it is important that one distinguish between the bisque molds and the plastic molds. Therefore, we have included the plastic trademark. The raised letters of the mold mark on the back shoulder indicates that the doll is hard plastic. The plastic dolls have a side seam on the head, body, and legs. Their feet have a line on the sole representing a heel. The plastic dolls were made in both painted eye and sleep eye plastic. When the company switched to plastic dolls at the end of 1947 and into 1948, the script "Nancy Ann Storybook Dolls" was added between the polka dots on the boxes, so be aware that dolls in this script-type box should be plastic, not bisque.

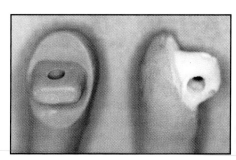

Story Book Dolls U.S.A. Trade Mark Reg.

Left: plastic arms have a square knob to string the elastic; right: bisque arms have a round, unpainted bisque knob.

Costume Construction and Design

"I cannot discover that anyone knows enough to say definitely what is and what is not possible."

Henry Ford

This quotation from Henry Ford is excellent to remember as one studies the clothing of the dolls from the Nancy Ann Storybook Doll Company. We have found that nothing, absolutely nothing, is sealed in stone when it comes to identifying a Nancy Ann Storybook Doll costume. The list of characters changed often, as new characters were added and others dropped from production. Over the years, the dolls were dressed as more than 125 characters. It has been reported that over 10,000 a day rolled out of the factory during the peak of this company's success. This was a business, so orders needed to be filled promptly and efficiently. We have interviewed employees from the factory and have a general sense of what it was like sewing numerous dresses each day and being paid by the piece. So if a trim or fabric was unavailable to the seamstress, we understand how easily a substitute was utilized, as the goal was to finish a costume. Consequently, small details, such as the lace or rickrack trim used may differ, and one should take this into account. Costume designs changed, as fabrics became unavailable, new ones were introduced, and price-cutting methods were initiated to keep up with the demand for these dolls. However, throughout this bisque era, Nancy Ann was insistent that quality of the doll and costume remain beyond reproach. Each doll would leave the factory meticulously dressed. Seams were checked for straightness, every strand of hair

was in place, each bow had to be tied correctly, and the face painted perfectly before packaging and shipping the dolls to stores and to their final destination, the hands of "wee collectors," as Nancy Ann advertising called them.

During a mold change at the factory, costumes were placed first on the discontinued mold until the remaining old stock was exhausted, and then on the new mold. The same held true with costume changes. Consequently, there was often overlapping as these changes occurred. Since we do not have any actual factory records dating individual costume introduction, the sequence of costumes for each character in this book is based on the following criteria: the mold of the doll and the costume construction, ribbons, fabrics, and the closures used for each costume. When applicable, we first illustrate the doll costumes for each character found on the imported Japanese dolls, then the American-made jointed leg dolls, and finally the American made frozen leg dolls.

Made in Japan 1146 – Japan – FAN8 – Japan

The clothing on the Japanese mold dolls has complex construction. These costumes were not yet mass produced, but instead were sewn by ladies doing piecework at home. On the Around the World Series we often see organdy blouses with large puffed sleeves and taffeta skirts. The storybook characters often have sprightly hats tied to the topknot of their painted hair heads. Under the dresses we regularly find separate slips without waistbands and wide-hemmed pantalets with large-scale elaborate trim and short panties with a front center seam. The costumes have a silver safety pin closure and a ribbon through the topknot on head. Particularly interesting construction and

Japanese bisque mold doll costume.

Japanese mold doll slip and pantalets.

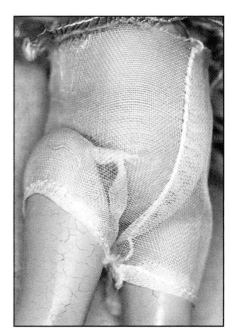

Japanese mold doll panties.

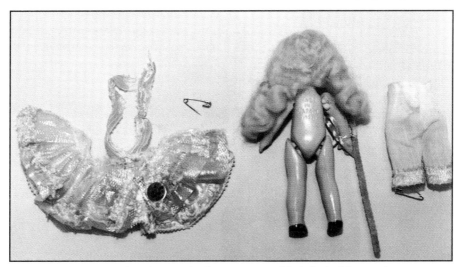

An example of an early Japanese mold doll clothing style.

style is found on the earliest costumes, consisting of tiny or non-existent bodices with straps of lace, ribbon, or fabric over shoulders with the skirt portion pulled high under the arms. If wigged, hair is at first the wool, often referred to as "dead" hair, as shown in the photo above. A hair ribbon often is tied to strands of hair at temple. The storybook characters regularly wear dimity rosebud print dresses with picot-hemstitch trim along with ribbon trim made into rosettes. Organdy and shadow print organdy fabric are frequently used. We repeatedly find separate aprons and separate skirts. These dolls have the "Nancy Ann Dressed Dolls" foil sticker with silver colored safety pin closures.

America

Cotton fabrics are used on many costumes on this mold, especially on the Around the World Series, which previously had used a profusion of taffeta fabric for the costumes. The Around the World Series dresses often have attached red vests decorated with crisscross stitching and organdy straight sleeves and neck insert. These early cotton fabrics are not colorfast and do fade, especially the blues to grays and greens to gold, so many costumes now have this color change. The company has yet to add an abundance of flowers to the storybook character, which become so prevalent in later years. Costumes on this mold may have center-seam short panties and a separate slip. Dolls have a silver-color safety pin closure. The dolls will have the "Judy Ann" foil sticker on clothes.

Judy Ann and Crude Mark

Until the factory stock was depleted, some of the early Judy Ann mold dolls still may have center seam panties on Around the World Series and the Flower Series. However, the late-in-production Judy Anns do not have center-seam panties. There is an occasional use of net trim on pantalets, sleeve edges, and the separate net slips. At this point we find some use of Lily of the Valley and fuzzy flowers. The brass safety pin closure is now introduced. Dolls have the "Storybook Doll" foil sticker and come in the sunburst box.

Molded Socks/Molded Bangs and Socks

The brass safety pin closure continues to be used for their costumes. Some of these costumes have layered net underskirt or slips, lace-trimmed pantalets, and panties have no front seam. There now is an increased use of the fuzzy flowers and marabou, and a brief attempt to use velvet ribbon trim. Dolls have the gold foil "Storybook Doll" sticker and come in colored boxes with tiny silver dots or large white polka dots.

Pudgy Tummy, Socket Head Months, and In Powder and Crinoline

The costumes have separate slips and either lace-trimmed or deeply hemmed pantalets of fine cotton. This is the end of the silver slippers and the white boots era, except on Scotch. The early Dolls of the Month Series have separate slips of crinoline, but the later costumes have the slip attached to the skirt. Dolls are now in the white box with colored dots. The foil sticker is discontinued and the heavy gold wrist tag is now introduced. The black oval sticker on hats of wool felt is introduced.

 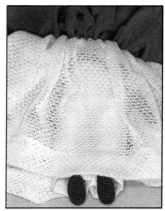

Separate slip and pantalet of fine cotton.   *Late costume with crinoline slip attached to skirt.*

19

Jointed Leg and Early Frozen Leg

Slips are now attached to the skirt and pantalets are of heavier cotton, either lace trimmed or deeply hemmed. The early imported ribbon is still used and dresses are sometimes fastened with this ribbon threaded through fabric instead of the safety pin due to the War. The silver slipper shoe is eliminated, but the high-top boots are still used on a few characters.

Later Frozen Leg

During the later part of the frozen leg period, some plastic and felt material is used and the ribbon changes to common florist ribbon. One observes a lot of net, satin, and plaid fabric. The sleeves and skirts frequently are not hemmed, and the pantalets have a narrow hem. The white box with colored dots continued throughout the remaining bisque period, with the label now placed in the left-hand corner. Although the majority of the

frozen leg dolls are still fastened with the safety pin, just before the transition to the painted-eye plastic mold, one can occasionally find the introduction of the small round gold snap fastener. By the plastic era all costumes will have this gold snap. A lighter weight gold foil wrist tag is used.

Teen Jointed Leg Mold

As this was such a transitional period, the same costume designs are often found either on the frozen leg or on this teen body mold, or even on the painted-eye plastic molds. They have the gold snap closure and florist ribbon.

Pinch Face Jointed Leg Mold

The same costume designs are often found on both the pinch-face bisque mold and the similar pinch-face painted-eye plastic mold. They have the gold snap closure and florist ribbon.

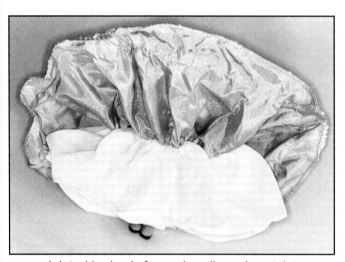

Jointed leg/early frozen leg slip and pantalet.

Jointed leg/early frozen leg with early imported ribbon.

Painted Shoes
Slipper-style Painted Shoes

Black. This is the basic black slipper-style shoe painted on the majority of Nancy Ann Storybook Dolls. No actual shoes were ever used. Left: molded socks mold; right: regular jointed leg painted black shoe. To coordinate with certain costumes, the color of the slipper shoes on the jointed-leg dolls, although infrequent, were found painted another color and even painted higher up to represent a boot-style shoe. Following are some of the uncommon painted shoes used.

Mary Jane style red-strap shoes on a Made in Japan 1146 mold representing Little Red Riding Hood. A similar black slipper-strap shoe is found on early imported Japanese mold Little Bo Peep and Mistress Mary.

Brown. Judy Ann mold #17 Dutch. The unusual brown shoes are painted a little higher up than the usual black slipper shoe, shaped to represent wooden shoes.

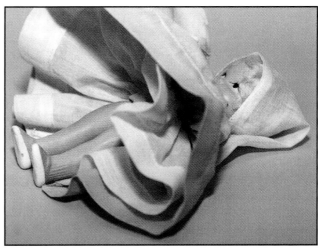

White. Used only on #70 Tennis and #83 Nurse (Nurse and Baby).

Silver. Molded socks silver slippers on left, and jointed leg silver slippers on right. A number of the imported Japanese molds and also the jointed leg molds made by the company are found with silver slippers. Among the characters found with silver slippers are the Bride, Bridesmaid, Snow White-Rose Red, Ballet Dancer, Cinderella, and Beauty.

Boots-Style Painted Shoes

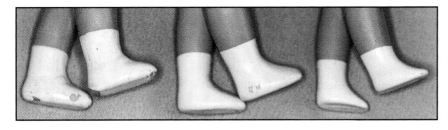

White boots. On the left is a pair of white molded socks boots, middle is the regular jointed leg pair, and right is the smaller 4½" Flower Girl white boots. On some of the very early molds, certain characters wore white boots, such as Skiing, Winter (in leggings), Sailing, Little Miss, Little Red Riding Hood, School Days in short dress, Mistress Mary in short dress, Goldilocks, Pussy Cat, Richman-Poorman, Jack and Jill, Eva, Clown, Margie Ann, Margie Ann in Party Dress, Margie Ann in Coat and Hat, Twin Sisters, Ring Bearer, Brother and Sister, Flower Girl, Geraldine Ann, and Audrey Ann.

White high-top boots. A taller white boot was used on Scotch. Most of the time Russian and Hungarian had these white boots, although the very early ones had black slippers.

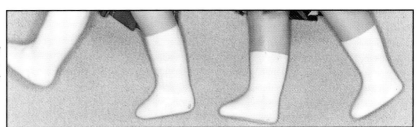

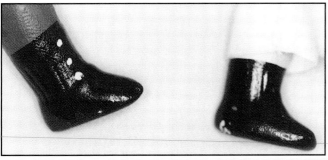

Black boots. Several characters used the black boots, usually this version. However, a few had boots painted even higher-up on the leg, such as Scotch. On the left, black boots have white dots painted on them to resemble buttons, such as we see on Topsy, Mammy, and One, Two, Button My Shoe. On the right, no white buttons; used on Cowboy, Pirate, Riding, East Side West Side, and the America mold Topsy.

Ribbons
Early Ribbon

The early ribbon imported from France and England is unique to the company and quickly identifies the doll as an early bisque jointed leg Nancy Ann. Used in abundance on the Japanese mold costumes, this ribbon continued to be used throughout the entire jointed leg era and even well into the frozen leg period. The most common ribbon used is the ¼" ribbon, but the ⅜" ribbon was also used, especially on the early doll molds. The early ribbon came in a multitude of colors, ranging from the pastel colors to the more intense red, black, and dark blue ribbon.

The weave of early imported ribbon.

Early ribbons.

Left. Once in a while during the early frozen leg era, the company used a two-tone version of this ribbon, usually white in the center and red or green on the outer edge of the ribbon or all white with ridges on the outer edge.

Right. During the MS/MB, MS, and PT era, although used rarely, velvet ¼" ribbon was utilized on dresses and as headbands.

Florist Ribbon

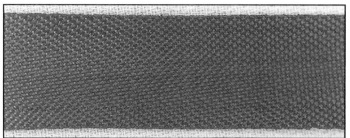

Left: The weave of common florist ribbon used on later frozen leg dolls, the teen jointed leg, and the pinch face molds.

Right. Toward the end of the bisque frozen leg period, the company switched to a ⅜" wide florist-type ribbon made here in the United States. This ribbon continued to be used throughout the later bisque era and throughout the plastic era.

Wigs
Wool Wigs

The early wool wigs look dull and frizzy, and sometimes are referred to as "dead" hair wigs by collectors. They were briefly used on the early "Made in Japan 1146" mold dolls.

Left. This early wool wig on Little Bo Peep is unusually long. Most wigs are shoulder length, except boys' wigs which were a short cut.

Right. Little Boy Blue. Early wool wig on Japanese boy doll has a shorter boy-style wig, just covering the ears.

Mohair Wigs

The mohair wigs, made of hair imported from England and France, were glued on securely and then given an over-coat of fixative to prevent the curls from loosing their perfect waves. Rubber bands around each head held the wigs in place until glue and fixative were dry. The mohair came in long strips and was cut at the factory to the correct length. A piece of muslin was sewn on the wig with white thread and the wig was placed on doll with the stitching making a right-side part. A few exceptions are the early Alice in Wonderland and some Alice through the Looking Glass who have a center part with bangs and most Goose Girls who have a center part with an extra long wig parted in center and tied at each end to represent pigtails.

  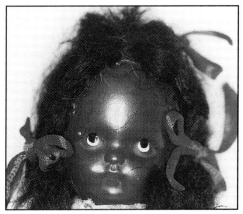

Left. The imported mohair wigs look shinier, have a nice wave, and were first introduced on the MIJ1146 molds. Center. Little Boy Blue. The shorter mohair wig for boys. Right. The wig for Mammy and Topsy is a coarse black wig parted in the center.

The wigs came in brown, auburn, and two shades of blond.

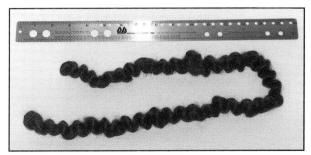

Mohair wigs were purchased from England and France in long strips and cut according to length desired for doll character.

•••Dating Bisque••• Nancy Ann Storybook Dolls

In 1936 Nancy Ann Abbott first started dressing baby dolls that she imported from Japan. However, at what precise time she advanced to dressing dolls in storybook costumes, we do not know, but certainly by 1937. We emphasis that since the company did not leave records dating the mold changes for the Storybook Doll, we can only catalog the approximate sequence we believe these changes transpired.

Circa 1936 – 1937
"Made in Japan 1146-48" molds
"FAN8 Japan" mold
"Japan" mold
Marble or sunburst box
Gold box label
No factory pamphlet
Silver pin safety closure
"NANCY ANN DRESSED DOLLS" sticker on clothing

Circa 1938 – early
"America" mold
Sunburst box
Gold box label
No pamphlet
Silver safety pin closure
"JUDY ANN" sticker on clothing

Circa 1938 – late
"Judy Ann USA" mold
"Story Book USA" (crude mark)
Sunburst box
Gold, transition to silver box label
No factory pamphlet
Brass safety pin closure
"STORYBOOK DOLLS" sticker on clothing

Circa 1939
"Story Book Doll USA" molded socks/molded bangs mold
Colored box, small silver dots
Silver box label
No factory pamphlet
Brass safety pin closure
"STORYBOOK DOLLS" sticker on clothing

Circa 1940
"Story Book Doll USA" molded socks mold
Colored box, white dots
Silver box label
Brass safety pin closure
"STORYBOOK DOLLS" sticker

Circa 1941 – 1942
"Story Book Doll USA" pudgy tummy mold
Transition to jointed leg (slim tummy) mold
White box, colored dots
Silver box label
Factory pamphlet
Brass safety pin closure
Foil wrist tag

Circa 1943 – 1945
"Story Book Doll USA" frozen-leg mold
White box, colored dots
Silver box label
Factory pamphlet
Either ribbon or silver or brass safety pin closure
Foil wrist tag

Circa 1946 – 1947
"PAT. APP. FOR" line added to frozen leg mold
White box, colored dots
Silver box label
Factory pamphlet
Safety pin closure
Foil wrist tag
Regular or florist ribbon

Circa 1946 – 1947
"Nancy Ann" added to mold
White box, colored dots
Silver box label
Factory pamphlet
Safety pin closure
Foil wrist tag
Regular or florist ribbon

Circa 1946 – 1947
"PAT. APP. FOR" teen jointed leg mold
White box, colored dots
Silver box label
Factory pamphlet
Gold snap closure
Foil wrist tag
Florist ribbon

Circa 1946 – 1947
Pinch face mold no mold mark
Silver box label
Factory pamphlet
Gold snap closure
Foil wrist tag
Florist ribbon

Babes in the Wood. See page 240.

● ● ● Pricing Bisque ● ● ●
Nancy Ann Storybook Dolls

For a Nancy Ann Storybook Doll to be called mint-in-box, the doll needs to have an original factory-mint costume, a factory pamphlet, either a wrist tag or identification sticker on the clothes, and be in its original box. Because so many of these dolls are now found without their boxes, the price listed after each doll in this book is for the *doll only.* For prices on the pamphlets, stickers, and boxes, please see individual sections for each.

The prices suggested for each character are based on a bisque doll wearing the complete costume in factory original condition on the correct unbroken bisque doll mold. The costume is extremely important, and is worth about 50% of the doll's value, depending on the doll mold and the costume's rarity and condition. Deduct accordingly if the costume has shelf dust, is faded, has tears, moth holes, stains, or has been crushed or ironed. All Nancy Ann Storybook dolls, except for a few boy characters, have some-

thing in their hair to coordinate with their costume, such as a ribbon, hat, or headband. If the headpiece is missing then deduct accordingly.

Prices indicated in this book are to be used only as a tool to help illustrate the average value of the doll, and not intended to set prices. The value of a doll is always an individual matter between buyer and seller. When consideration for rarity and condition, together with a willing buyer and seller, come together on a given day, a value is achieved. An emotional, financial, or nostalgic purchase for a doll does not guarantee that price is valid at another date, place, or time with another buyer and seller. A doll's selling price on the Internet, at auction houses, doll shows, and individual sales across the nation vary greatly and are too volatile to base reliable prices, and so should be used only as a guide. The authors and publisher assume no responsibility for losses incurred using this book as a price guide.

Old Women in the Shoe handmade by Eric Buckley, Jr. for his daughter Carolyn's childhood Nancy Ann Storybook Dolls.

The following list of dolls with stock numbers #6 through #24 were sold *before* the factory started printing pamphlets in 1940. These early stock numbers are located in the lower left corner of the gold label on the marble or sunburst design boxes. Starting in 1940, with the beginning of the printed pamphlet that was packaged in each doll box, the character's stock number was changed as follows.

Dolls in Salesman Sample Box

The numbers given each character in this box are handwritten, so it is unclear whether these numbers were actually issued by the company, or written by the salesman for his own personal use. See the photo on page 27. (Also see Salesman Sample Set section for further details on the dolls in this box.)

Early Numbers	Doll Name	Discontinued or Changed to the Following Numbers
#8	Little Red Riding Hood	#116
#9	School Days	#117
#10	Little Miss Muffet	#118
#11	Mistress Mary	#119
#12	All Dressed for a Party	Never listed in brochures; changed to #19

Other Characters with Early Numbers

Early Numbers	Doll Name	Discontinued or Changed to the Following Numbers
#6	Little Girl	Not listed — discontinued
#12	To Market	#120
#13	There Was a Little Girl	#130
#14	Jack and Jill	#175
#15	Jack Tar	Not listed — discontinued
#16	Snow White	#150
#17	Rose Red	#151
#17	Goldylocks and Bear (19)	#128
#18	Topsy and Eva	#176
#19	All Dressed for a Party	Not listed — discontinued; see photo pg. 27
#19	Goldilocks and Baby Bear (17)	#128
#19	Jack and Jill	#175
#19	Pussy Cat	#126
#20	Mary Had a Little Lamb	#152
#21	Little Bo Peep	#153
#22	Curly Locks	#154
#23	Cinderella	#155
#24	Hansel and Grethel	#177
#24	Tommy Tucker	Not listed — discontinued

For other early-numbered character information, please see the later stock numbers listed in pamphlet.

Salesman sample doll set.

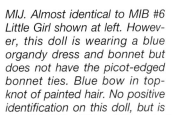

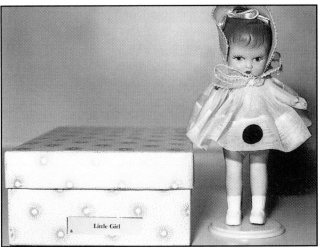

#6 Little Girl. MIJ. Painted hair with pink ribbon in topknot. Picot-edged pink organdy bonnet and dress, silver safety pin closure. NADD sticker. White boots. This character was never listed in factory pamphlets and is rare. Not enough examples have been found to price.

MIJ. Almost identical to MIB #6 Little Girl shown at left. However, this doll is wearing a blue organdy dress and bonnet but does not have the picot-edged bonnet ties. Blue bow in top-knot of painted hair. No positive identification on this doll, but is possibly Little Girl or #80 Judy Ann (see Margie Ann section). This character was never listed in factory pamphlets and is rare. Not enough examples have been found to price.

#12 and #19 All Dressed for a Party. Before the Judy Ann/Margie Ann Series developed, as early as the MIJ mold doll, the company created these two wonderful dolls. It is quite probable that the costume idea evolved later into two separate outfits, the Party Dress and the Hat and Coat costumes found in the later Judy Ann/Margie Ann Family Series. These characters were never listed in factory pamphlets and are rare. Not enough examples have been found to price.

#12 All Dressed for a Party. MIJ from Salesman Sample Set, sleeveless apricot chiffon skirt over taffeta underskirt. Picot edges with blue thread. Satin rosebud trim on skirt. Circle cut apricot chiffon hat, satin bud trim. NADD sticker.

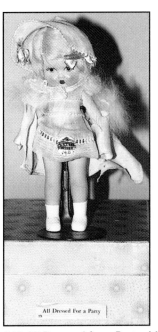

#19 All Dressed for a Party. MIJ. Early wool wig, silk coat, with marabou, picot-edged ties to hat. NADD sticker, sunburst box with gold label. $1,500.00+.

Left. #15 Jack Tar. Japan. White corded cotton two-piece sailor outfit. Matching sailor hat. Only one or two examples known so not enough examples to price.

Below. #24 Tommy Tucker. Body: Doll body appears to be actually the large Bye Baby Bunting baby mold with curved baby arms and one finger on right hand extended, slightly over five inches tall, marked "Made in Japan" with the backwards E in a circle. Gray painted eyes and painted reddish hair. Legs are the typical imported Japan legs with white boots for a toddler, not the baby mold. Costume: Short salmon-red cord cotton pants and matching sailor collar tied with red ribbon. Shirt is bright red cotton print, white circles with red line in circle. The costume seems too small for the baby body it was found on, so possibly this is not the correct body for this doll. The body and legs appear to be restrung. Until we find a mint-in-box example using this same combination of baby body and toddler legs, we can only surmise what is the correct factory version of this doll. Gold safety pin closure. NADD sticker. Gold sunburst box with label #24. Not enough examples to price.

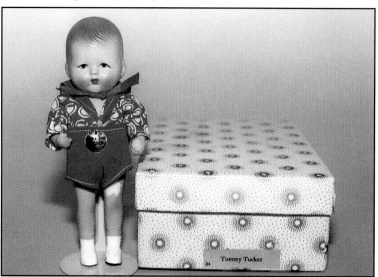

• • • Flower Series • • •
#1 – #6

The earliest example of the Flower Series is found on a Judy Ann mold. However, most early versions are on a MS/MB mold. Since the Flower Series was only produced through 1941, they are always bisque jointed leg dolls. The Flower Series dolls all wear short cotton underpants instead of pantalets.

Left: #1 Rose. MS/MB. Flower on skirt and in hair. Separate lace-edged slip. $500.00. Right: Two-tier dress, flower in hair. MS. $400.00. PT, short arms, no slip. $350.00.

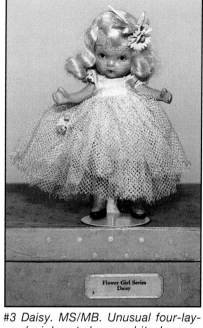

#2 Marguerite. Left: JA. Separate lace-edged white cotton slip. $600.00. Also found on a crude mark mold and MS/MB molds. $500.00. Right: PT. Attached shorter yellow taffeta slip. Note slight difference in the two flowers. $350.00.

#3 Daisy. MS/MB. Unusual four-layered pink net dress, white lace on sleeves, short pink panties. $600.00.

#3 Daisy. MS. Transition to long pink organdy dress. Attached pink taffeta slip. Early striped NA ribbon. $400.00.

#3 Daisy. MS. Net dress. Pink cotton panties. SB. sticker. $500.00.

#3 Daisy. PT. Long arm. $350.00.

#4 Black-eyed Susan. Left: MS. Net over attached yellow taffeta, lace on sleeves, yellow flower. SB. sticker. $450.00. Right: PT. Organdy over taffeta, white flower. WT. All versions have rare color brown painted eyes. $350.00.

#5 Lily. MS/MB. Green bodice, tiered net skirt, cotton slip. $500.00.

#5 Lily. PT. Green bodice, organdy ruffled overskirt. $350.00.

#6 Violet. MS/MB. Short green taffeta bodice and underskirt, longer lavender organdy overskirt. $450.00.

#6 Violet. PT. Short green taffeta bodice and underskirt, longer vivid purple organdy overskirt. $350.00.

The Around the World Series is one of the earliest series offered by the company, and has been found on all three Japanese molds. The series only continued through the slim joint leg period and then was discontinued. The Around the World Series dolls wear short panties, except Chinese. Most have sep-arate half-slips, although by the jointed leg mold period, some slips may be attached. The large #700 Around the World Box has flags for each of the countries in the box. It is possible, but has not been verified that individually sold Around the World Series characters also were sold with these flags.

Left. #25 French. MIJ. Wide black satin hair ribbon. Blue and red ribbon trim on skirt. Blouse and skirt are one piece. Same black satin ribbon used in hair is used for the black vest and attached to puffy organdy sleeves. Lace inserted in the center for the blouse. Taffeta skirt. Apron is separate. NADD sticker. $900.00.

Right. #25 French. Back view, picot edging on apron ties and separate slip.

#25 French. FAN8. Variation of trim on apron. $900.00.

Below, #25 French. MIJ. Two-piece outfit, skirt and apron attached. Puffy sleeved blouse sewn onto black taffeta cummer-bund, separate slip. $900.00.

Far right. #25 French. America. One-piece costume, cotton skirt and cummerbund. Judy Ann sticker. Separate slip. $1,000.00.

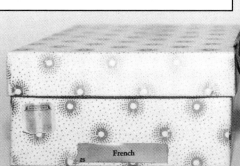  

#25 French. JA. Variation with SD sticker. $700.00.

#25 French. MS/MB and MS. Lace on sleeves. Black felt vest, separate slip. $350.00.

Left to right.

#25 French. JT. Red felt vest. Slip attached. $175.00.

#26 Swiss. MIJ. Organdy picot-trimmed puff sleeves, black cummerbund, print skirt, open crown large straw hat. Early wool wig, hair tied with red ribbon, print apron, ribbon trim. $1,200.00.

#26 Swiss. MIJ. Yellow print dress, rickrack trim on bodice and skirt, no cummerbund, white apron, and early wool wig. Open crown large straw hat. $1,200.00.

Left. #26 Swiss. MIJ. Two-piece costume, taffeta cummerbund. Open-crown straw hat with ribbon rosebud trim. Ribbon trim on skirt, lace on apron. Unusual yellow organdy puff sleeves. $1,200.00.

Right. #26 Swiss. JA. One-piece costume of cotton skirt, organdy blouse, red vest. Change to felt dunce-style hat. $850.00.

#26 Swiss. JA. Variation. $850.00.

#26 Swiss. JA. Variation. $850.00.

#26 Swiss. JA. Variation, felt vest, SB sticker. $850.00.

Left. #26 Swiss. MS/MB. No apron. Felt cummerbund. $450.00.

Right. #26 Swiss. MS. Print apron. $400.00.

Left. #26 Swiss. MS. Variation $400.00.

Below. #26 Swiss. MS. Variation. $400.00.

#26 Swiss. PT. Variation. $350.00.

#26 Swiss. JT. Variation. $200.00.

Below. #26 Swiss. JT. Variation. $200.00.

Right. #26 Swiss. JT. Variation. $200.00.

#27 Dutch. Japan. Cotton striped fabric dress with over-the-shoulder picot-edged organdy apron. Picot edged hat. NADD sticker. $900.00.

#27 Dutch. MIJ. Taffeta skirt, attached apron, separate picot-edged wrapped blouse, crossing in front. Picot-edged Dutch hat. Extra long wig tied with blue ribbons. Separate slip, front dart panties. $900.00.

#27 Dutch. JA. One-piece blue polished cotton dress, attached checked apron. Rare painted brown slipper shoes, separate cotton slip. $1,100.00.

#27 Dutch. MIJ. Variation in apron, large Dutch hat. $900.00.

Left. #27 Dutch. JA. Unusual skirt of two fabrics with black cotton over-the-shoulder vest. Two ribbons in hair. Also brown shoes. $1,100.00.

Right. #27 Dutch. JA. Unusual skirt of blue organdy and small check. Black slipper shoes. Change to black belt and white apron. $800.00.

#27 Dutch. MS/MB. Variation with larger check. $450.00.

#27 Dutch. MS/MB. Variation with diagonal check. $450.00.

#27 Dutch. MS. Change now to red felt belt and black apron. $350.00.

#27 Dutch. MS. $350.00.

#27 Dutch. MS. $350.00.

#27 Dutch. PT. $250.00.

#27 Dutch. JT. $175.00.

#27 Dutch. JT. $175.00.

#27 Dutch. JT. $175.00.

#28 Italian. MIJ. Early wool wig, rare marble box, gold label. Taffeta dress, headpiece of rectangle organdy picot trimmed edge with ribbon tie. NADD sticker. $2,000.00+.

Left. #28 Italian. MIJ. Variation in two-piece costume with attached print apron. Three rows of ribbon trim, early wool wig. $1,200.00.

Right. #28 Italian. MIJ. Variation in gold cotton, early wool wig. (Flag probably did not come with doll.) $1,200.00.

#28 Italian. MIJ. Variation in green taffeta one-piece dress, separate apron, NADD sticker, separate blue ribbon trimmed slip, mohair wig. $1,200.00.

#28 Italian. Japan. Variation with attached organdy apron to ribbon trimmed separate skirt, cummerbund attached to picot trimmed puff sleeves. $1,200.00.

#28 Italian. JA. No cummerbund. $900.00.

#28 Italian. Back view of hemmed organdy headpiece.

#28 Italian. CM. Cotton dress, matching trim on apron and hat. SBD sticker. $1,000.00.

#28 Italian. MS. $550.00.

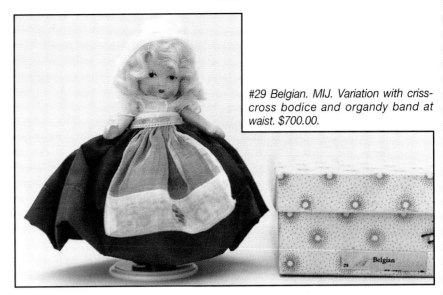

#29 Belgian. MIJ. Variation with criss-cross bodice and organdy band at waist. $700.00.

Above. #29 Belgian. MIJ. Picot edged scarf and ribbon ties, cranberry taffeta dress. $700.00.

Below. #29 Belgian. FAN8. White bodice, taffeta skirt. $700.00.

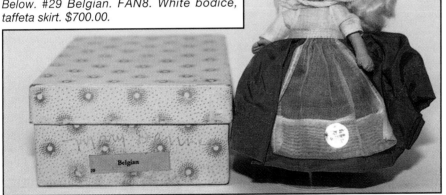

#29 Belgian. America. Change to polished cotton brown dress. $900.00.

Left. #29 Belgian. JA. Variation, longer dress. $700.00.

Right. #29 Belgian. JA. Variation, lace trim at neck and apron. $600.00.

Left. #29 Belgian. PT. Variation, lace straps on bodice. $200.00.

Right. #29 Belgian. JT. Variation, dark brown dress. $150.00.

#30 Spanish. MIJ. Early wool wig. Polished cotton dress. No bodice, just wide taffeta belt with v-shaped black lace. Separate black ribbon-trimmed half slip. Satin flower glued to side, under mantilla. Unusual red thread picot short front dart panties. Also found on Japan mold. $900.00.

#30 Spanish. JA. Variation on lace treatment. $700.00.

Left. #30 Spanish. America. Complete bodice with square lace trim. Mohair wig pulled to back of neck. JA sticker. Separate cotton white half-slip. $1,100.00+.

Right. #30 Spanish. MS/MB. Unusual organdy overskirt, cotton stripped underskirt. Black bodice. $400.00.

#30 Spanish. MS/MB. Unusual separate purple cotton slip. $400.00.

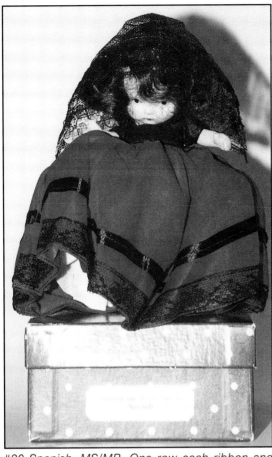

#30 Spanish. MS/MB. One row each ribbon and lace trim. $400.00.

#30 Spanish. MS/MB. Unusual brown eyes. $450.00.

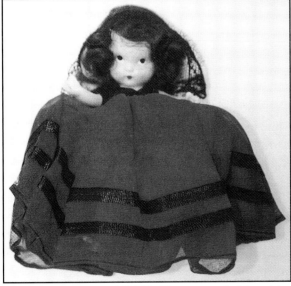

Above. #30 Spanish. MS/MB. Two rows of ribbon trim. $400.00.

Right. #30 Spanish. MS. Red cotton separate half-slip, starting with MS/MB mold. $300.00.

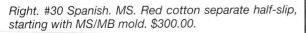

Left. #30 Spanish. JT. Large ruffled bottom of skirt. Black lace eliminated and mantilla discontinued. Poppy in hair. Some red cotton slips are still separate and then became attached. $150.00.

Right. #31 Portuguese. A Japan-made doll, but mold unknown. Print apron and rickrack trim. Early wool wig. Also similar costume, but in red taffeta, with yellow print matching apron and head scarf. $1,400.00.

#31 Portuguese. MIJ. Taffeta dress, separate apron. NADD sticker. Picot-edged scarf held by a wide black ribbon to form an Arabic-style headpiece. $1,400.00.

#31 Portuguese. Japan. Variation, taffeta dress. Variation also with yellow circle print apron and scarf. $1,400.00.

#31 Portuguese. America. Variation change to felt headband, organdy sleeves, red vest. $1,600.00+. Also JA. $1,000.00.

#31 Portuguese. MS/MB. Change to print dress. $700.00.

Portuguese. Variation. $700.00.

Left. #31 Portuguese. MS. Variation. $400.00.

Right. #31 Portuguese. MS. Variation. $400.00.

#31 Portuguese. MS. Change to long dress, ribbon trim at bottom of skirt. Discontinued Arabic head-dress, but flower in hair. Separate felt cummerbund and wool-fringed shawl added. $400.00.

#31 Portuguese. MS. Variation. $400.00.

#31 Portuguese. PT. Variation. $300.00.

#31 Portuguese. PT. Variation. $300.00.

#31 Portuguese. PT. Variation. $300.00.

#31 Portuguese. JT. Variation. $250.00.

#31 Portuguese. JT. Variation. $250.00.

#31 Portuguese. JT. Variation. $250.00.

#32 English Flower Girl. PT. Straw hat with flowers, cotton print, flower bouquet sewn in apron. Also found in pink print. $500.00.

#32 English Flower Girl. PT. Variation in blue with variety of flowers on wrist. $400.00. Also JT in white print. $350.00.

#32 English Flower Girl. PT. Organdy print, flowers on wrist, apron with straps over bodice. Straw hat discontinued, now ribbon in hair. $400.00.

#33 Chinese. MIJ. Black painted hair, Chinese painted features on face, two-piece taffeta outfit, long sleeves, yellow trim around jacket and sleeves with side tie. Topknot with yellow ribbon under skullcap with ribbon streamers. JA sticker. $1,300.00.

#33 Chinese. Japan. Brown eyes. Two-piece taffeta outfit. Ribbon trim all around jacket and sleeves. $1,300.00.

#33 Chinese. America. Center closure. Change to cotton kimono, center closure with gold trim. Skullcap without ribbon streamers. $1,400.00+.

#33 Chinese. JA. Skull cap discontinued, now ribbon headband with ribbon flowers. $1,000.00.

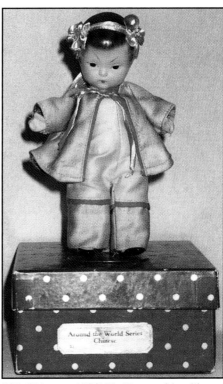

#33 Chinese. MS/MB. Vivid purple, aqua, and red trim. $1,200.00+ if color is this vivid and not faded.

#33 Chinese. MS/MB. Tan, gold, with red trim. $800.00.

#33 Chinese. MS. Variation. $700.00.

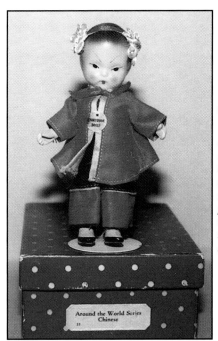

The hat for Irish is the typical organdy dust cap.

Left. #33 Chinese. MS. Variation. $700.00.

Right. #34 Irish. MIJ. Early wool wig. Taffeta skirt attached to sleeveless matching bodice. Short separate picot-edged white organdy apron and shawl, tucked into the apron. $800.00.

#34 Irish. Japan. Variation with ribbon trim on taffeta skirt, also green taffeta. $800.00.

#34 Irish. America. One-piece dress, SD sticker. $900.00+.

#34 Irish. JA. Variation. $700.00.

Left. #34 Irish. JA. Lace on apron. $700.00.

Right. #34 Irish. MS/MB. No lace on apron. $450.00. Also on MS $350.00. PT $200.00. JT $175.00.

Below. #35 Russian. MIJ. One-piece long burgundy taffeta, picot-edged puff sleeves. Ribbon trim on separate slip. Bandana tied in back. $1,100.00.

Right. #35 Russian. America. $1,400.00. Also JA mold. $1,000.00.

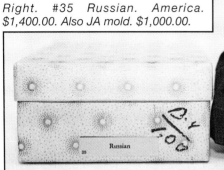

#35 Russian. JA. Polished cotton ¾ length dress, separate apron. $1,000.00.

#35 Russian. JA. Variation, change to red felt cummerbund, print skirt. Now rickrack trim on sleeves. $1,000.00. Also MS/MB. $850.00.

#35 Russian. CM. White high-top MS boots. Separate slip, red or blue bandana. $1,100.00+.

Left. #35 Russian. MS. Variation, red or green bandana. $700.00.

Right. #36 Hungarian. MIJ. Gold/tan taffeta skirt with row of ribbon trim. White organdy puff sleeves and cutwork on bodice and on long apron. $1,200.00+.

48

#36 Hungarian. America. Cotton skirt with attached blouse and vest, organdy headpiece and attached apron stitched with red thread. $1,300.00+. Also on JA mold. $1,000.00.

#36 Hungarian. CM. Change to organdy dress, green and red ribbons in hair. $1,100.00.

#36 Hungarian. MS/MB. Change to white high-top boots. $800.00.

#36 Hungarian. Crescent-shaped felt headpiece with red ribbon trim. White high top boots. $400.00. Also MS. $600.00. PT. $500.00.

#37 Swedish. Japan. Fan. Separate apron, sateen dress. $900.00.

#37 Swedish. Japan. Taffeta skirt, lace on sleeves and neck of cotton bodice, separate apron. Taffeta hat. $900.00.

#37 Swedish. JA. Change to black polished cotton vest and skirt. Rick-rack trim. Felt hat. $700.00.

#37 Swedish. Unusual yellow vest, mold unknown.

#37 Swedish. CM. Change to print apron, ribbon trim, elimination of lacing stitching on vest. $800.00.

#37 Swedish. MS/MB. $500.00.

#37 Swedish. MS. Variation. $350.00.

Left. #37 Swedish. MS. Variation. $350.00.

Right. #37 Swedish. JT. Variation. $175.00. PT $250.00.

#38 Scotch. All wear a kilt and matching scarf in a variety of tartan colors and white high-top painted boots. Only the very early costumes also sported a rabbit fur sporran.

Left. #38 Scotch. MIJ. Black taffeta jacket, no bodice. Taffeta hat with rosette of skirt material safety pinned to hair. A rabbit fur sporran is attached. $1,100.00.

Right. #38 Scotch. MIJ. Variation of tartan, scarf missing. If complete, $1,100.00.

#37 Swedish. JT. Variation. $175.00.

Left to right.

#38 Scotch. Japan. Felt hat with ribbon. JA. sticker. $1,000.00.

#38 Scotch. America and JA. Black polished cotton jacket and hat, ribbon rosette on hat, white cotton bodice. $1,100.00+.

#38 Scotch. JA. The sporran is now eliminated. Black felt jacket and hat. $900.00.

#38 Scotch. CM. $950.00.

#38 Scotch. MS. $400.00.

#38 Scotch. MS. $400.00.

#38 Scotch. MS. $400.00.

#38 Scotch. CM. $950.00.

#38 Scotch. MS. $400.00. PT. $250.00.

#38 Scotch. PT. $250.00.

Left. #38 Scotch. PT. $250.00.

Right. #38 Scotch. JT. $175.00.

Far left. #38 Scotch. PT. $250.00.

Left. #38 Scotch. JT. $175.00.

Right. #39 Mexican. JA. Three sequins on skirt, straw hat tied to doll with red ribbon. $900.00.

#39 Mexican. MS/MB. Sequins eliminated, straw hat. $350.00.

#39 Mexican. PT. Felt hat. $250.00.

#40 Norweign. America. Cotton skirt, cotton vest with white sequin, felt hat with three sequins, tied with black ribbon. JA sticker. $1000.00+.

#40 Norweign. JA. Lace on apron. $700.00.

#40 Norweign. JA. Print bodice, sequins eliminated. Various lace-trimmed aprons. Sequins now eliminated. $600.00.

#40 Norweign. MS. Change to red cotton skirt, various print bodices, blue felt hat. $400.00.

#40 Norweign. PT. Change to attached slip. $300.00.

#40 Norweign. JT. $200.00.

#40 Norweign. JT. $200.00.

#40 Norweign. JT. $200.00.

Poland is not found in any of the factory pamphlets. However, an empty Nancy Ann Storybook box has been found with a #41 Poland label, evidence that #41 Poland was sold. We have reason to believe that the dolls following are #41 Poland.

#41 Poland. Japan. Separate slip. One-piece costume of green (faded) cotton skirt, lace on organdy sleeves, attached print apron with tan ribbon. Judy Ann sticker. $1,300.00.

Left. #41 Poland. America. Variation, no lace on sleeves, red ribbon trim on apron. $1,600.00.

Right. #41 Poland. JA. Separate slip. One-piece costume of green cotton skirt, green ribbon trim. Stitching on bodice. $1,200.00.

Left. #41 Poland. JA. Variation of print scarf and apron. No stitching on bodice. $1,200.00.

Right. #41 Poland. JA. Variation with print skirt and bandana, and plain green apron, one row of ribbon trim. $1,200.00.

• • • American Girl Series • • •
#55 – #58

At first glance, most jointed leg #55 Quaker Maid costumes look the same. However, there are subtle details that changed over the early years. Early molds have collars tied in front with black ribbon. The dresses on the Japan through the molded-socks era have separate slips. Early organdy skullcap bonnets do not have a sewn hem over the face area, unlike the later bonnets, which have a deep hem along front brim. Bonnets changed from white organdy to white felt on the frozen leg dolls.

#55 Quaker Maid, jointed leg. Japan. NADD sticker. $800.00+.

#55 Quaker Maid, jointed leg. JA. Separate organdy collar tied with black ribbon. Separate cotton slip, cotton dress, SD sticker. $400.00.

#55 Quaker Maid, jointed leg. JA. Black ribbon trim on collar. $400.00.

#55 Quaker Maid, jointed leg. MS. Cotton dress, also MS/MB. $200.00.

#55 Quaker Maid, jointed leg. PT. Gray taffeta dress. $150.00.

#55 Quaker Maid, jointed leg. JT. Tan taffeta. $125.00.

#55 Quaker Maid, frozen leg. Gray silk dress. $50.00.

#55 Quaker Maid, frozen leg. Chiffon dress, felt hat. $40.00.

Colonial Dame wears a characteristic dress of the 1607 – 1776 colonial period of the United States. All wear a dust cap, except very last example.

Above. #56 Colonial Dame, jointed leg. Japan. Lace on pantalets, JA sticker. $800.00.

#55 Quaker Maid, frozen leg. Silk checked dress, felt hat. $40.00.

Left. #56 Colonial Dame, jointed leg. JA. $400.00.

Right. #56 Colonial Dame, jointed leg. JA. $400.00. MS/MB. $250.00.

#56 Colonial Dame, jointed leg. MS/MB. Unusual net shawl stitched to waist. $250.00. MS. $200.00.

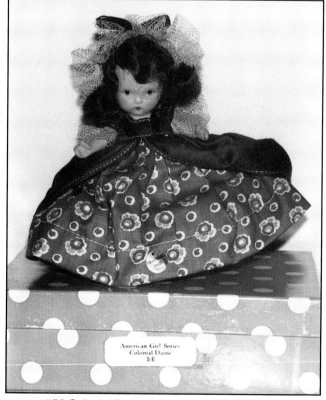

#56 Colonial Dame, jointed leg. MS. $250.00.

#56 Colonial Dame, jointed leg. MS/MB. $250.00.

#56 Colonial Dame, jointed leg. PT. $150.00.

#56 Colonial Dame, jointed leg. JT. $125.00.

#56 Colonial Dame, frozen leg. $50.00.

#56 Colonial Dame, frozen leg. $50.00.

#56 Colonial Dame, frozen leg. $50.00.

#56 Colonial Dame, frozen leg. $50.00.

#56 Colonial Dame, frozen leg. $50.00.

#56 Colonial Dame, frozen leg. $50.00.

Left. #57 Southern Belle, jointed leg. JA. Pale blue taffeta band of crinoline inside skirt, separate cotton slip, net collar. Also found on a MS/MB doll. $400.00.

Right. #57 Southern Belle, jointed leg. JA. Unusual net collar and rosette head-band. $400.00.

Left. #57 Southern Belle, jointed leg. MS/MB. Pink taffeta print, black lace on bodice and ribbon trim, separate slip. SB sticker, also in yellow taffeta. $350.00.

Above. #57 Southern Belle, jointed leg. Close-up of black felt bonnet with netting and rosette band.

Left. #57 Southern Belle, jointed leg. MS/MB. Variation, lace trim $350.00.

Right. #57 Southern Belle, jointed leg. MS. Yellow taffeta, floral print, separate cotton slip. $250.00.

#57 Southern Belle, jointed leg. PT. Blue taffeta, floral print, $150.00. Also on MS. $200.00.

#57 Southern Belle, jointed leg. JT. Tulip print, in pink or yellow, unusual black felt jacket. $125.00.

#57 Southern Belle, jointed leg. JT. Dotted swiss, red taffeta underskirt. $125.00.

#57 Southern Belle, frozen leg. Variation. $55.00.

#57 Southern Belle, frozen leg. Various prints with ribbon trim on skirts. $55.00 each. Bottom right. Close-up of hat.

#57 Southern Belle, frozen leg. Various prints with ribbon trim on skirts. $55.00 each.

#57 Southern Belle, frozen leg. Various prints with braid or rickrack trim. $50.00 each.

#57 Southern Belle, frozen leg. Various prints with braid or rickrack trim. $50.00 each.

Left. #58 Western Miss, jointed leg. JA. Yellow floral print. Organdy floral print, separate slip. Also in same print of either white or blue. $850.00+.

Right. Western Miss, jointed leg. Back view showing organdy bonnet with fabric brim.

Left. #58 Western Miss, jointed leg. JA. Cotton print. Black lace collar attached to felt hat, black lace parasol with pipe cleaner staff. $500.00.

Right. #58 Western Miss, jointed leg. MS/MB. Variation of print with red ribbons down front. Also costume with blue ribbons. $325.00.

#58 Western Miss, jointed leg. MS/MB. Variation of print, blue bows. $325.00.

#58 Western Miss, jointed leg. Back view of hat and collar.

Left. #58 Western Miss, jointed leg. MS/MB. Variation of print and ribbon down front, instead of bows, missing parasol. If complete $325.00.

Right. #58 Western Miss, jointed leg. MS/MB. Organdy skirt with cotton print bodice and ruffled bottom of skirt. Straw hat. $275.00.

#58 Western Miss, jointed leg. PT. Cotton print dress and matching hat with white streamers on each side. This same print is in yellow, blue, white, aqua, and pink floral print. $200.00.

#58 Western Miss, jointed leg. MS/MB and MS. Variation of print. $275.00.

#58 Western Miss, jointed leg. PT. Organdy ruche trim on bonnet and skirt. $200.00.

#58 Western Miss, jointed leg. MS. Ruche trim of ribbon on skirt. $225.00.

Left. #58 Western Miss, jointed leg. JT. Variation of print. $200.00.

Right. #58 Western Miss, jointed leg. Back view of streamers and sash.

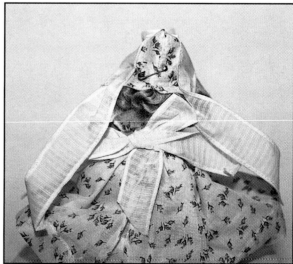

#58 Western Miss, jointed leg. PT. Magenta taffeta. $150.00.

#58 Western Miss, jointed leg. PT. Variation in deep wine taffeta print. $150.00.

#58 Western Miss, frozen leg. Also variation in apron and blue ribbon trim. $55.00.

#58 Western Miss, frozen leg. $55.00.

#58 Western Miss, frozen leg. $55.00.

#58 Western Miss, frozen leg. $55.00.

#58 Western Miss, frozen leg. Various organdy aprons. $55.00.

• • • Masquerade Series • • •
#60 – #63

This series appears only in the 1940 factory pamphlet. Examples are hard to find and are only on the Judy Ann, crude mark, MS/MB, and MS molds.

The earliest Gipsy found is on a Judy Ann mold. Gipsy has one-piece blouse and skirt. Early dolls have a black cotton vest, later dolls a red felt vest. Gipsy has brightly colored separate cotton slips and short panties. Earlier dolls have earrings. (Note uncommon spelling of Gypsy as Gipsy.)

Above left. #60 Gipsy. JA. Separate gold cotton slip. Gold earrings sewn to bandana. Plastic gold coins sewn to each side of black cotton vest. Attached purple skirt. Red with yellow bandana. $1,100.00+.

Above right. #60 Gipsy. JA. Variation with red flower-print scarf. $1,100.00+.

Left. #60 Gipsy. MS/MB. Attached yellow or white print skirt. Red felt vest with or without coins. Separate black ribbon holds earrings to each side of bandana. Red separate cotton slip. $1,000.00.

Right. #60 Gipsy. MS. Red felt vest. Bold multicolored print. Aqua separate cotton slip. No earrings. $900.00.

#60 Gipsy. MS. Variation with solid green scarf. $900.00.

#60 Gipsy. MS. Variation with yellow scarf, yellow separate cotton slip. $900.00.

A dashing Pirate with black painted boots topped with oilcloth cuffs is an excellent example of a detailed costume by this company. From our research, we believe the early Pirate probably came without a pirate hat. However, too few examples of this costume have been found to verify this. Several later pirates also have been found without a hat or without earrings. Were these lost, taken off, or never supplied by the company? At this point, because of the limited Pirates found MIB, we feel uncomfortable stating anything as a positive for this costume.

#61 Pirate. JA. Yellow shirt and dark blue short pants, both stretch material. Eye patch fastened with dark string under cotton print bandana. Earrings attached to bandana. $1,500.00+.

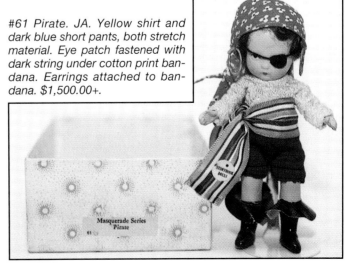

Left. #61 Pirate. MS. No earrings. $900.00.

Right. #61 Pirate. JA. Also MS/MB both with gold hoop earrings. Cotton shirt and pants. A soft black felt tri-fold hat with open crown slips over the color-ful bandana. $1,100.00+.

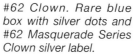

The #62 Clown is not listed in factory pamphlets. However, the #62 Clown has been found MIB with factory label and sticker. Thus, the costume was produced, if only for a short period. When the #62 Clown was discontinued, the #64 Cowboy was changed to #62 Cowboy.

#62 Clown. Rare blue box with silver dots and #62 Masquerade Series Clown silver label.

Left to right.

#62 Clown. JA. Separate white cotton tunic and long flared pants. Burgundy ruffled net collar, puffs of net at center of tunic and on dunce hat. White painted boots and SB sticker. $2,000.00.

#62 Clown. MS/MB. Clown with black net. $1,800.00.

#62 Clown. Back view.

Cowboy is listed under both #62 and #64. The early sunburst box label has #64 on the lower left of the box, whereas the later box label has #62 on the label. Cowboy has leather pants and trim, plaid cotton shirt, and black painted boots. Black felt cowboy hat. Small red neck scarf.

#64 Cowboy. MS/MB. Unusual three-Leaf leather decoration on leather chaps. SD sticker. $1,500.00+.

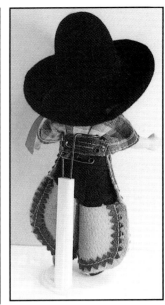

#62 and #64 Cowboy. Back view.

#62 Cowboy. MS/MB. Leather zigzag trim around edge of leather chaps. SD sticker. $1,500.00+.

#62 Cowboy. MS. $1,100.00.

Ballet Dancer has a short four-layer net skirt in either white, blue, yellow, or pink netting with attached cotton bodice, silver painted slippers, and short panties usually the color of the net tutu. The tutu in pastel colors is not as prevalent as the white tutu, so a higher price is warranted.

#63 Ballet Dancer. JA. White tutu. Sunburst box, gold label. $1,500.00.

Left. #63 Ballet Dancer. MS/MB. White tutu. Three sequins on bodice and two in netting. $1,300.00.

Right. #63 Ballet Dancer. MS/MB. Variation with ribbon headband with sequins. $1,100.00.

Left. #63 Ballet Dancer. Back view.

Right. #63 Ballet Dancer. MS/MB. Variation in blue tutu with blue underpants, sequins on bodice, and skirt/silver dot box, SBD sticker. $1,300.00.

Left. #63 Ballet Dancer. MS. Pink tutu, three sequins on bodice and two sequins in netting. $1,200.00.

Right. #63 Ballet Dancer. MS. Variation in yellow tutu with yellow panties. $1,200.00.

●●●Sports Series●●●
#70 – #73

This is a delightful series with each outfit truly an example of Nancy Ann Abbott's ability to design outfits in proportion to the scale of the doll. The Sports Series appears only in the 1940 factory pamphlet and then was discontinued. This series is on the molded sock mold or earlier.

  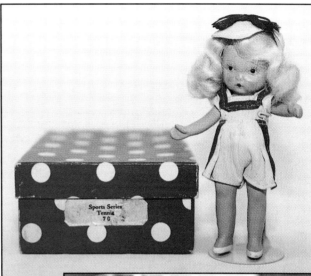

Left to right.

#70 Tennis. MS/MB. 1941. Two-piece white-corded cotton tennis outfit, red ribbon forming v-shape on bodice. Pleat on either side of pants. Matching white fabric cap, red ribbon bow under cap. White slipper shoes. $1,200.00+.

#70 Tennis. Back view shows red ribbon trim over shoulders.

#70 Tennis. MS. Variation, white slipper shoes. $1,200.00.

#70 Tennis. Red box with small silver dots and label.

Left to right.

#71 Sailing. MIJ. Two-piece sailor outfit of corded blue cotton. NADD sticker. Wool wig. Royal blue ribbon tie. $2,000.00+.

#71 Sailing. Back view.

#71 Sailing. America. Two-piece sailor outfit of cotton, attached collar. SD sticker, missing hat. $1,500.00.

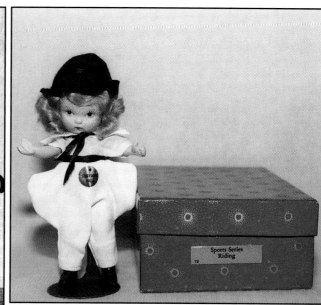

Above left to right.

#71 Sailing. JA. Red ribbon trim on collar and on sailor hat. SD sticker. White boots. $1,200.00+.

#71 Sailing. MS/MB. Blue ruffle on shirt. White boots. $1,200.00+.

#72 Riding. MS/MB. Starburst box. Black painted boots. White corded cotton jodhpurs with black ribbon waistband. Separate white organdy shirt with attached collar. Black ribbon neck scarf. Black felt riding hat with black ribbon. SD sticker. $1,350.00+.

Right. #72 Riding. MS. Variation with red ribbon neck scarf. $1,200.00+.

These costumes included a two-piece ski outfit plus ski cap, hair ribbon under ski cap, scarf and belt, and white painted boots.

Left. #73 Skiing. JA. Yellow and white ski outfit. $1,200.00.

Right. #73 Skiing. JA. Blue and red ski outfit. $1,200.00.

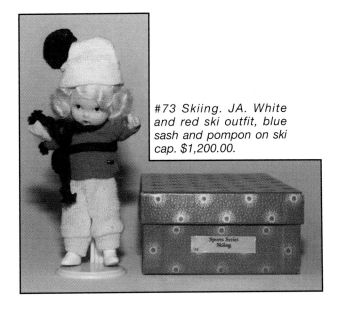

#73 Skiing. JA. White and red ski outfit, blue sash and pompon on ski cap. $1,200.00.

#73 Skiing. MS/MB. Red and blue ski outfit with white sash. $700.00.

#73 Skiing. MS. Blue and white ski outfit. $500.00.

#73 Skiing. Close-up of knit fabric.

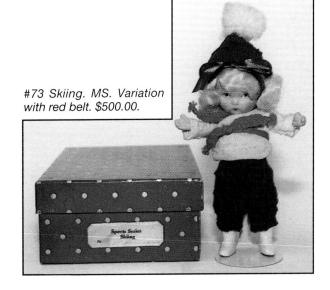

#73 Skiing. MS. Variation with red belt. $500.00.

••• Family Series ••• #78 – #89

The company used this broad heading for a progression of dolls wearing regular clothes. Over the years, it included the Judy Ann and the Margie Ann Series, Twin Sisters, Brother and Sister, Audrey Ann, The Bridal Party, Nurse and Baby, and Mammy, with and without a Baby.

The Margie Ann Series

As few actual factory specifics are known, we can only theorize what the company's business decisions over the years were regarding the Margie Ann series of little girl outfits. However, the company, systematically and sometimes even simultaneously, progressed from the Five Little Sisters, possibly because the interest in the famous Dionne Quintuplets had waned, to creating a series of little girl outfits. Earlier a MIJ mold doll in its box labeled "Judy Ann" had been marketed. With the implementation in 1938 of their own five inch bisque doll with the mold actually marked Judy Ann, the company had definitely christened a new series Judy Ann. The name, along with the doll mold, however, was soon dropped because of a Judy Ann name infringement.

If only we had factory records before 1940, we could piece together this ambiguity. However, probably by the end of 1939, the company had launched the next name change for this series, replacing the name Judy Ann with a new name, Margie Ann. If one compares the costumes for the very early dolls, #500 Five Little Sisters, #510 Five Little Sister in Playsuits, the #6 Little Girl, the #12 – #19 All Dressed for a Party, along with Family Series – Judy Ann costumes to the later Family Series – Margie Ann costumes, one can see the progression from this initial idea of little girls wearing various dresses, playsuits, and coats to the end result, the Margie Ann Series. Listed in the first pamphlet of 1940, we find #80 Margie Ann, #81 Margie Ann in Party Dress, and #82 Margie Ann in Coat and Hat. However, the stock numbers #500 Margie Ann in School Dress and #510 Margie Ann in Play Suit were not changed to #78 and #79, to flow in sequence with the other Margie Ann costumes, until 1941. The Margie Ann Series continued through 1942 and ended when the frozen leg mold was introduced in 1943.

FAMILY SERIES

STYLE No.	
80	Margie Ann
81	Margie Ann in Party Dress
82	Margie Ann in Coat and Hat
83	Mammy and Baby
84	Twin Sisters
85	Brother & Sister
86	Bride
87	Bridesmaid
87A	Flower Girl
88	Bridegroom
89	Mammy
500	Margie Ann in School Dress
510	Margie Ann in Play Suit
2000	Audrey Ann

This 1940 pamphlet lists #510 Margie Ann in Playsuit. The blue-eyed doll wears a solid-color cotton playsuit, found in various colors with a matching bonnet, similar to the earlier brown-eyed Five Little Sisters who also wore these solid-color broadcloth playsuits, but their eyes were painted brown. (For #500 Five Little Sisters and #510 Five Little Sisters in Playsuits, see separate section, Five Little Sisters.)

#510 Margie Ann in Playsuit. MS/MB. Yellow. $300.00.

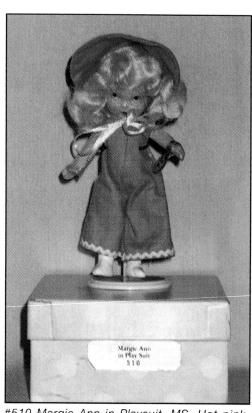

#510 Margie Ann in Playsuit. MS. Hot pink. $275.00.

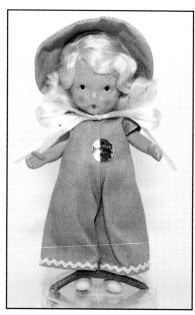

#510 Margie Ann in Playsuit. MS. Lavender. $275.00.

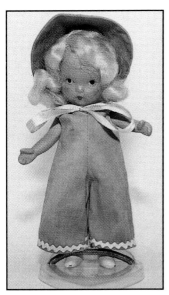
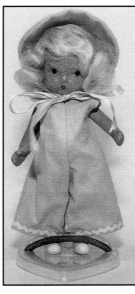

Left. #510 Margie Ann in Playsuit. MS. Blue. $275.00.

Right. #510 Margie Ann in Playsuit. PT. Light Pink. A transitional doll with #510 playsuit found on the PT mold, possibly should be on a MS mold. $260.00.

FAMILY SERIES

78	Margie Ann in Play Suit
79	Margie Ann in School Dress
80	Margie Ann
81	Margie Ann in Party Dress
82	Margie Ann in Coat and Hat
83	Mammy and Baby
84	Twin Sisters
85	Brother and Sister
86	Bride
87	Bridesmaid
88	Bridegroom
89	Flower Girl

The 1941 pamphlet shows that the number was changed to #78, and the solid-color playsuits gave way to various floral prints, checks, and polka dot playsuits on the pudgy tummy mold with the smooth white boots. At the pudgy tummy/jointed-leg transition in 1942, the white boots were discontinued, and the dolls had the common black slipper shoes.

#78 Margie Ann in Playsuit. PT. Blue/red polka dots. $250.00.

#78 Margie Ann in Playsuit. JT. White floral print in white box. $225.00.

#78 Margie Ann in Playsuit. PT. Blue and white. $250.00.

#78 Margie Ann in Playsuit. PT. Red/white check. $250.00.

#78 Margie Ann in Playsuit. PT. White/yellow floral. $250.00.

#78 Margie Ann in Playsuit. JT. Lavender floral. $225.00.

#78 Margie Ann in Playsuit. JT. Red/blue with white diamonds. $225.00.

Left to right.

#78 Margie Ann in Playsuit. JT. Aqua floral. $225.00.

#78 Margie Ann in Playsuit. JT. Blue floral. $225.00.

#78 Margie Ann in Playsuit. JT. Peach "teapot" print. $225.00.

Left to right.

#78 Margie Ann in Playsuit. JT. Pink floral. $225.00.

#78 Margie Ann in Playsuit. JT. Small white check. $225.00.

#78 Margie Ann in Playsuit. JT. Red with large white polka dots. $225.00.

This pink box has a label reading "#500 Margie Ann in School Dress" indicating that the name Margie Ann came into use probably as early as 1939 judging from the silver dot box. By 1940 it is listed as such in the 1940 factory pamphlet.

#500 Margie Ann in School Dress. An interesting doll, she wears a cotton print and matching bonnet on the MS/MB mold, indicating 1939. Although this same outfit is on both the crude mark and the Judy Ann mold with brown eyes, as Five Little Sisters, the same dress has also been found here on the MS/MB mold with blue eyes, indicating the transition/or simultaneous production of Five Little Sisters and Judy Ann/Margie Ann in School Dress on the later MS/MB mold. However, no box was with this doll for positive identification. $350.00.

Left. #500 Margie Ann in School Dress. MS. Apricot dress and matching bonnet. $300.00.

Below. #500 Margie Ann in School Dress. MS. Red dress and matching bonnet. Pink dots with large white dots has the label "#500 Margie Ann in School Dress." $300.00.

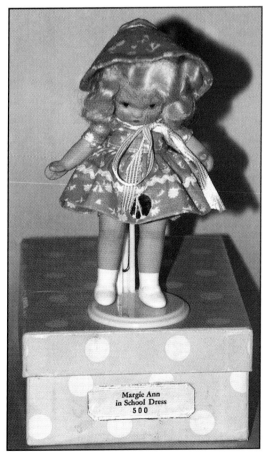

#500 Margie Ann in School Dress. MS. Pink print dress. $300.00.

The #500 Margie Ann in School Dress was changed to #79 in 1941.

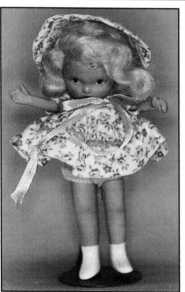  

#79 Margie Ann in School Dress. PT. Various cotton print dresses with matching hats and white boots. $275.00 each.

Left to right.

#79 Margie Ann in School Dress. PT. Various cotton print dresses with matching hats, with black slippers. $250.00.

#79 Margie Ann in School Dress. JT. Various cotton print dresses with matching hats, with black slippers $200.00.

#79 Margie Ann in School Dress. Long arms, dressed in short white flowered cotton sun dress with small lavender rickrack, matching sunbonnet. $200.00.

#79 Margie Ann in School Dress. JT. Various cotton print dresses with matching hats and black slippers $200.00 each.

#80 Family Series Judy Ann. Without factory records, we cannot pinpoint precisely when the Family Series Judy Ann started. However, a MIJ mold doll in a sunburst box labeled "Family Series Judy Ann" has been verified. The #80 Judy Ann character name was probably changed to #80 Margie Ann at the MS/MB period.

#80 Margie Ann. The basic Margie Ann is wigged, unlike the #80 Judy Ann character that has painted hair. She wears a short organdy dress with no trim, and short white lace-trimmed panties, white boots through the pudgy tummy period, and then black slipper shoes on the regular jointed-leg mold. The dresses came in white, the most common color, pink, yellow, peach, blue, light green, and lavender. One can see how these little dresses, although now extremely simplified, still remind us of the earlier Five Little Sisters.

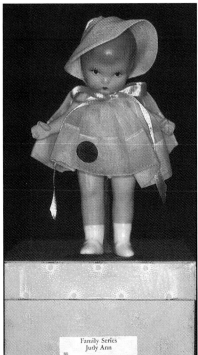

Below right. #80 Judy Ann on JA mold. Painted hair doll in a pink organdy dress and bonnet. $1,000.00.

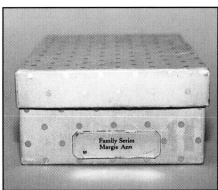

#80 Margie Ann. Silver-dot box probably from 1939 with label "Family Series #80 Margie Ann" now used at the MS/MB conversion from the #80 Judy Ann name character to the new #80 Margie Ann name

Above left. JA painted hair, blue organdy dress and bonnet, gold label, sunburst box reads "Family Series #80 Judy Ann." Although the picot-edge now is eliminated from the bonnet, this dress is similar to the two dolls illustrated in the Early Numbers section as #6 Little Girl. From this comparison, it is possible to recognize the progression from the early #6 Little Girl to #80 Judy Ann's costume. $1,000.00.

#80 Margie Ann. MS. Pink organdy dress, gathered at neck, in colored box/large dots of 1940. White panties with lace trim. White boots. $175.00.

Left to right. All #80 Margie Ann. MS. Yellow. $185.00. MS. Peach. $160.00. MS. Lavender. $325.00. JT. Blue. $125.00.

Left. #80 Margie Ann. MS. Light green. $400.00.

Right. #81 Judy Ann in Party Dress. JAPAN. This costume actually is unidentified, but is so similar to the pink dress on the Judy Ann mold wearing a similar Judy Ann in Party Dress, that we included it here for comparison to the dolls below. Doll wears a peach taffeta dress with wide lace creating the sleeves, rosebud trim at waist and white boots. What this interesting costume was called in this Japan-mold era is a not established, but the dress style certainly led right into the Judy Ann series, and the #81 Judy Ann in Party Dress pink taffeta dress. $900.00.

Left to right.

#81 Judy Ann in Party Dress. JA. White taffeta. Cap sleeves with lace trim. $500.00.

#81 Judy Ann in Party Dress. JA. Pink taffeta dress with lace-trimmed sleeves, rosebud trim at waist. $500.00.

#81 Judy Ann in Party Dress. MS/MB. Pink taffeta print dress with lace creating the sleeves. White boots. $400.00.

Right. #81 Margie Ann in Party Dress. JT. Pink floral print with aqua trim on skirt and bodice. Black slipper shoes. $250.00.

Below. #81 Judy Ann in Party Dress. MS/MB. Sold pink taffeta dress with fuzzy flowers at waist. "SBD" sticker. White boots. Pink sunburst box with the #81 Judy Ann in Party Dress label. $400.00.

#81 Margie Ann in Party Dress. JT. Similar to the Judy Ann in Party Dress taffeta dress, but with blue and red flower print, actual sleeves with lace trim. WT. #81 Party Dress White boots. $275.00.

A little trivia to note — the gold label on the sunburst box reads "Hat and Coat," yet, the 1940 factory pamphlet and later wrist tag for the #81 Margie Ann read the reverse, "Coat and Hat."

Right. #82 Judy Ann in Hat and Coat. Variation in yellow/white with two blue snaps. Storybook Sticker. $500.00.

Below. #82 Judy Ann in Hat and Coat. JA. Apricot/white knit coat with two white snaps and felt hat. Gold sunburst box with gold label "Family Series #82 Judy Ann in Hat and Coat." $500.00.

#82 Judy Ann in Hat and Coat. JA. Variation in aqua/white coat. Missing hat. Pink sunburst box with gold label "Family Series #82 Judy Ann in Hat and Coat." If complete, $500.00.

#82 Margie Ann in Hat and Coat. Pink box with silver dots with silver label "Family Series #82 Margie Ann in Hat and Coat."

#82 Margie Ann in Hat and Coat. MS. Pink felt coat with magenta pinked felt edge and matching hat. Underneath a pink organdy dress. White boots. $250.00.

Left. #82 Margie Ann in Hat and Coat. PT. White taffeta coat and hat with embroidery. Fuzzy flowers on hat brim and edged with a rickrack-looped trim. White organdy dress has white ribbon sews at neck. White boots. Wrist tag reads "Coat and Hat." $350.00.

Right. #82 Margie Ann in Hat and Coat. JT. Red felt coat and hat with red rickrack on edge of coat and hat. Black slipper shoes. $250.00.

#82 Margie Ann in Hat and Coat. Back view of the four coat and hat outfits. Notice the different style of the white taffeta hat with no center seam.

#83 Nurse and Baby. JA. The elusive #83 Nurse and Baby, boxed as a pair, is not listed in factory pamphlets. The Nurse wears a plain blue cotton ankle-length dress with attached apron. Her wig has been cut short, like a boy's wig and tucked under her pinned white cotton headpiece. She has a separate slip and short white panties. Most unusual, is that she has white slipper shoes (as does #70 Tennis). The 3½ inch star-hand baby that comes with the nurse has a short organdy dress with separate short half-slip, pinned diapers, and booties with pink ribbon ties. $2,000.00+.

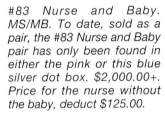

#83 Nurse and Baby. MS/MB. To date, sold as a pair, the #83 Nurse and Baby pair has only been found in either the pink or this blue silver dot box. $2,000.00+. Price for the nurse without the baby, deduct $125.00.

Mammy is brown painted bisque and has black painted high-top boots, usually with three white dots representing buttons. Baby is flesh-colored bisque and measures 3½ inches. They were sold as a pair in one box. The early baby has star hands, and later baby has closed fist and bent elbows. Babies wear a short white organdy dress, gathered at neck, separate slip, pinned diaper, and booties with ankle ribbons. Price for the Mammy without the baby, deduct $125.00. See #89 for Mammy sold separately without baby.

#83 Mammy and Baby. MS. Red/white cotton checked ankle-length dress. Separate apron, shawl, and bandana. Short panties, star-hand baby. $800.00.

#83 Mammy and Baby. PT. Variation, closed-fist baby. $600.00.

#83 Mammy and Baby. PT. Variation, Mammy with large checked print, baby dressed in unusual bonnet and dress not consistent with other examples. $600.00.

#83 Mammy and Baby. PT. Variation, Mammy with large diagonal print. $600.00.

#83 Mammy and Baby. PT. Variation, Mammy with small diagonal print, attached slip. $600.00.

#83 Mammy and Baby. JT. Variation, unusual polka dot fabric. $500.00.

Before company pamphlets, Twin Sisters had the early number 200. Starting with the first pamphlet in 1940, the Twin Sisters pair was renumbered under the Family Series as #84. They were sold as a pair, in same box.

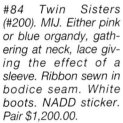

#84 Twin Sisters (#200). MIJ. Either pink or blue organdy, gathering at neck, lace giving the effect of a sleeve. Ribbon sewn in bodice seam. White boots. NADD sticker. Pair $1,200.00.

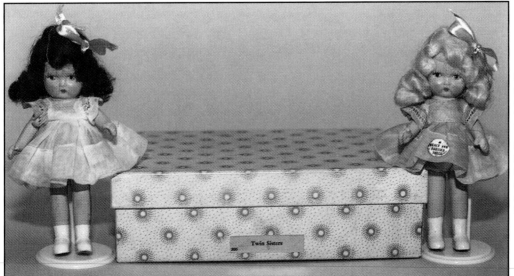

#84 Twin Sisters (#200). MIJ 1148. Rare #200 sunburst box. Top knot under wigs. White boots. Now with gathered cap sleeves, ribbon eliminated on bodice. White boots. Silver pin closures. NADD sticker. Pair $1,200.00.

#84 Twin Sisters (#200). One-piece teddy underwear for MIJ mold.

#84 Twin Sisters (#200). JA. Typical white organdy dresses with pink or blue ribbons, thought probably to be Twin Sisters. Pair $500.00.

Above. #84 Twin Sisters (#200). MS. pink and blue shadow print. Box label "Family Series Twin Sisters #84." Pair $450.00.

Left. #84 Twin Sisters (#200). PT. Pink and blue taffeta, white boots. Pair $400.00.

#84 Twin Sisters (#200). Japan. Variation with net sleeves. $500.00 each.

The #84 Ring Bearer character uses a small 4½ inch Storybook Doll USA, mold, some with the #10 stamped on back; the same mold was used for #85 Flower Girl, but this one has a short boy wig.

Price for only one of the pair from #85 Brother and Sister, deduct $50.00 or more, depending on rarity of mold.

Above left. #84 Ring Bearer. Two-piece bright blue taffeta shirt trimmed with lace and matching blue trousers. Brass snap fastener. Floral ribbon bow at neck. $200.00.

Above right. #84 Ring Bearer. Variation in very light blue, almost cream, taffeta. $150.00. (Same outfit also found on painted-eye plastic Ring Bearer.)

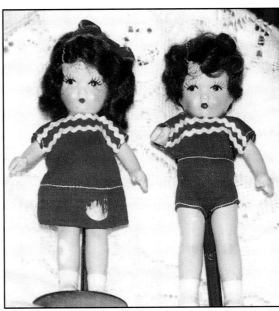

#85 Brother and Sister. MIJ. Red cotton cord fabric, white rickrack. Pair $1,000.00.

#85 Brother and Sister. America. Yellow cotton cord fabric, blue rickrack. Pair $1,100.00.

#85 Brother and Sister. JA. Pink cotton cord fabric, white rickrack. Pair $800.00.

#85 Brother and Sister. MS/MB. Blue cotton cord fabric, pink rickrack. Pair $600.00. Also JA. Pair $800.00.

#85 Brother and Sister. MS/MB. Variation in white, with red/blue rickrack. Pair $650.00.

#85 Brother and Sister. MS/MB. Variation in pink, with blue rickrack. $650.00. Also JA. Pair $800.00.

#85 Brother and Sister. MS. Red dotted swiss, with original box and SB stickers. Pair $600.00.

#85 Brother and Sister. MS. Polished cotton with star trim. Pair $450.00.

The #85 Flower Girl doll is on a 4½ inch mold with white boots, gold safety pin closure, and short plain panties. The Flower Girl was listed in the 1940 pamphlet as #87A. By 1941, the number had changed to #89. The early Flower Girl is referred to as Dee Dee Ann Flower Girl on the box, but only Flower Girl in the pamphlets. By 1943 Flower Girl had been deleted from the list and did not appear again until late 1947 – 1948, just before the introduction of plastic to the company, and was listed as #85 Flower Girl.

Above left. Flower Girl. MS. Dee Dee Ann Flower Girl #87A. Pink short sheer floral print dress. Fuzzy flower at waist. Blue hair ribbon. $185.00,

Above right. #85 Flower Girl. JT. Long white taffeta underskirt with net/lace overskirt. Lace bonnet with floral ribbon sash. Variation in pink and beige. $155.00. (This same long dress also appears on the transitional painted-eye plastic mold with gold snap.)

Left. #89 Flower Girl. JT. Short pink taffeta dress, net/lace skirt, fuzzy flower at waist, blue hair ribbon, wrist tag #89, white box with label "Dee Dee Ann Flower Girl #89." $275.00. An earlier version is in short blue taffeta dress with blue silver dot box, label reading "Dee Dee Ann Flower Girl #87A." $300.00.

#86 Bride, jointed leg. America. Separate net underskirt, over shorter taffeta gown, silver slippers. $500.00.

#86 Bride, jointed leg. JA. Variation, separate slip. $350.00.

#86 Bride, jointed leg. JA. Lace trimmed organdy skirt with attached lace, bodice, separate slip, silver slippers. (For JA Groom see #88) $350.00.

#86 Bride, jointed leg. MS. Variation, delicate tulle skirt, wide lace bottom. No ribbon trim on skirt, attached slip. $175.00.

#86 Bride, jointed leg. PT. Flocked dots, separate slip. Silver slippers. $150.00.

#86 Bride, jointed leg. JT. Large floral design satin gown. $125.00. Also frozen leg. $70.00.

Left. #86 Bride, jointed leg. MS. Satin underskirt, flocked daisy print gown, attached satin underskirt, separate slip, silver slippers. $175.00. Also PT. $150.00.

Right. #86 Bride, jointed leg. JT. variation in ecru. $125.00.

#86 Bride, jointed leg. JT. Two-tier dress. $125.00.

#86 Bride, frozen leg. Flocked sunburst design taffeta gown. $55.00.

#86 Bride, frozen leg. Flocked organdy floral gown. $55.00.

#86 Bride, frozen leg. Organdy gown, taffeta ruche trim. $50.00.

#86 Bride, frozen leg. Wide lace trim. $50.00.

#86 Bride, frozen leg. Variation with lily spray and Dutch-style hat. $50.00.

#86 Bride, frozen leg. Plastic arms. $45.00.

#86 Bride, frozen leg. Plastic arms. $45.00.

#285 Bride, Month Mold Size, frozen leg, 6½ inch. Satin bodice, flocked organdy over taffeta gown. This unusual larger size is not listed in any pamphlet as a larger mold. (Shown here with socket-head groom to illustrate size.) $60.00.

Left. #87 Bridesmaid, jointed leg. America. Attached fragile net at sleeves and bottom of skirt. Illustration is missing net headpiece. Silver slippers. $1,000.00.

Right. #87 Bridesmaid, jointed leg. JA. Yellow taffeta dress with wide pink net sewn at bottom and at sleeves. Two layers of circular net open-crown headpiece. Ribbon and flowers at bodice, separate slip, silver slippers. $450.00.

Left. #87 Bridesmaid, jointed leg. JA. Variation in lime green, pink net. $450.00.

Right. #87 Bridesmaid, jointed leg. JA. Variation in lavender, pink net. Illustration has hat missing. If complete, $450.00.

#87 Bridesmaid, jointed leg. JA. Variation in peach, pink net, but with lace instead of net on sleeves. $450.00.

#87 Bridesmaid, jointed leg. JA. Green organdy, two rows of ribbon trim, separate slips. A popular bridesmaid fashion that continued through the MS mold with six pastel colors making up the charming group of bridesmaids. $300.00.

#87 Bridesmaid, jointed leg. JA. Variation in lavender. $300.00.

#87 Bridesmaid, jointed leg. JA. Variation in pink. $300.00.

#87 Bridesmaid, jointed leg. MS. Variation in peach. $250.00.

#87 Bridesmaid, jointed leg. MS. Variation in blue. $250.00.

#87 Bridesmaid, jointed leg. MS. Variation in yellow. $250.00.

#87 Bridesmaid, jointed leg. MS. Lavender organdy flowered print with same fabric on circular hat with net, separate slip, silver slippers. $250.00.

#87 Bridesmaid, jointed leg. MS. Variation in pink. $250.00.

#87 Bridesmaid, jointed leg. PT. Variation in blue. $150.00.

#87 Bridesmaid, jointed leg. Close-up of Flower and Lace organdy print.

#87 Bridesmaid, jointed leg. PT. Ribbon print organdy in lavender, lace across bodice, separate slip, and silver slippers. $150.00.

#87 Bridesmaid, jointed leg. PT. Six pastel colors of ribbon print, peach, blue, pink, lavender, and yellow; some with lace across bodice and sliver slippers. $150.00.

#87 Bridesmaid, jointed leg. Close-up of ribbon print.

#87 Bridesmaid, jointed leg. PT. Peach large rose organdy print. $150.00.

#87 Bridesmaid, jointed leg. PT. Variation in pink. $150.00.

#87 Bridesmaid, jointed leg. JT. Variation in blue, pink underskirt and ribbon. $125.00.

#87 Bridesmaid, jointed leg. JT. Variation in blue and yellow. $125.00.

#87 Bridesmaid, jointed leg. JT. Variation in blue and pink. $125.00.

#87 Bridesmaid, jointed leg. JT. Small floral pink organdy print. Attached pink slip. $125.00.

#87 Bridesmaid, jointed leg. JT. Variation in color. $125.00.

#87 Bridesmaid, jointed leg. JT. Blue and red floral organdy print with bright pink taffeta bodice and attached slip. $100.00.

#87 Bridesmaid, jointed leg. JT. Variation with cream bodice, underskirt, and ribbon. $100.00.

#87 Bridesmaid, jointed leg. JT. Peach satin gown, attached white slip and peach pantalets. $75.00.

#87 Bridesmaid, jointed leg. Variation in pale green. $75.00.

#87 Bridesmaid, jointed leg. JT. One row of ribbon trim. Organdy overskirt, taffeta underskirt. Offered in various colors. $65.00. Transition to frozen-leg. $55.00.

#87 Bridesmaid, frozen leg. Taffeta print underskirt. Offered in various colors of organdy overskirt, one-row ribbon trim. $55.00.

#87 Bridesmaid, frozen leg. $55.00.

#87 Bridesmaid, frozen leg. $55.00.

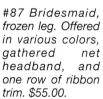

#87 Bridesmaid, frozen leg. Offered in various colors, gathered net headband, and one row of ribbon trim. $55.00.

#87 Bridesmaid, frozen leg. $55.00.

#87 Bridesmaid, frozen leg. $45.00.

#87 Bridesmaid, frozen leg. Various colors. $45.00.

#87 Bridesmaid, frozen leg. Satin. 450.00.

#87 Bridesmaid, frozen leg. Also in blue. $45.00.

Judy Ann mold Bride, Groom, and Bridesmaids.

#87 Flower Girl
Please see #85 Flower Girl

Only two versions of the bisque #88 Groom were issued. The smaller five inch groom, starting with the Judy Ann mold, was available through the pudgy tummy era. Then, the 6¼ inch month size socket head, jointed leg mold groom replaced the smaller version. There was not a change again until the painted-eye plastic groom and then the sleep-eye groom were introduced (not pictured).

   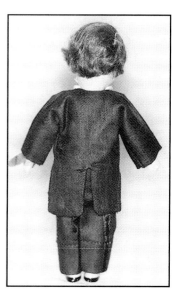

Left to right.

#88 Groom. JA. Five inch small-size groom. Black polished cotton tuxedo. Black ribbon down both sides of trousers. White corded cotton shirt, unhemmed sleeve edges. White ribbon at neck. $350.00. Also MS/MB $250.00, MS $225.00, and PT mold $200.00. #88 Groom. Back view of tuxedo with tails. #88 Groom. JT. 6¼" Groom, socket head. $150.00. #88 Groom. Back view of tuxedo with tails.

#89 Dee Dee Ann Flower Girl
Please see #85 Flower Girl

In the 1940 pamphlet both #83 Mammy and Baby and #89 Mammy without the baby were offered. Please see #83 for Mammy and Baby sold together as a pair.

Above left. #89 Mammy. JA. Small red/white gingham dress. Gold label #89 Mammy in sunburst box. $500.00.

Above right. #89 Mammy. M/S MB. Red box, silver dots, now with silver label #89 Mammy. $400.00.

#89 Mammy. JA. Variation in larger check. High-top black boots with three white dots, ankle-length small red/white gingham dress. Separate cotton apron, white shawl and bandana. Separate slip and short panties. $500.00.

FAMILY SERIES

STYLE No.

80	Margie Ann
81	Margie Ann in Party Dress
82	Margie Ann in Coat and Hat
83	Mammy and Baby
84	Twin Sisters
85	Brother & Sister
86	Bride
87	Bridesmaid
87A	Flower Girl
88	Bridegroom
89	Mammy
500	Margie Ann in School Dress
510	Margie Ann in Play Suit
2000	Audrey Ann

#2000 Audrey Ann. Audrey Ann has a blue organdy dress with a lace-edged square collar sewn across back shoulders of dress and a satin rosebud attached to collar. A wide pink ribbon is at her waist. Gold safety pin closure. Inside of box measures 6 inches, and the doll fits snuggly inside.

#2000 Audrey Ann is listed only in the 1940 pamphlet under the Family Series. The factory quickly discontinued this elusive larger jointed-leg doll for reasons unknown. Not enough examples are known to price.

Left. #2000 Audrey Ann. Variation in pale lavender organdy. Also found in pink and probably also came in other pastel colors as well.

Right. #2000 Audrey Ann. Comparison: Audrey Ann (right) is a taller, chunkier toddler-type girl than the regular storybook doll in the middle and the Japan mold to the left. Audrey Ann has molded socks, white boots, and measures approximately 5¾ inches. Doll is marked with a small number 12 placed below the regular "Storybook Doll USA" factory marking.

• • Seasons Series • • •
#90 – #93

#90 Spring, jointed leg. JA. Four-layer net skirt and sleeves. $1,000.00 +.

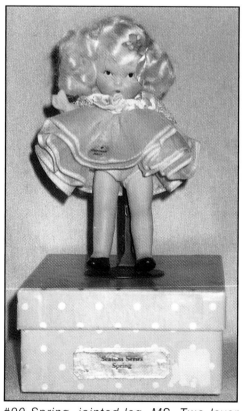

#90 Spring, jointed leg. MS. Two-layer organdy skirt. $600.00+.

#90 Spring, jointed leg. MS. Lime green and pink. $350.00.

#90 Spring, jointed leg. PT. $200.00.

#90 Spring, jointed leg. JT. $80.00.

#90 Spring, frozen leg. $45.00.

#90 Spring, frozen leg. $45.00.

#90 Spring, frozen leg. Silk underskirt. $45.00.

#90 Spring, frozen leg. Also in green/pink. $45.00.

#90 Spring, frozen leg. $45.00.

#90 Spring, frozen leg. $45.00.

#90 Spring, frozen leg. NA mold. Florist ribbon. $40.00.

#91 Summer, jointed leg. JA. Two-tier blue organdy dress $1,000.00+.

#91 Summer, jointed leg. Side view.

#91 Summer, jointed leg. MS/MB. $500.00.

#91 Summer, jointed leg. MS. Either wide or narrow daisy trim. $350.00.

#91 Summer, jointed leg. S. $350.00. PT in blue. $200.00.

#91 Summer, jointed leg. PT. Fan print. $200.00.

#91 Summer, jointed leg. PT. $200.00.

#91 Summer, jointed leg. JT. $80.00.

#91 Summer, jointed leg. JT. $80.00. Also on transition frozen leg. $45.00.

#91 Summer, frozen leg. Girl on a Swing print. $45.00.

#91 Summer, frozen leg. Ribbon print. $45.00.

#91 Summer, frozen leg. Blue organdy floral print. $45.00.

#91 Summer, frozen leg. Nylon floral. $45.00.

#91 Summer, frozen leg. $45.00.

#91 Summer, frozen leg. $45.00.

#91 Summer, frozen leg. $45.00.

#91 Summer, frozen leg. In pink or blue. $45.00.

#91 Summer, frozen leg. Pink checked. $45.00.

#91 Summer, frozen leg. Green/white plaid. $45.00.

#91 Summer, frozen leg. Also in blue. Start use of florist ribbon. $40.00.

#91 Summer, frozen leg. Also in pink. $40.00.

#91 Summer, frozen leg. $40.00.

#91 Summer, frozen leg. $40.00.

#91 Summer, frozen leg. $40.00.

#91 Summer, frozen leg. $40.00.

Left. #92 Autumn, jointed leg. JA. Calf-length orange taffeta dress. Fruit at waist. Variation with a red/yellow ribbon trim. $800.00. MS/MB variation in tan taffeta dress. $1,000.00.

Below. #92 Autumn, jointed leg. PT. Taffeta two-tier dress, felt leaves. Separate slip, pantalets, also found with short panties, $250.00. JT in chiffon $100.00. Frozen leg mold. $55.00.

#92 Autumn, jointed leg. MS. Fruit at waist. Long organdy skirt, with pink cotton floral print underskirt. $450.00.

#92 Autumn, jointed leg. $65.00.

#92 Autumn, frozen leg. $45.00.

#92 Autumn, frozen leg. $45.00.

#92 Autumn, frozen leg. $45.00.

#92 Autumn, frozen leg. $45.00.

#92 Autumn, frozen leg. $45.00.

#92 Autumn, frozen leg. Floral ribbon. $40.00.

#92 Autumn, frozen leg. Floral ribbon. $40.00.

#92 Autumn, frozen leg. Floral ribbon. $40.00.

#92 Autumn, frozen leg. NA mold. Floral ribbon, unusual trim. $45.00.

Left to right.

#93 Winter, jointed leg. MS/MB. Blue variation, red organdy dress. $800.00.

#93 Winter, jointed leg. JA. White organdy dress over white knit legging, matching hat and jacket. White boots. $1.500.00 +.

#93 Winter, jointed leg. JA. Red variation, unusual two snaps on jacket; also found with white pompon. $1.500.00+.

Left. #93 Winter, jointed leg. MS/MB. Red variation, white organdy dress. $800.00.

Right. #93 Winter, jointed leg. MS. Red velvet with attached white satin underskirt, velvet bonnet lined in satin. $350.00.

#93 Winter, jointed leg. MS. Velvet and taffeta dress. $350.00.

#93 Winter, jointed leg. MS. Peach velvet coat dress, matching silk lined velvet bonnet. (May not be correct. Dress is too long for the doll, yet it does not fit a month-size doll. March wears similar dress, but has a stiff black hat with feathers.) Not enough examples to price.

#93 Winter, jointed leg. PT. Flocked taffeta felt jacket and hat. Red taffeta underskirt. $200.00.

#93 Winter, jointed leg. PT. Red velvet gown, felt hat. $200.00.

#93 Winter, jointed leg. JT. Various trims. $130.00.

#93 Winter, jointed leg. JT. Polka dot overskirt. Now jacket eliminated. $100.00.

#93 Winter, frozen leg. White taffeta dress, also no jacket. $45.00.

#93 Winter, frozen leg. Red taffeta, red felt jacket once again. $45.00.

#93 Winter, frozen leg. Variation striped dress, $45.00.

#93 Winter, frozen leg. Taffeta with ribbon trim on skirt. $45.00.

#93 Winter, frozen leg. Variation iridescent silk. $45.00.

#93 Winter, frozen leg. Rayon faille skirt, cotton bodice. $45.00.

#93 Winter, frozen leg. $45.00.

#93 Winter, frozen leg. Net overskirt, taffeta bodice. Start of florist ribbon. $40.00.

#93 Winter, frozen leg. $40.00.

#93 Winter, frozen leg. $40.00.

#93 Winter, frozen leg. Variation light green. $40.00.

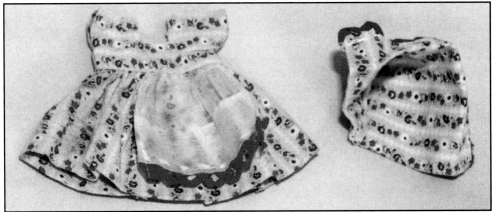

Left. #109 Little Betty Blue, Wore Her Holiday Shoe, jointed leg. MS. $150.00. PT. $135.00.

Above. #109 Little Betty Blue, Wore Her Holiday Shoe, jointed leg. Unusual yellow dress and hat. $155.00.

Left to right.

#109 Little Betty Blue, Wore Her Holiday Shoe, jointed leg. PT. $135.00.

#109 Little Betty Blue, Wore Her Holiday Shoe, jointed leg. PT. $135.00.

#109 Little Betty Blue, Wore Her Holiday Shoe, jointed leg. PT. $135.00. JT. $125.00.

Left to right.

#109 Little Betty Blue, Wore Her Holiday Shoe, jointed leg. PT. $135.00. JT. $125.00.

#109 Little Betty Blue, Wore Her Holiday Shoe, jointed leg. JT. $125.00.

#109 Little Betty Blue, Wore Her Holiday Shoe, frozen leg. $55.00.

#109 Little Betty Blue, Wore Her Holiday Shoe, frozen leg. $55.00 each.

Left. #109 Little Betty Blue, Wore Her Holiday Shoe, frozen leg. Plastic arms, florist ribbon. $50.00.

Right. #109 Little Betty Blue, Wore Her Holiday Shoe, frozen leg. Plastic arms, florist ribbon, matching pantalets. $50.00.

#109 Little Betty Blue, Wore Her Holiday Shoe, frozen leg. Plastic arms, florist ribbon, matching pantalets. $50.00.

#110 Little Miss, Sweet Miss, Blessings Light on You, jointed leg. PT. Picot-edged dress, white boots, short underpants. $140.00.

#110 Little Miss, Sweet Miss, Blessings Light on You, jointed leg. PT. Taffeta dress, rickrack trim. $135.00.

#110 Little Miss, Sweet Miss, Blessings Light on You, jointed leg. PT. Variation with cord trim. $135.00. Also on frozen leg. $115.00.

#110 Little Miss, Sweet Miss, Blessings Light on You, frozen leg. $55.00.

#110 Little Miss, Sweet Miss, Blessings Light on You, frozen leg. $55.00 each.

#110 Little Miss, Sweet Miss, Blessings Light on You. Teen JT. Plastic arms, gold snap closure, matching taffeta pantalets. $50.00.

#110 Little Miss, Sweet Miss, Blessings Light on You, frozen leg. Start of florist ribbon. $40.00.

Left to right.

#111 Here I Am Little Joan, jointed leg. PT. Short pink taffeta with print apron. $135.00.

#111 Here I Am Little Joan, jointed leg. PT. Variation. $135.00.

Here I Am Little Joan, jointed leg. JT. Variation. $130.00.

Left to right.

#111 Here I Am Little Joan, frozen leg. $55.00.

#111 Here I Am Little Joan, frozen leg. Variation iridescent silk. $55.00.

#111 Here I Am Little Joan, frozen leg. Cat print dress. $55.00.

#111 Here I Am Little Joan, frozen leg. Striped dress. $55.00.

#111 Here I Am Little Joan, frozen leg. $55.00.

#111 Here I Am Little Joan, frozen leg. $55.00.

Left. #111 Here I Am Little Joan, frozen leg. Florist ribbon. $40.00.

Right. #111 Here I Am Little Joan, frozen leg. NA mold mark. Plastic arms, florist ribbon. $40.00.

The #112 Dillar – A Dollar a Ten O'Clock Scholar character came as a boy on both the jointed leg and frozen leg molds. The girl came only on a frozen leg mold. The box does not designate whether it is a girl or a boy. Although they have coordinating outfits, both the boy and girl were in individual boxes, not as a pair.

#112 Dillar – A Dollar a Ten o'Clock Scholar, jointed leg, boy. MS. Cotton trousers, white shirt, yellow ribbon at neck, blue felt jacket. SD sticker. $225.00.

#112 Dillar – A Dollar a Ten o'Clock Scholar, jointed leg, boy. MS. Cotton trousers, Wide-striped shirt, white felt collar, red ribbon at neck. $160.00.

121

Left to right.

#112 Dillar – A Dollar a Ten o'Clock Scholar, jointed leg, boy. PT. Wide-width striped shirt. $150.00.

#112 Dillar – A Dollar a Ten o'Clock Scholar, jointed leg, boy. PT. Medium width stripes on shirt. $150.00.

#112 Dillar – A Dollar a Ten o'Clock Scholar, jointed leg, boy. JT. Medium width striped on shirt. $135.00.

Left to right.

#112 Dillar – A Dollar a Ten o'Clock Scholar, jointed leg, boy. JT. Narrow width stripes on shirt. $135.00.

#112 Dillar – A Dollar a Ten o'Clock Scholar, jointed leg, boy. PT. Cotton checked shirt, cotton trousers. $150.00. Also JT. $135.00.

#112 Dillar – A Dollar a Ten o'Clock Scholar, jointed leg, boy. JT. Polka dot shirt, red felt collar. $135.00.

#112 Dillar – A Dollar a Ten o'Clock Scholar, frozen leg, boy and girl. Green taffeta trousers and skirt, Boy has vertical pattern shirt. $65.00. Girl. $55.00.

#112 Dillar – A Dollar a Ten o'Clock Scholar, frozen leg, boy and girl. Variation in blue taffeta. Boy. $75.00. Girl. $65.00.

#112 Dillar – A Dollar a Ten o'Clock Scholar, frozen leg, boy and girl. Boy in green taffeta trousers, vertical pattern shirt. $65.00. Girl in green print skirt. $65.00.

#112 Dillar – A Dollar a Ten o'Clock Scholar, frozen leg, boy. Tan cotton trousers. Also comes with green print shirt. $60.00.

#112 Dillar – A Dollar a Ten o'Clock Scholar, frozen leg, boy. Red taffeta pants. $60.00.

#112 Dillar – A Dollar a Ten o'Clock Scholar, frozen leg, girls. Red or blue print, felt jacket. $50.00.

#112 Dillar – A Dollar a Ten o'Clock Scholar, frozen leg, girl. $50.00.

#112 Dillar – A Dollar a Ten o'Clock Scholar, frozen leg, girl. $50.00.

Left. #112 Dillar – A Dollar a Ten o'Clock Scholar, girl. Teen JT. Plastic arms, gold snap closure, matching pantalets. $45.00.

Right. #113 Roses Are Red Violets Are Blue (#123), jointed leg. MS. Organdy dress, cotton apron, SD sticker. $200.00. Also PT. $150.00.

123

Left to right.

#113 Roses Are Red Violets Are Blue (#123), jointed leg. PT. $135.00.

#113 Roses Are Red Violets Are Blue (#123), jointed leg. PT. $135.00.

#113 Roses Are Red Violets Are Blue (#123), jointed leg. JT. Variation in yellow. $125.00.

#113 Roses Are Red Violets Are Blue (#123), jointed leg. JT. $125.00. PT. $135.00.

#113 Roses Are Red Violets Are Blue (#123), jointed leg. JT. Taffeta print. $125.00.

#113 Roses Are Red Violets Are Blue (#123), frozen leg. Red taffeta dress, felt hat. $55.00.

#113 Roses Are Red Violets Are Blue (#123), frozen leg. Cotton skirt, taffeta bodice. $60.00.

#113 Roses Are Red Violets Are Blue (#123), frozen leg. Cotton shadow print dress. $55.00.

Left to right.

#113 Roses Are Red Violets Are Blue (#123), frozen leg. Variation in pink, no hat. $55.00.

#113 Roses Are Red Violets Are Blue (#123), frozen leg. Taffeta skirt, organdy apron, and bodice. $55.00.

#113 Roses Are Red Violets Are Blue (#123), frozen leg. Variation of apron print. $55.00.

Left. #113 Roses Are Red Violets Are Blue (#123), frozen leg. Variation pink taffeta dress. $55.00.

Right. #113 Roses Are Red Violets Are Blue (#123), frozen leg. Long organdy dress with blue felt bonnet, florist ribbon. $45.00.

The early Over the Hills dresses with the felt jackets are often confused with the #120 To Market character. However, after taking into consideration that errors do occur along with way with the factory, the storekeeper, the original owner, and after viewing several of these dolls with their boxes, we are listing the *short* felt jacket as #120 To Market and the *long* jacket as #114 Over the Hills. Similar striped and polka dot dresses with jackets are also found on East Side West Side, but these characters have the black boots with no white dots.

#114 Over the Hills, jointed leg. Long gray felt jacket and hat. Red ribbon trim runs up each opening side of jacket and ends with bow at the neck. $150.00.

#114 Over the Hills, jointed leg. MS. Red felt long jacket and hat. Red polka dot dress. $150.00.

#114 Over the Hills, jointed leg. MS. White organdy bodice with attached shirring waistband. $150.00.

#114 Over the Hills, jointed leg. PT. Variation, different print skirt. $135.00.

#114 Over the Hills, jointed leg. PT. Variation, different print skirt. $135.00.

Left to right.

#114 Over the Hills, jointed leg. PT. Variation with multicolored band at waist. $135.00.

#114 Over the Hills, jointed leg. PT. Long arms. $125.00.

#114 Over the Hills, jointed leg. JT. $125.00.

Left to right.

#114 Over the Hills, jointed leg. JT. $125.00.

#114 Over the Hills, jointed leg. JT. $125.00.

#114 Over the Hills, frozen leg. $55.00.

#114 Over the Hills, frozen leg. All frozen leg dolls are $55.00.

#114 Over the Hills, frozen leg. All with florist ribbon. $45.00 each.

Left. #115 Little Boy Blue Come Blow Your Horn (#7 and #142), jointed leg. MIJ. #7 from Salesman Sample Box. Wool wig. Not enough examples to price.

Below. #115 Little Boy Blue Come Blow Your Horn (#7 and #142), jointed leg. Japan. Early #7 starburst box. Corded cotton trousers, SD sticker, checked shirt. $1,000.00.

#115 Little Boy Blue Come Blow Your Horn (#7 and #142), jointed leg. MIJ. Wool wig, early #7, starburst box, NADD sticker. Corded cotton trousers, matching collar attached to striped shirt. Also with later mohair wig. $1,000.00.

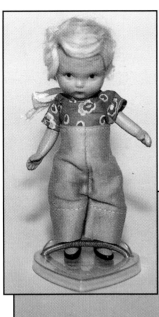

Left. #115 Little Boy Blue Come Blow Your Horn (#7 and #142), jointed leg. MS/MB. Polished cotton trousers. Red/blue print shirt. $450.00. JA. $550.00.

Below. #115 Little Boy Blue Come Blow Your Horn (#7 and #142), jointed leg. JA. Blue polished cotton trousers and short-sleeved multicolored leaf-shaped design shirt. White ribbon tie at neck. Sunburst box with #7 gold label. $800.00.

Above left. #115 Little Boy Blue Come Blow Your Horn (#7 and #142), jointed leg. MS/MB. SD sticker, polished cotton, organdy ruffled trim shirt. $450.00.

Above right. #115 Little Boy Blue Come Blow Your Horn (#7 and #142), jointed leg. MS. Satin with circle-crochet trim, SD sticker. $250.00.

Left to right.

#115 Little Boy Blue Come Blow Your Horn (#7 and #142), jointed leg. MS. Satin, variation with white spider web lace trim $200.00.

Second photo above. #115 Little Boy Blue Come Blow Your Horn (#7 and #142), jointed leg. PT. Variation, taffeta, blue spider web lace. $175.00.

#115 Little Boy Blue Come Blow Your Horn (#7 and #142), frozen leg. Cream taffeta trousers, also light blue trousers. Pink shirt, blue felt jacket. $60.00.

#115 Little Boy Blue Come Blow Your Horn (#7 and #142), frozen leg. Variation with taffeta floral print trousers, blue ribbon tie. $60.00.

129

#115 Little Boy Blue Come Blow Your Horn (#7 and #142), frozen leg. Variation, light blue felt jacket. Pink ribbon tie. $75.00.

#115 Lucy Locket (#124 and #134), jointed leg. MS. Organdy with locket on ribbon around doll's neck. Wide ribbon around waist. $350.00.

#115 Lucy Locket (#124 and #134), jointed leg. MS. Taffeta, with locket on ribbon around doll's neck. $275.00. PT. $260.00.

#115 Lucy Locket (#124 and #134), frozen leg. Plastic arms. $45.00.

#115 Lucy Locket (#124 and #134), frozen leg. $55.00 each.

#115 Lucy Locket (#124 and #134), frozen leg. Plastic arms. $45.00.

Two photos above. #115 Lucy Locket (#124 and #134), frozen leg. $55.00.

#8 Little Red Riding Hood Said to the Wolf

#116 Little Red Riding Hood Went through the Woods

Right. #116 Little Red Riding Hood (#8), jointed leg. MIJ. Black painted hair. Satin cape, NADD sticker, attached teddy underwear. Red painted shoes. $1,500.00.

Below. #116 Little Red Riding Hood (#8), jointed leg. JA. Hemstiching on the Judy Ann mold hoods are close to the edge of the hood making very narrow ruffle, hemstitching also on cape. White boots, Sunburst box with #8 gold label. $1,200.00.

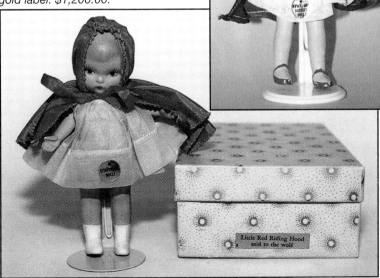

#116 Little Red Riding Hood (#8), jointed leg. MS/MB. Satin cape. $400.00.

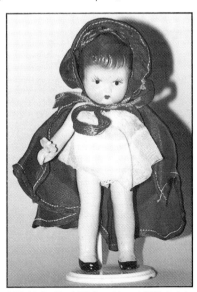

#116 Little Red Riding Hood (#8), jointed leg. MIJ. Red painted hair. Satin cape, hole in hand to hold flower. $1,000.00.

#116 Little Red Riding Hood (#8), jointed leg. MIJ. #8 in Salesman Sample box. NADD sticker, wool wig, red decorative stitching on dress. Hemstitching on edge of satin cape and hood. Not enough examples to price.

#116 Little Red Riding Hood (#8), jointed leg. JT. Felt cape. $125.00. Also frozen leg. $55.00.

#116 Little Red Riding Hood (#8), jointed leg. Left to right: MS/MB. $250.00. MS. $150.00. JT. Taffeta cape. $125.00.

#116 Little Red Riding Hood (#8), frozen leg. Mid-calf organdy dress. Left to right: taffeta, plastic, and felt capes. $55.00.

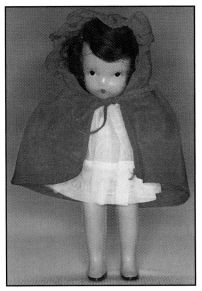

#116 Little Red Riding Hood (#8), frozen leg. $55.00.

#116 Little Red Riding Hood (#8), frozen leg. Variation in window-pane organdy dress. $55.00.

#116 Little Red Riding Hood (#8), frozen leg. $55.00.

#116 Little Red Riding Hood (#8), frozen leg. $55.00.

#116 Little Red Riding Hood (#8), frozen leg. Plastic arms. $45.00.

#116 Little Red Riding Hood (#8), frozen leg. Plastic arms, florist ribbon, also found on Teen JT mold. Gold snap enclosures. $45.00.

School Days only came as a girl on jointed leg molds. However, during the frozen-leg period, a boy School Days was also available. The box does not designate whether it is a girl or boy. They were not sold as pairs.

#117 School Days, Dear Old Golden Rule Days (#9), jointed leg, girl. MS/MB. Attached apron. White ribbons pull mohair wig to each side. Two versions of small red/white check. $350.00.

Left to right.

#117 School Days, Dear Old Golden Rule Days (#9), jointed leg, girl. MIJ. #9 in Salesman Sample box, wool wig. White collar with red picot edge. Not enough examples to price.

#117 School Days, Dear Old Golden Rule Days (#9), jointed leg, girl. Japan. White corded collar. NAAD sticker. $1,200.00.

#117 School Days, Dear Old Golden Rule Days (#9), jointed leg, girl. MS/MB. $350. MS. $250.00. JA. $400.00. Blue/white checked dress. Dark blue ribbons pull mohair wig to each side.

#117 School Days, Dear Old Golden Rule Days (#9), jointed leg, girl. MS. Attached eyelet-trimmed apron. Red/white checked dress, white boots. $250.00.

Left to right.

#117 School Days, Dear Old Golden Rule Days (#9), jointed leg, girl. MS. $250.00. JT. White boots. $175.00.

#117 School Days, Dear Old Golden Rule Days (#9), jointed leg, girl. MS. Blue/white with attached apron. $250.00.

#117 School Days, Dear Old Golden Rule Days (#9), jointed leg, girl. PT. $135.00.

#117 School Days, Dear Old Golden Rule Days (#9), jointed leg, girl. PT or JT. Various combinations of red check and pink solid. $125.00.

Left to right.

#117 School Days, Dear Old Golden Rule Days (#9), jointed leg, girl. JT. $125.00.

#117 School Days, Dear Old Golden Rule Days (#9), frozen leg, girl. Red dress. Blue print apron and bodice, also in all blue. $55.00.

#117 School Days, Dear Old Golden Rule Days (#9), frozen leg, girl. Variation in bodice and apron. $55.00.

Left to right.

#117 School Days, Dear Old Golden Rule Days (#9), frozen leg, girl. Blue checked dress. $55.00.

#117 School Days, Dear Old Golden Rule Days (#9), frozen leg, girl. Red polka dot, white apron. $55.00.

#117 School Days, Dear Old Golden Rule Days (#9), frozen leg, girl. Red/white checked apron. $55.00.

Left to right. #117 School Days, Dear Old Golden Rule Days (#9), frozen leg, girl. $55.00 each.

Left to right. #117 School Days, Dear Old Golden Rule Days (#9), frozen leg, girl. $55.00.

#117 School Days, Dear Old Golden Rule Days (#9), girl. Teen JT. Plastic arms, gold snap closure, florist ribbon. $45.00.

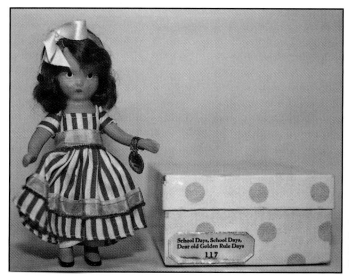

#117 School Days, Dear Old Golden Rule Days (#9), frozen leg, girl. Florist ribbon. $45.00.

Left to right.

#117 School Days, Dear Old Golden Rule Days (#9), frozen leg, boy. Red/white checked shirt. $75.00.

#117 School Days, Dear Old Golden Rule Days (#9), frozen leg, boy. Taffeta trousers, polka dot shirt. $75.00.

#118 Little Miss Muffet Sat on a Tuffet (#10), jointed leg. MIJ. Long dress, lace sleeves, ribbon waistband on lace apron. Black painted hair. Black shoes with strap. NADD sticker. $1,500.00.

Left. #118 Little Miss Muffet Sat on a Tuffet (#10), jointed leg. MIJ. #10 from Salesman Sample Box. Not enough examples to price.

Below. #118 Little Miss Muffet Sat on a Tuffet (#10), jointed leg. Japan. Separate apron, ribbon trim, pink organdy picot edged dust cap with eyelet openings. Pink ribbon trim on pantalets. $1,200.00.

#118 Little Miss Muffet Sat on a Tuffet (#10), jointed leg. JA. Variation in blue; also in lavender and pink print. $1,000.00.

Little Miss Muffet
sat on a tuffet
10

#118 Little Miss Muffet Sat on a Tuffet (#10), jointed leg. MS/MB. Yellow print, found in JA in Fairyland box. $500.00.

Right. #118 Little Miss Muffet Sat on a Tuffet (#10), jointed leg. MS. Variation in print, no bow on dust cap. Found in JA in Fairyland box; also with yellow ribbon. $350.00.

Below. #118 Little Miss Muffet Sat on a Tuffet (#10), jointed leg. MS. SD sticker, blue print. $250.00.

#118 Little Miss Muffet Sat on a Tuffet (#10), jointed leg. MS. SD sticker, pink floral print. $250.00.

#118 Little Miss Muffet Sat on a Tuffet (#10), jointed leg. MS. Blue print with red/white flowers. $250.00.

Right. #118 Little Miss Muffet Sat on a Tuffet (#10), jointed leg. PT. $175.00.

Below. #118 Little Miss Muffet Sat on a Tuffet (#10), jointed leg. PT. $175.00.

Left to right.

#118 Little Miss Muffet Sat on a Tuffet (#10), jointed leg. PT. $175.00.

#118 Little Miss Muffet Sat on a Tuffet (#10), jointed leg. Variation in print. $175.00.

#118 Little Miss Muffet Sat on a Tuffet (#10), jointed leg. JT. $125.00.

#118 Little Miss Muffet Sat on a Tuffet (#10), frozen leg. $55.00 each.

#118 Little Miss Muffet Sat on a Tuffet (#10), frozen leg. $55.00 each.

#118 Little Miss Muffet Sat on a Tuffet (#10), frozen leg. Plastic arms. $45.00.

#119 Mistress Mary, Quite Contrary, How Does Your Garden Grow? (#11 and #25), jointed leg, front and back view. MIJ. Skimpy sun suit, separate skirt. Black Mary Jane shoes with strap. Shiny black painted hair with bangs. $2,000.00.

Left. #119 Mistress Mary, Quite Contrary, How Does Your Garden Grow? (#11 and #25), jointed leg. MIJ. #11 from Salesman Sample box. Although the early Mistress Mary dolls have painted hair, this doll from the Salesman Sample Box has a wig. Not enough examples to price.

Right. #119 Mistress Mary, Quite Contrary, How Does Your Garden Grow? (#11 and #25), jointed leg. MIJ. NADD sticker. Long yellow dotted swiss dress. Marble box; back of box marked in pencil "#7 Maize." Inside of box, top, reads, "Mistress Mary Quite Contrary, how does your garden grow?" $2,000.00.

Left to right.

#119 Mistress Mary, Quite Contrary, How Does Your Garden Grow? (#11 and #25), jointed leg. MIJ 1146. Variation, blue wilth larger white polka dots. Black Mary Jane-type shoes. $2,000.00.

#119 Mistress Mary, Quite Contrary, How Does Your Garden Grow? (#11 and #25), jointed leg. MIJ. Variation, blue print. $1,500.00.

#119 Mistress Mary, Quite Contrary, How Does Your Garden Grow? (#11 and #25), jointed leg. MIJ. Yellow print, wide lace trimmed pantalets, rickrack inside hat brim. Lace sleeves. Bow in loop on head. NAAD sticker. $1,500.00.

#119 Mistress Mary, Quite Contrary, How Does Your Garden Grow? (#11 and #25), jointed leg. Variation in blue checked, rickrack on pantalets, missing hat. If complete, $1,200.00.

Above left. #119 Mistress Mary, Quite Contrary, How Does Your Garden Grow? (#11 and #25), jointed leg. MIJ. Sunburst box. Yellow checked dress, organdy hat and apron. $1,200.00.

Above right. #119 Mistress Mary, Quite Contrary, How Does Your Garden Grow? (#11 and #25), jointed leg. Japan. Variation, pink checked. Ribbon trim on panteletes. Sunburst box, gold label #11. $1,500.00.

#119 Mistress Mary, Quite Contrary, How Does Your Garden Grow? (#11 and #25), jointed leg. JA. Blue print. Net on sleeves and inside bonnet, separate apron. $800.00.

Left. #119 Mistress Mary, Quite Contrary, How Does Your Garden Grow? (#11 and #25), jointed leg. JA. Cream print. Net trim eliminated. Attached apron. $800.00.

Below. #119 Mistress Mary, Quite Contrary, How Does Your Garden Grow? (#11 and #25), jointed leg. JA. Variation in green print. Also found in pink print. $800.00.

Left to right.

#119 Mistress Mary, Quite Contrary, How Does Your Garden Grow? (#11 and #25), jointed leg. JA. Green dotted swiss. $800.00.

#119 Mistress Mary, Quite Contrary, How Does Your Garden Grow? (#11 and #25), jointed leg. JA. Lavender flowered print, yellow ribbon trim. White boots. $800.00.

#119 Mistress Mary, Quite Contrary, How Does Your Garden Grow? (#11 and #25), jointed leg. MS/MB. Yellow print, lavender bonnet, yellow ribbon on skirt. White boots. Brown eyes. $400.00.

Left to right.

#119 Mistress Mary, Quite Contrary, How Does Your Garden Grow? (#11 and #25), jointed leg. MS/MB. Variation with yellow organdy bodice, sleeves and waist trimmed in yellow ribbon, cream print, no trim on skirt. $350.00.

#119 Mistress Mary, Quite Contrary, How Does Your Garden Grow? (#11 and #25), jointed leg. MS/MB and MS. Pink print. White boots. $350.00.

#119 Mistress Mary, Quite Contrary, How Does Your Garden Grow? (#11 and #25), jointed leg. MS/MB. Green print. White boots. $350.00.

Left to right.

#119 Mistress Mary, Quite Contrary, How Does Your Garden Grow? (#11 and #25), jointed leg. MS. Peach print. White boots. $275.00.

#119 Mistress Mary, Quite Contrary, How Does Your Garden Grow? (#11 and #25), jointed leg. MS. Pink print, lavender ribbon. White boots. $275.00.

#119 Mistress Mary, Quite Contrary, How Does Your Garden Grow? (#11 and #25), jointed leg. MS. Blue print, lavender ribbon. White boots. $275.00.

Left to right.

#119 Mistress Mary, Quite Contrary, How Does Your Garden Grow? (#11 and #25), jointed leg. PT. Purple print. $250.00.

#119 Mistress Mary, Quite Contrary, How Does Your Garden Grow? (#11 and #25), jointed leg. PT. $250.00.

#119 Mistress Mary, Quite Contrary, How Does Your Garden Grow? (#11 and #25), jointed leg. PT and MS. Variation with blue flowers and hat. $250.00.

Left to right.

#119 Mistress Mary, Quite Contrary, How Does Your Garden Grow? (#11 and #25), jointed leg. PT. Mid-calf dress. MS with dress shorter length. $200.00.

#119 Mistress Mary, Quite Contrary, How Does Your Garden Grow? (#11 and #25), jointed leg. PT. $175.00.

#119 Mistress Mary, Quite Contrary, How Does Your Garden Grow? (#11 and #25), jointed leg. PT. Variation in blue. $175.00.

Left. #119 Mistress Mary, Quite Contrary, How Does Your Garden Grow? (#11 and #25), jointed leg. PT. $175.00.

Below. #119 Mistress Mary, Quite Contrary, How Does Your Garden Grow? (#11 and #25), jointed leg. PT. $175.00.

Above left. #119 Mistress Mary, Quite Contrary, How Does Your Garden Grow? (#11 and #25), jointed leg. PT. $175.00.

Above right. #119 Mistress Mary, Quite Contrary, How Does Your Garden Grow? (#11 and #25), jointed leg. JT. $125.00.

#119 Mistress Mary, Quite Contrary, How Does Your Garden Grow? (#11 and #25), jointed leg. JT. $125.00 each.

#119 Mistress Mary, Quite Contrary, How Does Your Garden Grow? (#11 and #25), jointed leg. JT. $125.00 each.

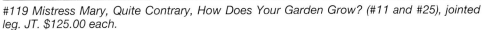

#119 Mistress Mary, Quite Contrary, How Does Your Garden Grow? (#11 and #25), frozen leg. $55.00.

Left to right.

#119 Mistress Mary, Quite Contrary, How Does Your Garden Grow? (#11 and #25), frozen leg. $55.00.

#119 Mistress Mary, Quite Contrary, How Does Your Garden Grow? (#11 and #25), frozen leg. $55.00.

#119 Mistress Mary, Quite Contrary, How Does Your Garden Grow? (#11 and #25), frozen leg. Variation. $55.00.

Left to right.

#119 Mistress Mary, Quite Contrary, How Does Your Garden Grow? (#11 and #25), frozen leg. $55.00.

#119 Mistress Mary, Quite Contrary, How Does Your Garden Grow? (#11 and #25), frozen leg. $50.00.

#119 Mistress Mary, Quite Contrary, How Does Your Garden Grow? (#11 and #25), frozen leg. $50.00.

#119 Mistress Mary, Quite Contrary, How Does Your Garden Grow? (#11 and #25), frozen leg. NA. Plastic arms. Tag reads #25. $45.00.

#119 Mistress Mary, Quite Contrary, How Does Your Garden Grow? (#11 and #25), frozen leg. Wrist tag and box read #25. $45.00.

#120 To Market, to Market to Buy a Fat Hen (#12), jointed leg, front and side view. JA. Pink cotton dress and matching sunbonnet. Black polished cotton purse. Outside bonnet is solid black cotton, inside matches dress. $1,000.00.

Left to right.

#120 To Market, to Market to Buy a Fat Hen (#12), jointed leg. JA. Variation in orange print. Black felt purse. Lace edged separate slip. $1,000.00.

#120 To Market, to Market to Buy a Fat Hen (#12), jointed leg. MS/MB. Variation in yellow or pink organdy with print apron. Red felt purse. Costume used in JA in Fairyland Box Set. $500.00.

#120 To Market, to Market to Buy a Fat Hen (#12), jointed leg. MS. Matching short felt jacket and hat, red cotton print dress. $250.00.

#120 To Market, to Market to Buy a Fat Hen (#12), jointed leg. JA. Yellow print dress and bonnet, #12 starburst box. Missing purse. If complete $900.00.

#120 To Market, to Market to Buy a Fat Hen (#12), jointed leg. JA or MS/MB. In white, peach, or yellow organdy dress. Red felt purse. $500.00.

Left. #120 To Market, to Market to Buy a Fat Hen (#12), jointed leg. PT. $135.00.

Below. #120 To Market, to Market to Buy a Fat Hen (#12), jointed leg. MS. Matching short felt jacket and hat, red/white striped dress. (Dolls wearing dresses with long felt jackets are Over the Hills.) $250.00.

#120 To Market, to Market to Buy a Fat Hen (#12), jointed leg. PT. $135.00.

Left to right.

#120 To Market, to Market to Buy a Fat Hen (#12), jointed leg. PT. Variation. Print apron. $135.00.

#120 To Market, to Market to Buy a Fat Hen (#12), jointed leg. PT. Variation. Print apron. $135.00.

#120 To Market, to Market to Buy a Fat Hen (#12), jointed leg. JT. Variation. Print apron. $125.00.

#120 To Market, to Market to Buy a Fat Hen (#12), jointed leg. JT. Variation. Solid red apron. $125.00.

#120 To Market, to Market to Buy a Fat Hen (#12), frozen leg. $55.00 each.

#120 To Market, to Market to Buy a Fat Hen (#12), frozen leg. $55.00 each.

Left and center. #120 To Market, to Market to Buy a Fat Hen (#12), frozen leg. Matching pantalets. Plastic arms. $50.00.

Right. #120 To Market, to Market to Buy a Fat Hen (#12), frozen leg. Taffeta dress with striped pantalets, gold snap. Plastic arms. $50.00.

Left to right.

#121 He Loves Me (#1), jointed leg. MS. Peach two-layers organdy dress. Lace-trimmed pantalets. SD sticker. Also in pink organdy. $175.00.

#121 He Loves Me (#1), jointed leg. PT. Sheer print, separate slip and pantalets trimmed in lace. $135.00.

Left to right.

#121 He Loves Me (#1), jointed leg. JT. Two-tier taffeta print with red dots, short panties. $125.00.

#121 He Loves Me (#1), jointed leg. JT. Variation. Two-tier aqua taffeta print dress. $125.00.

#121 He Loves Me (#1), frozen leg. Yellow taffeta print. $55.00.

Left. #121 He Loves Me (#1), frozen leg. Yellow taffeta dress, flower tied with ribbon at edge of skirt. Also in lavender and white organdy floral print. $55.00.

Right. #121 He Loves Me (#1), frozen leg. White organdy shade print skirt, insert of lavender taffeta. White daisy felt flower on hat and skirt. Also in blue panel with pink felt flower. $50.00.

Left to right.

#121 He Loves Me (#1), frozen leg. White taffeta with circle and square felt on skirt. Also in organdy daisy print with pink braid trim. $50.00.

#121 He Loves Me (#1), frozen leg. Pale lavender taffeta dress, florist ribbon. $45.00.

#121 He Loves Me (#1), frozen leg. Satin bodice, taffeta underskirt, wrist tag #21. $45.00.

Left to right.

#122 Alice Sweet Alice (#22), jointed leg. JT. Net collar. $125.00.

#122 Alice Sweet Alice (#22), frozen leg. $55.00.

#122 Alice Sweet Alice (#22), frozen leg. $55.00.

#122 Alice Sweet Alice (#22), frozen leg. $55.00 each.

#122 Alice Sweet Alice (#22), frozen leg. $55.00 each.

#122 Alice Sweet Alice (#22), frozen leg. Wrist tag now reads #22. $45.00.

Left. #122 Alice Sweet Alice (#22), frozen leg. Plastic arms. $45.00.

Right. #122 Alice Sweet Alice (#22), frozen leg. NA mold mark. Plastic arms, wrist tag #22. $45.00.

Left. #123 One-Two, Button My Shoe (113), jointed leg. PT. Longer jacket, matching trim on hat, jacket, and dress. $150.00.

Below. #123 One-Two, Button My Shoe (113), jointed leg. MS. Also MS/MB. Short black felt jacket, eyelet sewn on both sides. Straw hat. $350.00.

#123 One-Two, Button My Shoe (113), jointed leg. PT. Variation in trim. $150.00.

Left to right.

#123 One-Two, Button My Shoe (113), jointed leg. JT. Variation in trim. $125.00.

#123 One-Two, Button My Shoe (113), frozen leg. Variation. Green taffeta dress. $65.00.

#123 One-Two, Button My Shoe (113), frozen leg. Variation. Yellow taffeta dress. $65.00.

#123 One-Two, Button My Shoe (113), frozen leg. Striped seersucker dress. $55.00.

Left to right.

#123 One-Two (113), Button My Shoe, frozen leg. Checked seersucker skirt; no trim on jacket and hat. $55.00.

#123 One-Two (113), Button My Shoe, frozen leg. Checked gingham dress; no trim on jacket and hat. $55.00.

#123 One-Two (113), Button My Shoe, frozen leg. Jacket eliminated. $50.00.

Left to right.

#123 One-Two, Button My Shoe (113), frozen leg. $50.00.

#123 One-Two, Button My Shoe (113), frozen leg. $50.00.

#123 One-Two, Button My Shoe (113), frozen leg. $50.00.

#123 One-Two, Button My Shoe (113), frozen leg. Gold snap, plastic arm. $45.00.

#124 Pretty as a Picture (#24 & #115), jointed leg. JT. Two variations. $125.00.

154

Left to right.

#124 Pretty as a Picture (#24 & 115), jointed leg. JT. Variation in creams, five-petal flowers. $125.00.

#124 Pretty as a Picture (#24 & 115), jointed leg. JT. Also with blue hat and light pink print. $125.00.

#124 Pretty as a Picture (#24 & 115), jointed leg. JT. $125.00.

#124 Pretty as a Picture (#24 & 115), frozen leg. $55.00 each.

Left. #124 Pretty as a Picture (#24 & 115) , frozen leg. Florist ribbon. $45.00.

Right. #124 Pretty as a Picture (#24 & 115), frozen leg. Long dress, plastic arms, wrist tag #24. $45.00.

#125 Alice in Wonderland and Alice through the Looking Glass (#119)

This character was first called Alice in Wonderland. In 1942 the name was changed to Alice through the Looking Glass. The wigs for Alice during the jointed-leg mold period did not have the usual side part, but were placed on the center of the head with bangs, the only character to have a wig with bangs. The wig used had exceptionally long golden locks. Later in the frozen leg period the usual the side-part wig was used. Alice is always dressed in blue.

#125 Alice in Wonderland, jointed leg. MS/MB. Blue cotton print, ribbon on bodice, eyelet apron. $250.00.

#125 Alice in Wonderland, jointed leg. JA. Blue taffeta with attached organdy apron. $400.00.

#125 Alice in Wonderland, jointed leg. MS/MB and MS. Ribbon on bodice. $250.00.

Left. #125 Alice in Wonderland, jointed leg. MS. $225.00.

Below. #125 Alice in Wonderland, jointed leg. MS. Variation in apron. $250.00.

#125 Alice in Wonderland, jointed leg. MS. No ribbon on bodice. $225.00.

#125 Alice in Wonderland, jointed leg. PT. $150.00.

#125 Alice through the Looking Glass (119). PT. $135.00. JT. $150.00.

#125 Alice through the Looking Glass (119), frozen leg. $55.00 each.

#125 Alice through the Looking Glass (119), frozen leg. $55.00 each.

#125 Alice through the Looking Glass (119), frozen leg. NA mold. Plastic arms. $45.00.

#125 Alice through the Looking Glass (119), frozen leg. Number changed to #119. Plastic arms, gold snap closure. $45.00.

#126 Pussy Cat, Pussy Cat
#126 I Have a Little Pet

The #126 was first used for Pussy Cat, Pussy Cat. The dolls had white painted boots, short white panties, and came with a white cat either pinned or attached with ribbon to the doll's arm.

#126 Pussy Cat, Pussy Cat (19), jointed leg. MS/MB. Blue dotted swiss skirt, variation, organdy bodice now has actual lace-trimmed sleeves. White pipe cleaner cat. $700.00.

#126 Pussy Cat, Pussy Cat (19), jointed leg. MS. Blue dotted swiss, trim on apron matches trim on bodice. Came in both pink and blue dotted swiss and also on PT mold. $600.00.

#126 Pussy Cat, Pussy Cat (19), jointed leg. JA. Pink dotted swiss skirt. Organdy bodice, extended down to make lace-trimmed apron, with tiny lace around neck and lace cap sleeves. Ribbon at waist, furry cat that may or may not be original, as only example seen. $800.00.

At the end of the pudgy tummy mold and starting with the regular jointed-leg mold, the #126 was changed to read I Have a Little Pet. The company then started offering the character with a variety of animals, such as a dog, lamb, and also a black pipe cleaner cat. The costume and animal combination often varied. Pictured below are only some of the combinations, but there could be others. The later era I Have a Little Pet no longer had white painted boots, but the regular black slipper shoes and wore pantalets instead of short white panties. This character was discontinued at the end of the jointed-leg period.

#126 Pussy Cat, Pussy Cat (19), jointed leg. MS. Organdy dress, no apron. $600.00.

#126 I Have a Little Pet, jointed leg. PT. White floral taffeta dress, with black-eared dog. $500.00.

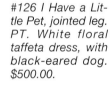

#126 I Have a Little Pet, jointed leg. PT. Pink taffeta with rosebud print apron. Holding lamb. $500.00.

Left. #126 I Have a Little Pet, jointed leg. JT. Blue taffeta print dress. Found with both poodle. $450.00.

Below. #126 I Have a Little Pet, jointed leg. JT. Variation in pink tulip print dress with lamb. $550.00.

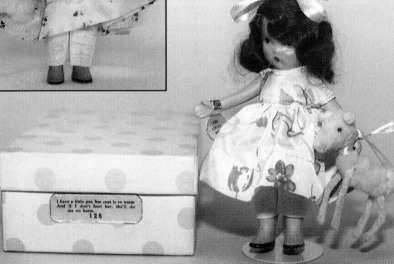

#126 I Have a Little Pet, jointed leg. JT. White taffeta tulip print dress, with poodle. $450.00.

Left. #126 I Have a Little Pet, jointed leg. JT. Variation of print, with black cat. $700.00.

Right. #126 I Have a Little Pet, jointed leg. JT. Variation of print, with lamb. $450.00.

Left. #126 I Have a Little Pet, jointed leg. JT. Variation of print, with black pipe cleaner cat. $700.00.

Right. #126 I Have a Little Pet, jointed leg. JT. Variation with another example of cat that may or may not be original. $450.00.

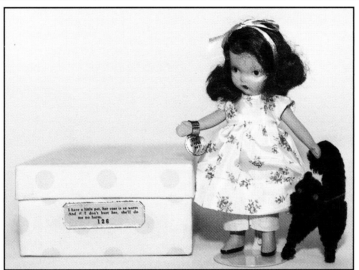

#126 was originally used for Pussy Cat, Pussy Cat and then later I Have a Little Pet. This character was discontinued and the character Going a Milking then used #126. Since this is a later doll, there were no bisque jointed-leg Going a Milking dolls.

#126 Going a Milking (#28), frozen leg. $55.00 each.

#126 Going a Milking (#28), frozen leg. $55.00 each.

#126 Going a Milking (#28), frozen leg. $55.00.

#126 Going a Milking (#28), frozen leg. Wrist tag. #26. $45.00.

Left to right.

#127 Richman, Poorman, jointed leg. JA. Blue cotton dress, four material-covered buttons. $900.00.

#127 Richman, Poorman, jointed leg. JA. Apricot cotton dress with crocheted buttons. (Missing hat-style unknown.) If complete, $900.00.

#127 Richman, Poorman, jointed leg. JA. Rose print organdy dress. Replaced hat. If all original, $1,100.00.

Left. #127 Richman, Poorman, jointed leg. MS. Blue print dress. $800.00.

Right. #127 Richman, Poorman, jointed leg. Variation in pink. $800.00.

The character #127 One, Two, Three, Four Mary at the Cottage Door, replaced #127 Richman, Poorman. This is the only version of this character we have found.

#127 One, Two, Three, Four Mary at the Cottage Door. PT. Pink taffeta dress. $500.00.

#127 Merry Little Maid replaced #127 Richman, Poorman and One, Two, Three, Four.

Left to right.

#127 Merry (Merrie) Little Maid (#27), jointed leg. JT. $125.00.

#127 Merry (Merrie) Little Maid (#27), frozen leg. $55.00.

#127 Merry (Merrie) Little Maid (#27), frozen leg. $55.00.

#127 Merry (Merrie) Little Maid (#27), frozen leg. $55.00 each.

#127 Merry (Merrie) Little Maid (#27), frozen leg. Long dress, satin bodice. Wrist tag reads #27. $45.00.

#127 Merry (Merrie) Little Maid (#27), frozen leg. Long dress. Wrist tag reads #27. $45.00.

#17 and #19 Goldylocks and the Baby Bear
#128 Goldylocks and the Baby Bear
#128 Goldilocks and #28 Goldilocks

Left. #17 Goldylocks and the Baby Bear (19 & 128), jointed leg. MIJ. Short organdy dress, wide ruffle over each shoulder in pinafore style with picot edge. NADD sticker. Pink ribbon rosette. Also with blue ribbon rosette. White pipe cleaner bear. Pink starburst box, gold label. Right. #19 Goldylocks and Baby Bear, jointed leg. Japan mold variation with either white or blue ribbon rosette. White starburst box, gold label. Each doll $2,100.00+.

#17 Goldylocks and the Baby Bear (19 & 128), jointed leg. America. Mold variation with extra-wide lace on edge of sleeves. Lace trimmed panties with front seam. JA sticker. $1,500.00+.

#128 Goldylocks and the Baby Bear (17 & 19), jointed leg. JA. Mold variation with smaller lace on sleeves. SB sticker. $800.00.

#128 Goldylocks and the Baby Bear (17 & 19), jointed leg. JA. Pink or blue ribbon across skirt, rosette eliminated. SB sticker. $800.00.

#128 Goldylocks and the Baby Bear (17 & 19), jointed leg. CM. Dimity dress. Floral band across bodice. $750.00.

#128 Goldylocks and the Baby Bear (17 & 19), jointed leg. MS/MB. Variation in pink organdy dress. $700.00.

#128 Goldylocks and the Baby Bear (17 & 19), jointed leg. MS/MB. Pink dotted swiss dress. $700.00.

#128 Goldylocks and the Baby Bear (17 & 19), jointed leg. MS. Blue organdy with rickrack. $600.00.

#128 Goldylocks and the Baby Bear (17 & 19), jointed leg. MS. Variation in shadow print. $600.00.

#128 Goldylocks and the Baby Bear (17 & 19), jointed leg. MS. Taffeta floral print. $500.00.

Left to right.

#128 Goldylocks and the Baby Bear (17 & 19), jointed leg. PT. Apron added, matching bodice. $450.00.

#128 Goldylocks and the Baby Bear (17 & 19), jointed leg. JT. Yellow taffeta print. $400.00.

#128 Goldylocks and the Baby Bear (17 & 19), jointed leg. JT transition. Some with brown bear holding plastic cereal bowl and spoon. $400.00.

Left. #128 Goldilocks, jointed leg. JT. Bear eliminated at this point. $100.00.

Right. #128 Goldilocks, frozen leg. Variation aqua apron. $65.00.

#128 Goldilocks and the Baby Bear (17 & 19), jointed leg. JT. $375.00.

Left. #128 Goldilocks, frozen leg. Variation, solid yellow dress. $65.00.

Right. Florist ribbon. #128 Goldilocks, frozen leg. $45.00.

#128 Goldilocks, frozen leg. $55.00 each.

#28 Goldilocks. Wrist tag, label changed to #28 Goldilocks, florist ribbon. Also with rickrack trim. $45.00.

#128 Goldilocks, frozen leg. Floral print, plastic arms. $45.00.

#129 East Side, West Side All around the Town. This character has all-black high-top boots with no white buttons painted on shoe. The dolls have short felt jackets. East Side, West Side was probably made for only two years, then discontinued. Then, #129 Annie at the Garden Gate replaced this character.

Right. #129 East Side, West Side All around the Town, jointed leg. MS/MB. Blue or red striped dress with blue knit tam. Short black felt jacket. $700.00. Also found on a JA with a black derby-style hat like Riding wears. $725.00.

#129 East Side, West Side All around the Town, jointed leg. MS. Red polka dot dress with short red felt hat and jacket. $400.00.

Above. #129 East Side, West Side All around the Town, jointed leg. MS/MB. Straw hat. Narrow red or blue striped dress. Short black felt jacket. $700.00.

#129 East Side, West Side All around the Town, jointed leg. MS/MB. Straw hat. Wide red/white striped dress. Short black felt jacket $700.00.

#129 was first used for two years for East Side, West Side. When this character was discontinued, #129 then was used for Annie at the Garden Gate.

Left to right.

#129 Annie at the Garden Gate (#29), jointed leg. MS. $135.00.

#129 Annie at the Garden Gate (#29), jointed leg. PT. $125.00.

#129 Annie at the Garden Gate (#29), frozen leg. $55.00.

#129 Annie at the Garden Gate (#29), frozen leg. $55.00 each.

#129 Annie at the Garden Gate (#29), frozen leg. $55.00 each.

#129 Annie at the Garden Gate (#29), frozen leg. Long dress, florist ribbon. $50.00.

#129 Annie at the Garden Gate (#29), frozen leg. Long dress, florist ribbon. Plastic arms. Wrist tag reads #29. $45.00.

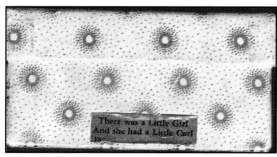

Left to right.

#130 There Was a Little Girl, and She Had a Little Curl (#13). Early box with character as #13.

#130 There Was a Little Girl, and She Had a Little Curl (#13), jointed leg. MS/MB. Variation, blue ribbon. $1,200.00+.

#130 There Was a Little Girl, and She Had a Little Curl (#13), jointed leg. MS/MB. Variation, pink ribbon. $1,200.00+.

#130 There Was a Little Girl, and She Had a Little Curl (#13), jointed leg. MS/MB. Silver-dot box #130 on label. Apricot organdy short dress, lace on sleeves and on panties, ribbon rosebud trim at waist and on bonnet; lavender ribbon. Also in yellow organdy dress. Ribbon rosebud trim on hat and at waist. White boots. $1,200.00+.

#130 There Was a Little Girl has now been replaced by #30 Dainty Dolly, Pink and Blue, which first appears in the 1941 factory pamphlet.

#130 Dainty Dolly, Pink and Blue, No Knife Can Cut Our Love in Two (#30), jointed leg. PT. Also on MS. Matching pantalets. $150.00.

#130 Dainty Dolly, Pink and Blue, No Knife Can Cut Our Love in Two (#30), frozen leg. Pale blue taffeta. Spideweb lace on hat and dress. $55.00.

#130 Dainty Dolly, Pink and Blue, No Knife Can Cut Our Love in Two (#30), jointed leg. JT. Pink or blue print. $125.00.

#130 Dainty Dolly, Pink and Blue, No Knife Can Cut Our Love in Two (#30), frozen leg. Variation. Dark or light blue taffeta, pink ribbon, rickrack, light or deep pink hat with either large or small flower on hat. $55.00.

#130 Dainty Dolly, Pink and Blue, No Knife Can Cut Our Love in Two (#30), frozen leg. $55.00.

#130 Dainty Dolly, Pink and Blue, No Knife Can Cut Our Love in Two (#30), frozen leg. $55.00 each.

#130 Dainty Dolly, Pink and Blue, No Knife Can Cut Our Love in Two (#30), frozen leg. $55.00.

#130 Dainty Dolly, Pink and Blue, No Knife Can Cut Our Love in Two (#30), frozen leg. Change to #30 label. Florist ribbon. Plastic arms. $45.00.

Left. #130 Dainty Dolly, Pink and Blue, No Knife Can Cut Our Love in Two (#30), frozen leg. Variation. Trim and florist ribbon. Plastic arms. $45.00.

Right. #130 Dainty Dolly, Pink and Blue, No Knife Can Cut Our Love in Two (#30), frozen leg. Pink oval hat with blue felt flower. Also with bow on hat. $45.00.

172

#130 Dainty Dolly, Pink and Blue, No Knife Can Cut Our Love in Two, frozen leg. Tag reads #30. Florist ribbon, satin bodice. $45.00.

#131 Elsie Marley (#31), jointed leg. PT. Pink satin dress. $150.00.

#131 Elsie Marley (#31), jointed leg. PT. Satin dress, matching pantalets. $125.00.

#131 Elsie Marley (#31), jointed leg. PT. Variation in white satin. $150.00.

#131 Elsie Marley (#31), frozen leg. $55.00.

#131 Elsie Marley (#31), frozen leg. $55.00 each.

#131 Elsie Marley (#31), frozen leg. $55.00 each.

#131 Elsie Marley (#31), frozen leg. Plastic arms. Gold Snap closure. Tag reads #31. $40.00.

#131 Elsie Marley (#31), frozen leg. Also with ribbon instead of bonnet. Wrist tag reads #31. $55.00.

#132 When She Was Good (#32), jointed leg. MS. $200.00.

Left to right.

#132 When She Was Good (#32), jointed leg. PT. $150.00.

#132 When She Was Good (#32), frozen leg. $60.00.

#132 When She Was Good (#32), frozen leg. $55.00.

#132 When She Was Good (#32), frozen leg. Sheer print skirt, various trims. $55.00.

#132 When She Was Good (#32), frozen leg. Variation. Cotton print skirt. $55.00.

#132 When She Was Good (#32), frozen leg. $55.00.

#132 When She Was Good (#32), frozen leg. NA mold mark. Box label and wrist tag reads #32. $45.00.

> #133 Little Polly Flinders
>
> #134 or #146 Old Mother Hubbard
>
> #143 or #145 Mother Goose
>
> The above character names are listed in factory pamphlets. However, to our knowledge, these dolls have never been found and possibly were never made.

•••Storybook Series•••
Fairyland
#150 – #163

Snow White is not listed on any known factory pamphlet, but has been found in the early gold label sunburst box (see photo below, right) as #16, and also in the later small silver dot box (see photo below, left) with silver label as #150. It is an early doll, rarely found in its original box. Although thought of as a pair, Snow White and Rose Red were sold separately.

#150 Snow White (#16), jointed leg. Blue box with silver dots. Silver label.

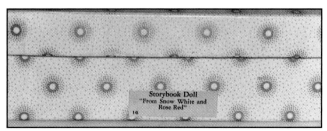

#150 Snow White (#16), jointed leg. Snow White Sunburst box with gold label reads #16.

150 Snow White (#16), jointed leg. MS/MB. No pearls on skirt. Silver dot box label changes to #150. $700.00.

#150 Snow White (#16), jointed leg. JA. (#16) Silver slippers. Four-layer net attached to taffeta bodice. Net at sleeves. Three pearls sewn to top layer of net skirt. SBD sticker. Matching dunce cap, matching bodice, with trail of white net streaming almost to hem of skirt. $800.00.

Rose Red is not listed on any known factory pamphlet, but has been found in the early gold label sunburst box as #17 and in the later small silver dot box with silver label as #151. Along with Snow White, Rose Red also is an early doll, rarely found in its original box.

#151 Rose Red (#17), jointed leg. Sunburst box with gold label reads #17.

#151 Rose Red (#17), jointed leg. America. Silver slippers. Four-layer net skirt attached to taffeta bodice. Matching dunce cap, with trail of magenta net streaming almost to hem of skirt. Three pearls sewn on skirt. SD sticker. Lace edged pantalets. Separate slip. $1,200.00.

#151 Rose Red (#17), jointed leg. Pink box with silver dots. Silver label now changes to #151.

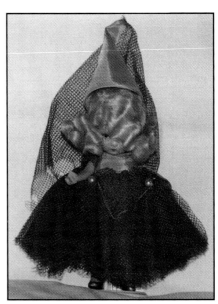

#151 Rose Red (#17), jointed leg. MS/MB. #151 Silver slippers. Dusty rose three or four-layer net skirt attached to satin bodice. Satin dunce cap, matching bodice with trail of rose net. $900.00.

#151 Rose Red (#17), jointed leg. MS. Transition with dusty rose bodice and hat with magenta net skirt and pearls on skirt. $800.00.

#152 Mary Had a Little Lamb, Its Fleece Was White as Snow (#20), jointed leg. MIJ. Probably Mary had a little lamb, but not verified. Also seen with pinafore-style dress with picot on apron and bodice, no sleeves. Straw hat with rosebud ribbon trim. NADD sticker. $1,000.00.

#152 Mary Had a Little Lamb, Its Fleece Was White as Snow (#20), jointed leg. Front and side view. America. Silver slippers, JA sticker. $1,100.00.

Left. #152 Mary Had a Little Lamb, Its Fleece Was White as Snow (#20), jointed leg. MS/MB. Pink dotted swiss dress, organdy inset in straw hat. $600.00.

Right. #152 Mary Had a Little Lamb, Its Fleece Was White as Snow (#20), jointed leg. MS/MB. Blue organdy dress, blue trim on straw hat. $600.00. Also MS. Pink trim on hat. $500.00. Also JA with blue trim on hat in starburst box with #20 gold label. $600.00.

#152 Mary Had a Little Lamb, Its Fleece Was White as Snow (#20), jointed leg. MS/MB. $500.00. Also MS. $400.00.

#152 Mary Had a Little Lamb, Its Fleece Was White as Snow (#20), jointed leg. MS. Felt hat, still has separate slip of earlier dolls. Also found in pink floral print. $400.00.

#152 Mary Had a Little Lamb, Its Fleece Was White as Snow (#20), jointed leg. PT. Taffeta rose print, feather on pink felt hat. $250.00. Also JT in various rose prints with tiny flowers or pink poppy on felt hat. $175.00.

#152 Mary Had a Little Lamb, Its Fleece Was White as Snow (#20), jointed leg. JT. $85.00.

Left. #152 Mary Had a Little Lamb, Its Fleece Was White as Snow (#20), frozen leg. $55.00.

Right. #152 Mary Had a Little Lamb, Its Fleece Was White as Snow (#20), frozen leg. $55.00 each.

#152 Mary Had a Little Lamb, Its Fleece Was White as Snow (#20), frozen leg. $55.00 each.

#152 Mary Had a Little Lamb, Its Fleece Was White as Snow (#20), frozen leg. $55.00.

#152 Mary Had a Little Lamb, Its Fleece Was White as Snow (#20), frozen leg. Unusual green sprig attached. $55.00.

#152 Mary Had a Little Lamb, Its Fleece Was White as Snow (#20), frozen leg. $55.00.

#152 Mary Had a Little Lamb, Its Fleece Was White as Snow (#20), frozen leg. Shadow print and blue organdy. $55.00.

A very popular character through the years of the company, the jointed-leg Little Bo Peep carried a pipe cleaner staff, which was discontinued at the frozen-leg period.

#153 Little Bo Peep Has Lost Her Sheep (#21), jointed leg. MIJ. One-piece elaborate satin panniers and net costume. Bright satin squares sewn to blue netting, shiny black painted bobbed hair with bangs, top knot. Painted black Mary Jane shoes. NADD sticker. Also in pale pink satin panniers. $1,200.00+.

#153 Little Bo Peep Has Lost Her Sheep (#21), jointed leg. Side view. Tear-shaped satin headpiece tied to top knot, ruffled pale blue ribbon. Separate blue satin slip with pink ribbon at hem. Lace trimmed organdy pantalets, painted black strapped shoes.

#153 Little Bo Peep Has Lost Her Sheep (#21), jointed leg. Front and side view. MIJ 1148. NADD sticker. Painted red hair, hat tied to topknot. Lace pannier, taffeta underskirt. Painted hair, no actual sleeves, gathered at neck, painted black shoes. $1,200.00+.

#153 Little Bo Peep Has Lost Her Sheep (#21), jointed leg. MIJ. Early wool wig, pink organdy panniers with blue fringed trim. No actual bodice, picot-edged strips over shoulders. Lace for sleeves. Oval woven straw hat trimmed with ribbon rosettes. Rare marble design box, gold label #21. $1,100.00.

Above left. #153 Little Bo Peep Has Lost Her Sheep (#21), jointed leg. MIJ. Wool wig. Rayon panniers attached to pink satin picot short underskirt. Sheer pantalets, pink picot-edged trim on each cuff. No actual bodice, picot edged straps over each shoulder. NADD sticker. Headpiece missing, style unknown. If complete with hat, $1,100.00.

Above right. #153 Little Bo Peep Has Lost Her Sheep (#21), jointed leg. Japan. Variation with yellow organdy panniers trimmed in lavender ribbon, lavender rickrack on bodice and skirt. Yellow fringed pantalets, narrower lace from sleeves. $1,100.00.

#153 Little Bo Peep Has Lost Her Sheep (#21), jointed leg. MIJ. Sunburst box #21. Lace straps over organdy insert to form bodice. Pink organdy pannier trimmed in variegated blue ribbon, cotton blue floral dress, lace trimmed pantalets. Straw pancake-style hat trimmed with ribbon rosettes. $1,100.00.

Above left. #153 Little Bo Peep Has Lost Her Sheep (#21), jointed leg. Japan. Same print. Attached to waistband of pale pink organdy, no sleeves, small bodice with organdy ruffle at neck. Pale pink picot edge strip attached around neck. NADD sticker. No trim on panniers. Lace on pantalets. $900.00.

Above right. #153 Little Bo Peep Has Lost Her Sheep (#21), jointed leg. Japan. Yellow floral dress, now with organdy bodice and actual lace sleeves, matching lace on pantalets, ribbon trim on panniers. $900.00.

Right. #153 Little Bo Peep Has Lost Her Sheep (#21), jointed leg. MB/MB. Lace on sleeves and tiny rope trim on neck and at skirt hem. $300.00.

Below. #153 Little Bo Peep Has Lost Her Sheep (#21), jointed leg. Japan. Variation in pink floral print with variegated ribbon neckline, actual organdy bodice with inset sleeves. $900.00.

#153 Little Bo Peep Has Lost Her Sheep (#21), jointed leg. JA. Unusual net trim on pantalets. Lace on sleeves. SD sticker. Also dress in reverse design with floral panniers and solid organdy dress. $500.00.

#153 Little Bo Peep Has Lost Her Sheep (#21), jointed leg. MS/MB. Net lace on sleeves. Also with pink floral panniers and blue dress. Straw oval hat with ribbon rosebud. Also hat with ruche trim. $300.00.

#153 Little Bo Peep Has Lost Her Sheep (#21), jointed leg. Straw hat with pink ribbon ruche trim. $300.00.

Left. #153 Little Bo Peep Has Lost Her Sheep (#21), jointed leg. MS/MB. Unusual long organdy floral print pannier with blue organdy underskirt with separate slip. Straw hat with rosebud ribbon trim. SD sticker. Also in white underskirt, pink ribbon with pink ruche trimmed straw hat. $300.00.

Right. #153 Little Bo Peep Has Lost Her Sheep (#21), jointed leg. MS. Taffeta print dress, straw hat. $250.00.

Left. #153 Little Bo Peep Has Lost Her Sheep (#21), jointed leg. PT. Change to oval felt hat. $150.00.

Right. #153 Little Bo Peep Has Lost Her Sheep (#21), jointed leg. JT. Oval felt hat. $125.00.

Left. #153 Little Bo Peep Has Lost Her Sheep (#21). JT. $125.00.

Right. #153 Little Bo Peep Has Lost Her Sheep (#21), frozen leg. Long yellow taffeta dress. The pipe-cleaner shepherd's staff is now discontinued. $55.00.

#153 Little Bo Peep Has Lost Her Sheep (#21), frozen leg. $55.00 each.

#153 Little Bo Peep Has Lost Her Sheep (#21), frozen leg. $55.00.

#153 Little Bo Peep Has Lost Her Sheep (#21), frozen leg. Gold snap closure, plastic arms, florist ribbon. $45.00.

#153 Little Bo Peep Has Lost Her Sheep (#21), frozen leg. NA. Florist ribbon. $45.00.

#153 Little Bo Peep Has Lost Her Sheep (#21), frozen leg. Plastic arms. Florist ribbon. $45.00.

Left to right.

#154 Curly Locks, Curly Locks, Wilt Thou Be Mine (#22), jointed leg. Japan. Sunburst box #22. $1,100.00.

#154 Curly Locks, Curly Locks, Wilt Thou Be Mine (#22), jointed leg. JA. Sunburst box #22. Also in blue print fabric. $500.00.

#154 Curly Locks, Curly Locks, Wilt Thou Be Mine (#22), jointed leg. JA. Variation in pink. $500.00.

#154 Curly Locks, Curly Locks, Wilt Thou Be Mine (#22), jointed leg. MS/MB. $300.00.

#154 Curly Locks, Curly Locks, Wilt Thou Be Mine (#22), jointed leg. MS/MB. Two-tier blue taffeta bodice and underskirt. SB sticker. $350.00.

#154 Curly Locks, Curly Locks, Wilt Thou Be Mine (#22), jointed leg. PT. $150.00. Also JT. $130.00.

#154 Curly Locks, Curly Locks, Wilt Thou Be Mine (#22), jointed leg. Variation in pink organdy. Separate pink net underskirt. $300.00.

#154 Curly Locks, Curly Locks, Wilt Thou Be Mine (#22), jointed leg. JT. Also in pink. $110.00.

#154 Curly Locks, Curly Locks, Wilt Thou Be Mine (#22), jointed leg. JT. $100.00.

#154 Curly Locks, Curly Locks, Wilt Thou Be Mine (#22), frozen leg. $55.00.

#154 Curly Locks, Curly Locks, Wilt Thou Be Mine (#22), frozen leg. $55.00 each.

Left. #22 Curly Locks, Curly Locks, Wilt Thou Be Mine, frozen leg. $55.00 each.

Right. #155 Cinderella (#23), jointed leg. MIJ. Taffeta dress with black lace vertically on bodice and skirt. Ribbon rosebud headband and trim on skirt. Mohair wig. $2,000.00+.

Left. #155 Cinderella (#23), jointed leg. MIJ. Yellow taffeta dress. Black lace for sleeves and over bodice, matching lace on skirt. Blue ribbon v-shape trim on bodice. Ribbon rosebud headband and trim on skirt. Sunburst box with #23 on label. $2,000.00+.

Right. #155 Cinderella (#23), jointed leg. Variation. Wide lace both on slip and pantalets. $2,000.00.

#155 Cinderella (#23), jointed leg. CM. Variation in peach. Black lace for sleeves and over bodice, matching lace on skirt. Blue ribbon v-shape trim on bodice. Blue ribbon in hair with rosebuds. Lace trimmed slip and pantalets. $1,500.00.

#155 Cinderella (#23), jointed leg. JA. White lace square trim on bodice. Gathered on both sides with satin bud trim. Pink taffeta attached underskirt, separate half slip, lace edged pantalets, silver slippers, #23 sunburst box. Also in white satin dress. $500.00.

#155 Cinderella (#23), jointed leg. MS/MB. Variation in white. $400.00.

#155 Cinderella (#23), jointed leg. MS/MB. Pink organdy overskirt with embroidered center panel trimmed in pink ribbon. Pink taffeta underskirt. Lace circle headpiece with flowers and blue ribbon. Lace on sleeves and slip Blue ribbon at side and at side gatherings. Silver slippers #153 blue silver dot box. $400.00.

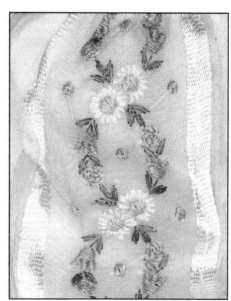

#155 Cinderella (#23), jointed leg. Close-up of panel insert.

#155 Cinderella (#23) MS. Two layers of net underskirt. Silver slippers. (Although our inclination is to identify this doll as Cinderella, it has also been found with tag/box as #156 Beauty). $250.00.

#155 Cinderella (#23), jointed leg. "Poor" Cinderella dress used in Geraldine in Movieland Box. Not sold individually, as far as we know.

#155 Cinderella (#23), jointed leg. MS. Blue satin print, two-layer blue net underskirt, silver slippers, blue cotton pantalets. Also in pink. $250.00.

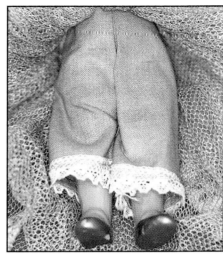

Right. #155 Cinderella (#23), jointed leg. Close-up of blue cotton pant.

#155 Cinderella (#25), jointed leg. MS. Satin dress with net overskirt, spider web lace crown and trim on skirt. Silver slippers. This doll found in "Cinderella" box, but only example of costume found, so would like more verification that this is Cinderella. $250.00.

#155 Cinderella (#23), jointed leg. MS. Embroidered pink taffeta gown, separate slip, silver slippers, also in blue taffeta. $250.00.

#155 Cinderella (#23), jointed leg. MS/MB. Pink satin overskirt, shadow print organdy underskirt. Three-layer pink net attached slip. Silver slippers. Also in blue and deep pink. $300.00.

#155 Cinderella (#23), jointed leg. PT. Silver flocked organdy dress. Separate lace trimed slip and pantalets. $150.00.

#155 Cinderella (#23), jointed leg. PT. Also on JT. Silver flocked overskirt edged in taffeta ruche trim, taffeta underskirt. $125.00.

#155 Cinderella (#23), jointed leg. JT. Variation, satin print overskirt. $100.00.

#155 Cinderella (#23), jointed leg. JT. Variation, silver flocked polka dot overskirt. $100.00.

#155 Cinderella (#23), jointed leg. JT. Variation in flocked print and flower in hair. $100.00.

#155 Cinderella (#23), frozen leg. Variation in dotted swiss overskirt. Pink ribbon with silver trim and feather in hair. $55.00.

191

#155 Cinderella (#23), frozen leg. $55.00.

#155 Cinderella (#23), frozen leg. $55.00.

#155 Cinderella (#23), frozen leg. Also in white. $45.00.

#155 Cinderella (#23), frozen leg. $45.00.

#156 Beauty (from Beauty and the Beast), jointed leg. MS. Separate gauze slip. Two vertical panels of lace sewn over the dress. $250.00.

#156 Beauty (from Beauty and the Beast), jointed leg. MS. Blue satin/lace inset panel. Separate slip. $225.00.

#156 Beauty (from Beauty and the Beast), jointed leg. PT. $180.00.

#156 Beauty (from Beauty and the Beast), jointed leg. PT. $180.00.

#156 Beauty (from Beauty and the Beast), jointed leg. PT. Variation in print, long arms. Separate slip. $155.00.

#156 Beauty (from Beauty and the Beast), jointed leg. PT. Long arms. $155.00.

#156 Beauty (from Beauty and the Beast), jointed leg. PT. Variation in blue. $155.00.

#156 Beauty (from Beauty and the Beast), jointed leg. JT. $125.00.

193

#156 Beauty (from Beauty and the Beast), jointed leg. JT. $125.00.

#156 Beauty (from Beauty and the Beast), frozen leg. $55.00.

#156 Beauty (from Beauty and the Beast), frozen leg. $55.00 each.

#156 Beauty (from Beauty and the Beast), frozen leg. $55.00.

#156 Beauty (from Beauty and the Beast), frozen leg. Also found in reversed fabrics with felt hat. $45.00.

#156 Beauty (from Beauty and the Beast), frozen leg. $45.00.

#156 Beauty (from Beauty and the Beast), frozen leg. $45.00.

#156 Beauty (from Beauty and the Beast), frozen leg. Lavender. Also in yellow and pink. $45.00.

195

#156 Beauty (from Beauty and the Beast), frozen leg. Plastic arms. $45.00.

#157 Queen of Hearts, jointed leg. MS. Three-layer net skirt, satin bodice. Lace at sleeves, separate lace edged cotton slip and pantalets. $275.00.

#157 Queen of Hearts, jointed leg. MS. Ivory taffeta, separate lace edged cotton slip and pantalets. $250.00.

#157 Queen of Hearts, jointed leg. MS. Ivory taffeta, open weave separate slip. $225.00.

#157 Queen of Hearts, jointed leg. PT. White flocked skirt, wagon-wheel lace trim at edge. $140.00.

#157 Queen of Hearts, jointed leg. PT. Ecru print organdy underskirt. $150.00.

#157 Queen of Hearts, jointed leg. PT. White print organdy underskirt. Also with no lace trim on hat. $150.00.

#157 Queen of Hearts, jointed leg. PT. Variation of trims on skirt. Organdy pantalets. $140.00.

#157 Queen of Hearts, jointed leg. JT. $110.00.

#157 Queen of Hearts, frozen leg. $55.00.

#157 Queen of Hearts, frozen leg. $55.00.

#157 Queen of Hearts, frozen leg. $55.00.

#157 Queen of Hearts, frozen leg. $55.00.

#157 Queen of Hearts, frozen leg. Bisque. Also with plastic arms and NA mold mark. $45.00.

#157 Queen of Hearts, frozen leg. Plastic arms. $45.00.

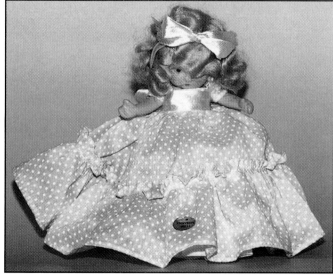

#158 Sugar and Spice and Everything Nice, jointed leg. MS. Light blue dotted swiss, SBD sticker. $225.00.

#158 Sugar and Spice and Everything Nice, jointed leg. PT. Variation in medium blue. $150.00.

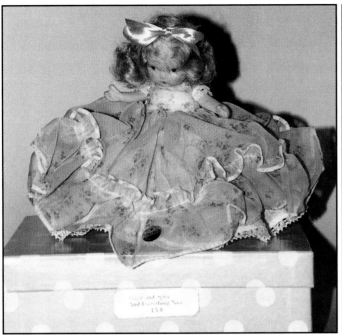 

Above left. #158 Sugar and Spice and Everything Nice, jointed leg. MS. Organdy print, SBD sticker. $250.00.

Above right. #158 Sugar and Spice and Everything Nice, jointed leg. MS. Blue shadow print. Also in pink. SBD sticker. $250.00.

#158 Sugar and Spice and Everything Nice, jointed leg. PT. Shadow print. $150.00.

#158 Sugar and Spice and Everything Nice, jointed leg. JT. $125.00.

#158 Sugar and Spice and Everything Nice, jointed leg. JT. $125.00.

#158 Sugar and Spice and Everything Nice, jointed leg. JT. $125.00.

#158 Sugar and Spice and Everything Nice, jointed leg. JT. $125.00.

#158 Sugar and Spice and Everything Nice, frozen leg. $55.00.

#158 Sugar and Spice and Everything Nice, frozen leg. $55.00 each.

#158 Sugar and Spice and Everything Nice, frozen leg. $55.00 each.

#158 Sugar and Spice and Everything Nice, frozen leg. $55.00 each.

#158 Sugar and Spice and Everything Nice, frozen leg. $55.00.

#158 Sugar and Spice and Everything Nice, frozen leg. Plastic arms. $45.00.

#159 Ring Around the Rosy, jointed leg. MS. Organdy. Ribbon rosettes on skirt, bodice, and hair. Separate blue net half slip. $275.00.

#159 Ring Around the Rosy, jointed leg. MS. Variation in peach. $275.00.

#159 Ring Around the Rosy, jointed leg. MS. Variation in striped organdy. $275.00.

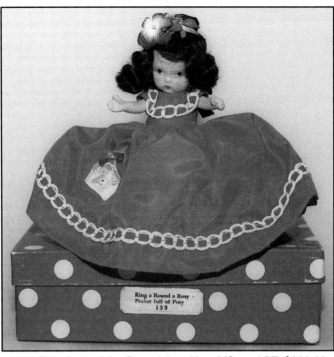

#159 Ring Around the Rosy, jointed leg. MS. and PT. $200.00.

#159 Ring Around the Rosy, jointed leg. PT. $135.00.

#159 Ring Around the Rosy, frozen leg, with apron. Cotton print, green hair ribbon. $55.00.

#159 Ring Around the Rosy, frozen leg, with apron. Cream, pink, or lavender taffeta print. $55.00.

#159 Ring Around the Rosy, frozen leg, with apron. Cotton print of blue and lavender. $55.00.

#159 Ring Around the Rosy, frozen leg, with apron. Large flowers, yellow cotton print. $55.00.

#159 Ring Around the Rosy, frozen leg, with apron. Variation in blue print. $55.00.

#159 Ring Around the Rosy, frozen leg, with apron. Silk type rose print fabric. $55.00.

#159 Ring Around the Rosy, frozen leg, with apron. Variation with organdy skirt. $45.00.

#159 Ring Around a Rosy, frozen leg, without apron. $45.00 each.

#159 Ring Around a Rosy, frozen leg, without apron. $45.00 each.

#159 Ring Around the Rosy, frozen leg, with apron. Plastic apron, dotted swiss skirt. $45.00.

#159 Ring Around the Rosy, frozen leg, with apron. Purple taffeta (no flower in pocket). $45.00.

#159 Ring Around a Rosy, frozen leg, without apron. $45.00 each.

#159 Ring Around a Rosy, frozen leg, without apron. $45.00 each.

#160 Pretty Maid, jointed leg. MS. Delicate shadow print with two rows of taffeta ruching. Net underskirt. $250.00.

#160 Pretty Maid, jointed leg. PT. Separate lace-trimmed slip, flocked dots print. $160.00.

#160 Pretty Maid, jointed leg. MS. Variation, blue organdy. $250.00.

#160 Pretty Maid, jointed leg. PT. Variation. Daisy print flocked, attached slip. Also in blue. $160.00.

#160 Pretty Maid, jointed leg. JT. Floral print. $125.00.

#160 Pretty Maid, frozen leg. Taffeta underskirt, organdy overskirt. White organdy apron with scalloped edge. Also with organdy apron with rose print. $55.00.

#160 Pretty Maid, frozen leg. Solid pink underskirt, and apron variation. $55.00.

#160 Pretty Maid, frozen leg. Variation. Daisy print. $55.00.

#160 Pretty Maid, frozen leg. White flocked parasol print dress. $55.00.

#160 Pretty Maid, frozen leg. Variation, blue, flocked polka dots fabric. $55.00.

#160 Pretty Maid, frozen leg. $55.00.

#160 Pretty Maid, frozen leg. Florist ribbon. $45.00.

#160 Pretty Maid, frozen leg. Blue sheer dress with felt bonnet, also in pink with headband $45.00. Also on NA mold, plastic arms. $40.00.

#161 Jennie Set the Table, jointed leg. PT. Green dotted swiss with separate apron. $135.00. Also with attached apron. $125.00.

#161 Jennie Set the Table, jointed leg. JT. $125.00.

#161 Jennie Set the Table, frozen leg. Variation. $55.00.

#161 Jennie Set the Table, frozen leg. Variation. $55.00.

#161 Jennie Set the Table, frozen leg. Variation of fabric on page 208, bottom left, but frozen leg. $55.00.

#161 Jennie Set the Table, frozen leg. Variation. $55.00.

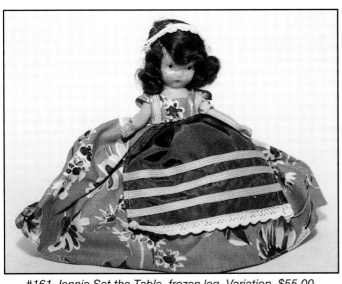

#161 Jennie Set the Table, frozen leg. Variation. $55.00.

#161 Jennie Set the Table, frozen leg. Variation. $55.00.

#161 Jennie Set the Table, frozen leg. Plaid taffeta, matching apron and headband. $55.00.

#161 Jennie Set the Table, frozen leg. Cotton polka dot dress. Also with crochet-type trim. $55.00.

#161 Jennie Set the Table, frozen leg. Two variations of green striped taffeta dress. $55.00.

#161 Jennie Set the Table, frozen leg. Variation in print, with crochet-type trim. $55.00.

#161 Jennie Set the Table, frozen leg. Black-checked skirt. $45.00.

#161 Jennie Set the Table, frozen leg. Variation. Green-checked skirt, braid trim. $45.00.

#161 Jennie Set the Table, frozen leg. Variation in apron and bodice. Eyelet-trimmed headband. $45.00.

#161 Jennie Set the Table, frozen leg. Taffeta plaid dress, florist ribbon. $45.00.

#162 Princess Rosanie, jointed leg. PT. $125.00.

#162 Princess Rosanie, jointed leg. JT. $125.00.

#162 Princess Rosanie, frozen leg. $55.00.

#162 Princess Rosanie, frozen leg. $55.00 each.

#162 Princess Rosanie, frozen leg. $55.00.

#162 Princess Rosanie, frozen leg. Paper crown. $65.00.

#162 Princess Rosanie, frozen leg. $55.00.

#162 Princess Rosanie, frozen leg. $55.00.

#162 Princess Rosanie, frozen leg. Florist ribbon. $45.00.

#162 Princess Rosanie, frozen leg. Florist ribbon. $45.00.

#162 Princess Rosanie, frozen leg. Florist ribbon. Plastic arms. $40.00.

#163 Little Miss Donnet, jointed leg. PT. Separate slip. $150.00.

#163 Little Miss Donnet, jointed leg. PT. Separate slip. $150.00.

#163 Little Miss Donnet, jointed leg. JT. $125.00.

#163 Little Miss Donnet, frozen leg. $55.00 each.

#163 Little Miss Donnet, frozen leg. $55.00 each.

#163 Little Miss Donnet, frozen leg. $55.00.

#163 Little Miss Donnet, frozen leg. NA mold. Plastic arms. $40.00.

#163 Little Miss Donnet, frozen leg. Plastic arms. $40.00.

•••Storybook Series•••
Nursery Rhyme
#168 – 179

#168 Silks and Satin, jointed leg. JT. Pink taffeta, satin insert panel. $95.00. Also on frozen-leg mold. $60.00.

#168 Silks and Satin, frozen leg. Fabric with painted striped. $45.00.

#168 Silks and Satin, frozen leg. Pink satin. Also in white. Floral ribbon. $45.00.

#168 Silks and Satin, frozen leg. $45.00.

216

#168 Silks and Satin, frozen leg. NA mold. $40.00.

#169 Goose Girl, frozen leg. Heavy blue skirt. Organdy Dutch-style hat. $65.00.

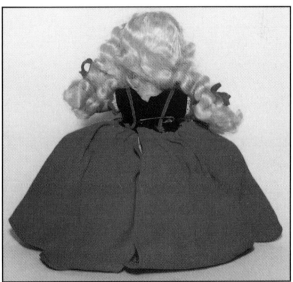

Front and back view. #169 Goose Girl, frozen leg. Exceptionally long wavy blond wig, part in the center. Each side tied with red ribbons. Heavy cotton skirt. This doll did not come with a hat. $65.00.

#169 Goose Girl, frozen leg. Red/white taffeta. $65.00.

#169 Goose Girl, frozen leg. Plaid taffeta. $65.00.

#169 Goose Girl, frozen leg. Transition to regular length wig. Lace hat and apron. Plaid taffeta dress. $55.00.

#169 Goose Girl, frozen leg. Cotton print. $55.00.

#169 Goose Girl, frozen leg. NA mold. Plastic arms. $45.00.

#169 Goose Girl, frozen leg. NA mold. Plastic arms. $45.00.

#170 Rain Rain, Go Away, frozen leg. $55.00 each.

#170 Rain Rain, Go Away, frozen leg. $55.00 each.

#170 Rain Rain, Go Away, frozen leg. $55.00.

#170 Rain Rain, Go Away, frozen leg. NA mold. $45.00.

#170 Rain Rain, Go Away, frozen leg. NA mold, plastic arms. $45.00.

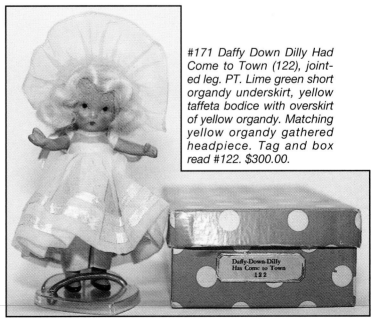

#171 Daffy Down Dilly Had Come to Town (122), jointed leg. PT. Lime green short organdy underskirt, yellow taffeta bodice with overskirt of yellow organdy. Matching yellow organdy gathered headpiece. Tag and box read #122. $300.00.

Right. #171 Daffy Down Dilly Had Come to Town (122), jointed leg. Back view of bonnet.

Below. #171 Daffy Down Dilly Had Come to Town (122), jointed leg. PT. Lime green taffeta underskirt. Yellow organdy Dutch-style organdy bonnet with yellow ribbon. $250.00.

#171 Daffy Down Dilly Had Come to Town (122), frozen leg. Variation, felt hat, with ruffled brim. $55.00.

#171 Daffy Down Dilly Had Come to Town (122), frozen leg. Long lime green taffeta underskirt, flocked overskirt. $55.00.

#171 Daffy Down Dilly Had Come to Town (122), frozen leg. Variation in flocked overskirt. $55.00.

171 Daffy Down Dilly Had Come to Town (122), frozen leg. Variation, short taffeta overskirt. $55.00.

#171 Daffy Down Dilly Had Come to Town (122), frozen leg. Yellow taffeta. Short flocked overskirt. $55.00.

#171 Daffy Down Dilly Had Come to Town (122), frozen leg. $55.00.

#171 Daffy Down Dilly Had Come to Town (122), frozen leg. Light green organdy underskirt. $55.00.

#171 Daffy Down Dilly Had Come to Town (122), frozen leg. Floral ribbon. $45.00.

#171 Daffy Down Dilly Had Come to Town (122), frozen leg. Floral ribbon. $45.00.

#171 Daffy Down Dilly Had Come to Town (122), frozen leg. Floral ribbon. $45.00.

#172 Snow Queen, frozen leg. Two-tier dress, flocked and lace. Paper crown with net. $60.00.

#172 Snow Queen, frozen leg. Feather in hair. Variation with flower in hair. $55.00.

#172 Snow Queen, frozen leg. Plastic arms. $45.00.

#172 Snow Queen, frozen leg. NA mold. Unusual wrist tag reads "The Queen Snow," plastic arms. $45.00.

#173 Polly Put the Kettle on, jointed leg (#161). PT. Original wooden kettle attached to wrist. Tag reads #161. $175.00.

#173 Polly Put the Kettle on, jointed leg (#161). PT. Original wooden kettle attached to wrist. Tag reads #161. $175.00.

#173 Polly Put the Kettle on (#161), frozen leg (changed to #173). Red taffeta skirt, red/white check bodice, and dotted swiss apron. $55.00.

#173 Polly Put the Kettle on (#161), frozen leg (changed to #173). Black taffeta dress. At least four different organdy aprons. $55.00.

#173 Polly Put the Kettle on (#161), frozen leg (changed to #173). Floral ribbon. $45.00.

#173 Polly Put the Kettle on (#161), frozen leg (changed to #173). Variation of apron, plastic arms. $45.00.

#174 Flossie Came from Dublin Town, frozen leg. $55.00 each.

#174 Flossie Came from Dublin Town, frozen leg. $55.00 each.

#174 Flossie Came from Dublin Town, frozen leg. Plaid taffeta, floral ribbon. $45.00.

#174 Flossie Came from Dublin Town, frozen leg. Floral ribbon. $45.00.

#174A Florie Came from Dublin Town, frozen leg. Floral ribbon. $45.00.

#174A Florie Came from Dublin Town, frozen leg. NA mold, plastic arms. $45.00.

#175 Jack and Jill Went Up the Hill (#19 and #14). Jack and Jill were sold as a pair in one box with divider insert to hold both dolls securely in box. Not found on frozen leg mold, the pair Jack and Jill were dropped from stock, and #175 was replaced with the frozen leg Maiden Bright and Gay. $600.00 pair.

#175 Jack and Jill Went Up the Hill (#19 and #14), jointed leg. MIJ 1146. Early wool wigs. Jack has cotton cord short blue pants. Owner feels confident that these are Jack and Jill. Only pair in this outfit found so far. $1,200.00 pair.

#175 Jack and Jill Went Up the Hill (#19 and #14), jointed leg. Japan. Jack has blue polished cotton short pants, white shirt with three rows of rickrack trim. Jill has matching dress with separate apron with two rows or rickrack, tied with red ribbon, matching red ribbon in hair, front dart underpants. Also found with white boots. $1,100.00 pair.

#175 Jack and Jill Went Up the Hill (#19 and #14), jointed leg. JA. Variation, both with white boots. Box reads #14. $1,000.00 pair.

#175 Jack and Jill Went Up the Hill, jointed leg. JA and MS/MB. $900.00 pair.

#175 Jack and Jill Went Up the Hill, jointed leg. MS/MB. $1,000.00 pair.

#175 Jack and Jill Went Up the Hill, jointed leg. MS. Variation, but in yellow. $1,000.00 pair.

#175 Jack and Jill Went Up the Hill, jointed leg. MS/MB and MS. Ruffled organdy sleeves have inset all the way to waist. $900.00 pair.

#175 Jack and Jill Went Up the Hill, jointed leg. PT. Two sizes of red polka dots. White box. #175 wrist tag. $600.00 pair.

#175 Maiden Bright and Gay, frozen leg. Pink flocked dress. $55.00.

#175 Maiden Bright and Gay, frozen leg. Blue flocked dress, satin inset panel. $55.00.

#175 Maiden Bright and Gay, frozen leg. Blue flocked skirt, satin bodice. $55.00.

#175 Maiden Bright and Gay, frozen leg. Floral ribbon. $45.00.

#175 Maiden Bright and Gay, frozen leg. Blue and pink. $45.00.

#175 Maiden Bright and Gay, frozen leg. $55.00.

#175 Maiden Bright and Gay, frozen leg. Plastic arms. $45.00.

> **#176 Topsy and Eva pair**
>
> #18 early number sold as a pair
> Topsy #26 and #137 later numbers sold separately.
> Eva #27 and #138 later numbers sold separately.

Topsy and Eva were sold as a pair through 1941. In 1942 they were discontinued. However, in 1944 through 1946 they were again listed in the factory pamphlets, only this time separately as #137 and #138 and with the "Temporarily out of Stock" notation. They were again launched in 1947 – 48 and listed separately again as #26 and #27. Topsy has black boots with white dot buttons, until the frozen leg period. Eva has white boots until the molded sock period. When Topsy and Eva were discontinued, #176 became Nellie Bird.

#176 Topsy and Eva, jointed leg. Japan. Topsy, unusual green/white check variation. Japan 1146. Eva has gathered collar. $2,000.00 pair.

229

Right. #176 Topsy and Eva, jointed leg. Japan. Topsy variation in unusual blue/white check. $1,000.00.

Left. #176 Topsy and Eva, jointed leg. Japan. Pair with topknot under wig. Topsy, brown bisque, frizzy black center-part wig. Sleeveless red/white check dress, separate apron. Eva has white painted boots, a dress gathered at neck, and lace at sleeve openings. $1,800.00 pair.

Left. #176 Topsy and Eva, jointed leg. America. Topsy, no apron. $500.00. JA Topsy. $400.00.

Right. #176 Topsy and Eva, jointed leg. Japan. Variation. Eva with ribbon at waist and unusual wider lace at hemline and Topsy has actual sleeves. $1,700.00 pair.

#176 Topsy and Eva, jointed leg. MS/MB. $900.00 pair.

#176 Topsy and Eva, jointed leg. JA. Topsy, separate apron. Also CM mold. Eva, unusual yellow picot-edged gathered collar and ruffled skirt. White or blue bow in hair. $1,100.00 pair.

#176 Topsy and Eva, jointed leg. MS. Topsy, plaid, Eva in pink print, now with black slippers. Also MS/MB. $900.00 pair.

#176 Topsy and Eva, jointed leg. MS. Topsy dress variation. $800.00.

#176 Topsy and Eva, jointed leg. MS. $800.00 pair.

#176 Topsy and Eva, jointed leg. JT. Topsy, dress red, white, and blue. Eva, blue print variation. Eva's dress also comes in pink. $700.00 pair.

#176 Topsy and Eva, frozen leg. Topsy, long taffeta plaid. $85.00. Eva, pinch face. Both with plastic arms. Gold snap closure. Eva. $65.00. Topsy and Eva now sold separately, label reads "Fairytale Series #Topsy #26" and "Fairytale Series Eva #27."

#176 Topsy and Eva, jointed leg. JT. Topsy dress variation. $700.00 pair.

#176 Nellie Bird, frozen leg. Broom attached to wrist. $60.00.

#176 Nellie Bird replaces #176 Topsy and Eva.

#176 Nellie Bird, frozen leg. No longer comes with broom. $50.00.

#176 Nellie Bird, frozen leg. Variation, missing broom. If complete $55.00.

#176 Nellie Bird, frozen leg. No longer comes with broom. $50.00.

#176 Nellie Bird, frozen leg. No longer comes with broom. $50.00.

#176 Nellie Bird, frozen leg. Plastic apron. $45.00.

#176 Nellie Bird, frozen leg. Variation in lavender. $45.00.

Hansel and Grethel were sold together as a pair in one box. The early number for this character is #24. They have coordinating fabrics. Early Hansel has a lined jacket, a ribbon around neck, and no hat. The early Grethel has a ribbon in her hair. Later Grethels have felt hats and Hansels have short felt jackets, and the last version Hansel has no jacket. In 1944 the spelling of Grethel was changed to Gretel. This pair was discontinued at the end of the jointed-leg period and #177 later was used for See Saw, Marjorie Daw on a frozen leg mold.

#177 Hansel & Grethel (#24), jointed leg. JA. Grethel has blue polished cotton vest, inset sleeves of the bright leaf pattern fabric of skirt, red polished cotton apron, and red ribbon trim at edge of skirt. Hansel has long blue felt jacket lined with print fabric, coordinating with Grethel. His jodhpurs and her skirt are of the same print fabric. $1,200.00 pair.

#177 Hansel & Grethel (#24), jointed leg. JA. Grethel, bodice and skirt of floral print skirt with red cotton vest sewn onto bodice. Edge of skirt has strip of red polished cotton matching vest. Attached apron matches Hansel's jodhpurs, probably was bright blue, now faded to gray. His long jacket lined with Grethel's floral print dress fabric. $1,200.00 pair.

#177 Hansel & Grethel (#24), jointed leg. JA. Variation. Grethel has red bodice, two rows of ribbon trim on skirt, no apron. Hansel has red jacket and solid blue jodhpurs, SBD sticker. $1,200.00 pair.

#177 Hansel & Grethel (#24), jointed leg. JA. Short red felt jacket on Hansel. Grethel wears red felt hat. Yellow print dress with brown leaves, one row of ribbon trim. $1,100.00. Also found in MS/MB mold in small silver dot box. SBD sticker. $1,000.00.

#177 Hansel & Grethel (#24), jointed leg. MS. Aqua print dress and shirt. $700.00 pair.

#177 Hansel & Grethel (#24), jointed leg. MS. Hansel no longer wears jacket. $700.00 pair.

#177 Hansel & Grethel (#24), jointed leg. MS/MB. Hansel, blue jodhpurs, felt jacket. Purple/green flowers, yellow print matching Grethel's dress and Hansel's shirt. Grethel now wears red felt hat. SBD sticker. $1,100.00 pair.

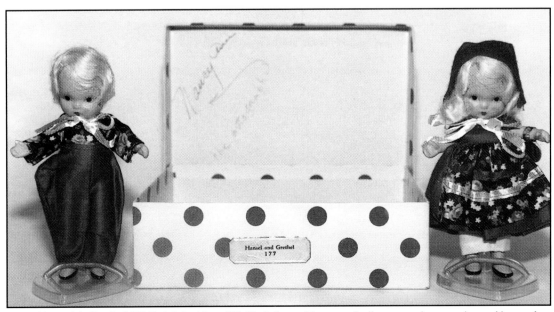

#177 Hansel & Grethel (#24), jointed leg. PT. Variation with green jodhpurs and green dress. Nancy Ann Abbott's signature on box lid. $700.00 pair. Value of original signature, add $200.00 more.

#177 Hansel & Grethel (#24), jointed leg. MS/MB. Yet another yellow print pair variation, with Hansel is dark green jodhpurs. Small silver dot box. SBD sticker. $1,100.00 a pair.

#177 Hansel & Grethel (#24), jointed leg. MS. Aqua floral print. $700.00 pair.

The #177 See-Saw, Marjorie Daw character now replaces Hansel & Grethel (Gretel).

#177 See-Saw, Marjorie Daw, frozen leg. Cotton dress, satin floral print front panel. $55.00.

#177 See-Saw, Marjorie Daw, frozen leg. Variation. Blue polka dot flocked dress, taffeta rosebud insert. $55.00.

#177 See-Saw, Marjorie Daw, frozen leg. Solid blue taffeta dress. $55.00.

#177 See-Saw, Marjorie Daw, frozen leg. Variation. Magenta and striped fabrics. $55.00.

#177 See-Saw, Marjorie Daw, frozen leg. Silk underskirt, net overskirt. $55.00.

#177 See-Saw, Marjorie Daw, frozen leg. Florist ribbon. Pale apricot taffeta dress. $45.00.

#177 See-Saw, Marjorie Daw, frozen leg. Floral ribbon. Satin bodice. $45.00.

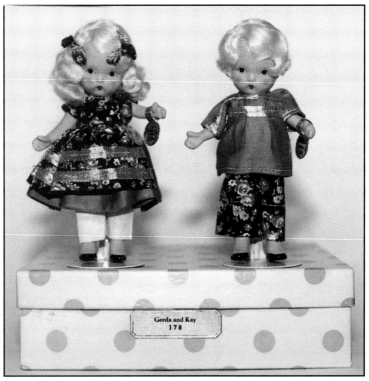

#178 Gerda and Kay, jointed leg. PT. This pair was sold together as a pair. This is the only outfit found for Gerda and Kay. Kay wears polished cotton navy floral print long pants. Shirt is blue with front tuck trimmed in pink ribbon. Gerda has matching blue floral bodice and apron, with blue skirt. Gerda has two bright blue ribbons in her hair. Kay does not wear a hat. Gerda and Kay were offered briefly and quickly discontinued, and replaced with #178, Give Me a Lassie on the frozen leg mold. $1,200.00+ for pair.

The #178 Give Me a Lassie as Sweet as She's Fair character replaced #178 Gerda and Kay.

#178 Give Me a Lassie as Sweet as She's Fair, frozen leg. $55.00.

#178 Give Me a Lassie as Sweet as She's Fair, frozen leg. Variation in beige. $55.00.

#178 Give Me a Lassie as Sweet as She's Fair, frozen leg. $55.00.

#178 Give Me a Lassie as Sweet as She's Fair, frozen leg. $55.00.

#178 Give Me a Lassie as Sweet as She's Fair, frozen leg. $55.00.

#178 Give Me a Lassie as Sweet as She's Fair, frozen leg. Florist ribbon. $45.00.

#178 Give Me a Lassie as Sweet as She's Fair, frozen leg. Florist ribbon. $45.00.

#178 Give Me a Lassie as Sweet as She's Fair, frozen leg. Florist ribbon. $45.00.

239

#179 The Babes in the Wood, jointed leg. PT. This boy and girl pair were made only in this outfit and sold together as a pair in red polka dot, white box with double dividers, large enough to accommodate both dolls. Silver box label reads "The Babes in the Wood #179." Red/white checked matching cotton outfits with one patch of blue print material sewn on each doll. Girl wears pointed hat trimmed in red felt and ribbon. Boy does not wear hat. This pair was offered briefly and quickly discontinued, replaced with Daisy Belle, Daisy Belle only on a frozen leg mold. $1,000.00 pair.

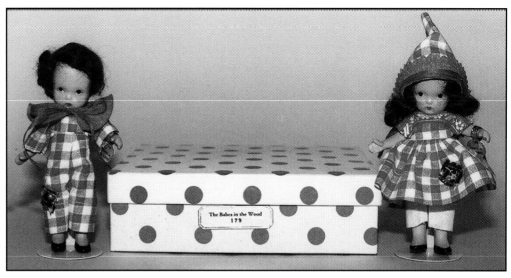

The #179 Daisy Belle, Daisy Belle character replaced #179 The Babes in the Wood.

#179 Daisy Belle, Daisy Belle, frozen leg. $55.00.

#179 Daisy Belle, Daisy Belle, frozen leg. $55.00.

#179 Daisy Belle, Daisy Belle, frozen leg. Felt daisy on skirt and hat. $55.00.

#179 Daisy Belle, Daisy Belle, frozen leg. Variation in yellow. $55.00.

#179 Daisy Belle, Daisy Belle, frozen leg. Magenta, daisies on skirt, dress also in white. Florist ribbon. $45.00.

#179 Daisy Belle, Daisy Belle, frozen leg. Plastic arms. $45.00.

•●● Dolls of the Day Series ●●•
#180 – #186

This was one of the most successful series for the company, especially though the late 1940s. A popular gift for a little girl's birthday, The Days of the Week Series was listed first in the 1941 factory pamphlet. However, some Days of the Week were marketed as early as 1940 on the molded sock mold. The name "Birthday Dolls" was trademarked for these dolls in 1945 – 1946. However, the series was officially still called Dolls of the Day Series on the boxes and labels. The Days of the Week continued to be offered through the balance of the bisque era and continued throughout the plastic era.

#180 Monday's Child Is Fair of Face, jointed leg. PT. Dotted swiss, various taffeta print underskirts, some with separate slips. $125.00.

#180 Monday's Child Is Fair of Face, jointed leg. MS. Pink taffeta, found with pink or blue velvet ribbon trim, two-layer separate net or cotton slip. Silver or black slippers. $250.00.

#180 Monday's Child Is Fair of Face, jointed leg. PT. Dotted swiss, pink taffeta underskirt, two vertical gathers. $125.00.

#180 Monday's Child Is Fair of Face, frozen leg. $55.00.

#180 Monday's Child Is Fair of Face, jointed leg. PT. Variation of above, flocked fabric. $125.00.

#180 Monday's Child Is Fair of Face, frozen leg. $55.00.

#180 Monday's Child Is Fair of Face, frozen leg. $55.00.

#180 Monday's Child Is Fair of Face, frozen leg. $55.00.

#180 Monday's Child Is Fair of Face, frozen leg. $45.00.

#180 Monday's Child Is Fair of Face, frozen leg. $45.00.

243

#180 Monday's Child Is Fair of Face, frozen leg. $45.00.

#181 Tuesday's Child Is Full of Grace, jointed leg. MS. Blue satin bodice and over-skirt with three-layer separate net front panel, ribbon rosebud trim, and headband. Net sleeves. Also in white satin. $250.00.

#181 Tuesday's Child Is Full of Grace, jointed leg. PT. Magenta taffeta. Also on JT. $125.00.

#181 Tuesday's Child Is Full of Grace, jointed leg. PT. Magenta taffeta. Also on JT. $125.00.

#181 Tuesday's Child Is Full of Grace, frozen leg. Blue flocked large floral print. Also in pink flocked. $65.00.

#181 Tuesday's Child Is Full of Grace, frozen leg. Variation in solid white, but same trim. $65.00.

#181 Tuesday's Child Is Full of Grace, frozen leg. Dress design in a variety of different flocked fabrics and ribbons with print or plain taffeta inset panel. $55.00.

#181 Tuesday's Child Is Full of Grace, frozen leg. Lavender taffeta underskirt, flocked overskirt. $55.00.

#181 Tuesday's Child Is Full of Grace, frozen leg. $55.00.

#181 Tuesday's Child Is Full of Grace, frozen leg. Florist ribbon. $45.00.

#182 Wednesday's Child Is Full of Woe, jointed leg. PT. Two-tier organdy. $150.00.

#182 Wednesday's Child Is Full of Woe, jointed leg. Variation. Polka dot taffeta underskirt. $125.00. Also with no lace or flowers on hankerchief. $100.00.

All the bisque Wednesday's Child costumes come with a handkerchief attached to her wrist.

#182 Wednesday's Child Is Full of Woe, jointed leg. MS. Two layers each of black and pink net. $250.00.

#182 Wednesday's Child Is Full of Woe, jointed leg. PT. Floral print taffeta underskirt, organdy overskirt. $150.00.

#182 Wednesday's Child Is Full of Woe, frozen leg. $55.00.

246

#182 Wednesday's Child Is Full of Woe, frozen leg. $55.00.

#182 Wednesday's Child Is Full of Woe, frozen leg. $55.00.

#182 Wednesday's Child Is Full of Woe, frozen leg. $55.00.

#182 Wednesday's Child Is Full of Woe, frozen leg. $45.00.

Above left. #183 Thursday's Child Has Far to Go, jointed leg. MS. Taffeta gown. Separate black lace shawl and separate pink net slip. $300.00.

Above right. #183 Thursday's Child Has Far to Go, jointed leg. View of separate black lace shawl.

#183 Thursday's Child Has Far to Go, jointed leg. MS. Separate white lace stole. $300.00.

#183 Thursday's Child Has Far to Go, jointed leg. PT. $135.00.

#183 Thursday's Child Has Far to Go, jointed leg. PT. Cherries on hat, multicolored fringe trim, long arm. $135.00.

#183 Thursday's Child Has Far to Go, jointed leg. Variation of left, slim and frozen leg. $125.00.

#183 Thursday's Child Has Far to Go, frozen leg. Donut print dress. $55.00.

#183 Thursday's Child Has Far to Go, frozen leg. Spruce silk dress, brown silk ribbon, flowers attached to ribbon dress at hem, plum felt bonnet. $60.00.

#183 Thursday's Child Has Far to Go, frozen leg. Variation. Pumpkin silk. $60.00.

#183 Thursday's Child Has Far to Go, frozen leg. Variation. Ivory silk. $60.00.

#183 Thursday's Child Has Far to Go, frozen leg. Variation. Heliotrope silk, yellow silk ribbon. $60.00.

#183 Thursday's Child Has Far to Go, frozen leg. Variation. Burgundy silk. $60.00.

#183 Thursday's Child Has Far to Go, frozen leg. Variation. Bronze silk. $60.00.

#183 Thursday's Child Has Far to Go, frozen leg. Variation. Blue/green iridescent silk, rust ribbon. $60.00.

#183 Thursday's Child Has Far to Go, frozen leg. Variation. Sage silk, rust ribbon. $60.00.

#183 Thursday's Child Has Far to Go, frozen leg. Variation. Raisin silk, peach grosgrain ribbon. $60.00.

#183 Thursday's Child Has Far to Go, frozen leg. Variation of silk dress, but in gold taffeta. Also in burgundy taffeta. $55.00.

#183 Thursday's Child Has Far to Go, frozen leg. Yellow taffeta, red bows. $55.00.

#183 Thursday's Child Has Far to Go, frozen leg. Variation in salmon taffeta, blue bows. $60.00.

#183 Thursday's Child Has Far to Go, frozen leg. Yellow eyelet inset panel. $55.00.

#183 Thursday's Child Has Far to Go, frozen leg. Red plaid, florist ribbon. $45.00.

#183 Thursday's Child Has Far to Go, frozen leg. Satin gown. Florist ribbon. $45.00.

#183 Thursday's Child Has Far to Go, frozen leg. NA mold. Plastic arms. $45.00.

All Friday's Child costumes have a wrapped "gift" made of paper tied to the wrist.

#184 Friday's Child Is Loving and Giving, jointed leg. MS. Pink taffeta print with blue paper gift. Velvet ribbon trim and headband. $250.00.

#184 Friday's Child Is Loving and Giving, jointed leg. PT. Variation in white taffeta print, velvet ribbon trim, and headband. $200.00.

#184 Friday's Child Is Loving and Giving, jointed leg. MS. Variation in white taffeta print with blue paper gift. Velvet ribbon trim and headband. $250.00.

#184 *Friday's Child Is Loving and Giving, jointed leg. MS. Sheer pink "large sunflower-daisy" flocked overskirt $200.00. Pink gift. Also PT. $150.00.*

#184 *Friday's Child Is Loving and Giving, jointed leg. PT. Variation in pink small daisy flocked overskirt. $150.00.*

#184 *Friday's Child Is Loving and Giving, jointed leg. Taffeta floral, blue gift. $125.00.*

#184 *Friday's Child Is Loving and Giving, jointed leg. JT. Royal blue taffeta. $125.00.*

#184 *Friday's Child Is Loving and Giving, frozen leg. $55.00.*

#184 Friday's Child Is Loving and Giving, frozen leg. $55.00.

#184 Friday's Child Is Loving and Giving, frozen leg. Florist ribbon. $45.00.

#184 Friday's Child Is Loving and Giving, frozen leg. Florist ribbon. $45.00.

#185 Saturday's Child Must Work for a Living, jointed leg with broom. MS. Separate net or cotton slip, net dust cap. $250.00.

#185 Saturday's Child Must Work for a Living, jointed leg with broom. MS or PT. Separate cotton slip. $250.00.

#185 Saturday's Child Must Work for a Living, jointed leg with broom. JT. Separate cotton slip. $150.00.

#185 Saturday's Child Must Work for a Living, jointed leg with broom. JT. Dotted swiss, now attached slip. $125.00.

#185 Saturday's Child Must Work for a Living, jointed leg with broom. JT. Red/white checked taffeta. $125.00.

#185 Saturday's Child Must Work for a Living, jointed leg with broom. JT. Variation of photo above. $105.00. Also frozen leg with white rickrack trim. $65.00.

#185 Saturday's Child Must Work for a Living, frozen leg with broom. Variation of top photo. $75.00.

#185 Saturday's Child Must Work for a Living, frozen leg with broom. Variation of top photo. $75.00.

#185 Saturday's Child Must Work for a Living, frozen leg with broom. Heavy cotton with flower or red-star trim. $75.00.

#185 Saturday's Child Must Work for a Living, frozen leg with broom. Seersucker. $75.00.

#185 Saturday's Child Must Work for a Living, frozen leg without broom. $55.00.

#185 Saturday's Child Must Work for a Living, frozen leg without broom. Blue and white gingham, organdy apron and hat, dutch style hat; variation in dotted Swiss apron and hat and blue organdy dress with no apron. $55.00.

#185 Saturday's Child Must Work for a Living, frozen leg without broom. Yellow taffeta with eyelet apron, florist ribbon. $45.00.

#185 Saturday's Child Must Work for a Living, frozen leg without broom. Red dotted swiss. Bow in hair. $55.00.

#185 Saturday's Child, frozen leg. Without broom. $55.00.

#186 The Child that Was Born on the Sabbath, jointed leg. MS. Satin underskirt, separate net or cotton slip. $250.00.

#186 The Child that Was Born on the Sabbath, jointed leg. PT. Two-tier organdy, separate cotton slip. $175.00.

#186 The Child that Was Born on the Sabbath, jointed leg. MS. Taffeta underskirt, separate cotton slip. $250.00. JT. $175.00.

#186 The Child that Was Born on the Sabbath, jointed leg. JT. Flocked organdy. $125.00.

#186 The Child that Was Born on the Sabbath, jointed leg. JT. Striped organdy. $125.00.

#186 The Child that Was Born on the Sabbath, jointed leg. JT. Dotted Swiss. $125.00.

#186 The Child that Was Born on the Sabbath, jointed leg. JT. Daisy flocked organdy. $125.00.

#186 The Child that Was Born on the Sabbath, frozen leg. $55.00.

#186 The Child that Was Born on the Sabbath, frozen leg. $45.00.

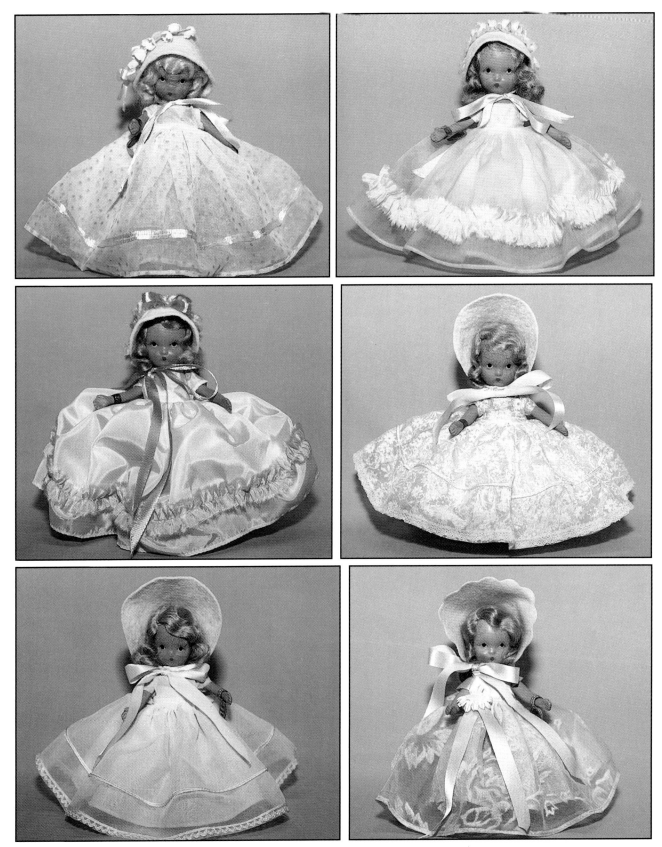

#186 The Child that Was Born on the Sabbath, frozen leg. $45.00.

#187 A January Merry Maid for New Year, jointed leg, socket head. Inserted front panel, multi-striped satin. $125.00.

#187 A January Merry Maid for New Year, jointed leg, socket head. Variation. Multi-striped taffeta panel. $125.00.

#187 A January Merry Maid for New Year, frozen leg, socket head. Two rows red taffeta ruche trim vertically down dress. Multicolor striped taffeta dress. $100.00.

#187 A January Merry Maid for New Year, frozen leg, socket head. Variation. Red and white stripe trim. $100.00.

#187 A January Merry Maid for New Year, frozen leg, socket head. Variation. Black ruche trim. $100.00.

#187 A January Merry Maid for New Year, frozen leg, socket head. Two rows of ribbon trim at bottom of skirt. $100.00.

#187 A January Merry Maid for New Year, frozen leg. Two rows of ribbon trim, either pink or blue ribbon trim. $65.00.

#187 A January Merry Maid for New Year, frozen leg. Variation with gold ribbon. $65.00.

#187 A January Merry Maid for New Year, frozen leg. Red chiffon overskirt. Change to black felt hat with ribbon bow. $65.00.

#187 A January Merry Maid for New Year, frozen leg. Green/yellow combination. Variation in yellow chiffon. Variation with green taffeta overskirt and yellow taffeta underskirt with red/green ribbon trim. $65.00.

Left. #187 A January Merry Maid for New Year, frozen leg. Red taffeta skirt, blue cord trim. $60.00.

Right. #187 A January Merry Maid for New Year, frozen leg. Variation, black cord trim. $60.00.

Left. #187 A January Merry Maid for New Year, frozen leg. Plaid skirt. Florist ribbon. $50.00.

Right. #187 A January Merry Maid for New Year, frozen leg. Multi-color polka-dot skirt. Plastic arms. Florist ribbon. $45.00.

#187 A January Merry Maid for New Year, frozen leg. Striped overskirt. Plastic arms. Florist ribbon. $45.00.

#187 A January Merry Maid for New Year, frozen leg. Green felt half-hat. Plastic arms. Florist ribbon. $45.00.

#187 A January Merry Maid for New Year, frozen leg. Hat discontinued, now ribbon in hair, plastic arms. Florist ribbon. $45.00.

#188 A February Fairy Girl for Ice and Snow, jointed leg, socket head. Satin with ecru dots on inserted sheer fabric panel. Unhemmed net ruche trim at hem, trimmed in wide vertical lace. $125.00.

#188 A February Fairy Girl for Ice and Snow, jointed leg, socket head. Variation with flocked daisy pattern. Also found with plain sheer panel. $125.00.

#188 A February Fairy Girl for Ice and Snow, jointed leg, socket head. Variation with larger sparkle-dot fabric in panel. $125.00.

#188 A February Fairy Girl for Ice and Snow, frozen leg, socket head. Circular light blue taffeta flocked polka dot dress, taffeta ruche trim at hem. Also in white taffeta. $100.00.

#188 A February Fairy Girl for Ice and Snow, frozen leg, socket head. Circular white taffeta, flocked flowers, taffeta ruche trim at hem. $100.00.

#188 A February Fairy Girl for Ice and Snow, frozen leg, socket head. Variation, light blue with blue feather, slip attached. $100.00.

#188 A February Fairy Girl for Ice and Snow, frozen leg. $65.00.

#188 A February Fairy Girl for Ice and Snow, frozen leg. $65.00.

#188 A February Fairy Girl for Ice and Snow, frozen leg. $65.00.

#188 A February Fairy Girl for Ice and Snow, frozen leg. Plastic arms. Florist ribbon. $45.00.

All the socket-head March dolls wear the same style dress, but in different fabrics.

Left. #189 A Breezy Girl and Arch for Worship Me Through March, jointed leg, socket head. Peach velvet. $150.00.

Right. #189 A Breezy Girl and Arch for Worship Me Through March, jointed leg, socket head. Variation, taffeta. $125.00. Also on frozen-leg socket mold. $100.00.

#189 A Breezy Girl and Arch for Worship Me Through March, frozen leg, socket head. Variation, satin shadow print. $100.00. Also on frozen-leg mold. $75.00.

#189 A Breezy Girl and Arch for Worship Me Through March, frozen leg, socket head. Variation, shadow print. $100.00. Also frozen leg. $75.00.

#189 A Breezy Girl and Arch for Worship Me Through March, frozen leg, socket head. Variation flocked taffeta. $100.00. Also frozen leg with trim variation. $75.00.

#189 A Breezy Girl and Arch for Worship Me Through March, frozen leg. Dress style has changed. No longer the stylish black hat, but a typical bonnet. $65.00.

#189 A Breezy Girl and Arch for Worship Me Through March, frozen leg. Various eyelet panels, various trimmed felt bonnets, either flowers or feather. $65.00.

#189 A Breezy Girl and Arch for Worship Me Through March, frozen leg. Cat print. $75.00.

#189 A Breezy Girl and Arch for Worship Me Through March, frozen leg. Pink ruche trim on organdy dress. $65.00.

#189 A Breezy Girl and Arch for Worship Me Through March, frozen leg. Sheer lavender dress, florist ribbon. $45.00.

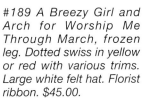

#189 A Breezy Girl and Arch for Worship Me Through March, frozen leg. Dotted swiss in yellow or red with various trims. Large white felt hat. Florist ribbon. $45.00.

#189 A Breezy Girl and Arch for Worship Me Through March, frozen leg. Black and white checked. Florist ribbon. $45.00.

#189 A Breezy Girl and Arch for Worship Me Through March, frozen leg. Satin. Florist ribbon. $45.00.

All April dolls have a fabric umbrella with pipe cleaner staff.

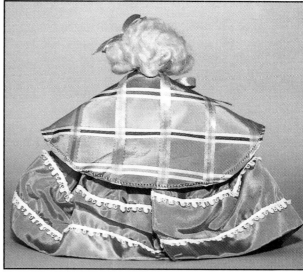

#190 A Shower Girl for April, jointed leg, socket head. Front and back view. Variation. Plaid cape. Umbrella missing. With umbrella, $150.00.

#190 A Shower Girl for April, jointed leg, socket head. Floral taffeta cape with matching umbrella. $125.00.

#190 A Shower Girl for April, frozen leg, socket head. Trim on bodice, flower; also flower on umbrella. Also found with smaller lace, no trim on bodice, no flowers. Also on frozen leg with no lace on bodice and tatting trim on skirt. $100.00.

#190 A Shower Girl for April, frozen leg, socket head. Ivory eyelet. $75.00.

#190 A Shower Girl for April, frozen leg. $85.00.

#190 A Shower Girl for April, frozen leg. $85.00.

#190 A Shower Girl for April, frozen leg. $65.00.

#190 A Shower Girl for April, frozen leg. $65.00.

#190 A Shower Girl for April, frozen leg. In pink, lavender, or blue taffeta. $65.00.

#190 A Shower Girl for April, frozen leg. Lace umbrella. Also in blue. $55.00.

#190 A Shower Girl for April, frozen leg. Plastic arms. $55.00.

#191 A Flower Girl for May, jointed leg, socket head. Floral print. $125.00.

#191 A Flower Girl for May, jointed leg, socket head. Unusual floral print, organdy ruche trim. $145.00.

#191 A Flower Girl for May, jointed leg, socket head. Rosebud print. $150.00.

#191 A Flower Girl for May, jointed leg, socket head. Pale blue flocked dress. $125.00. Also found on socket head, frozen leg. $100.00.

271

#191 A Flower Girl for May, frozen leg, socket head. Variation with large floral flocked dress. $100.00.

#191 A Flower Girl for May, frozen leg, socket head. Variation in blue flocked dress. $100.00.

#191 A Flower Girl for May, frozen leg, socket head. Variation in cream flocked dress. $100.00.

#191 A Flower Girl for May, frozen leg. Peach floral print. $65.00.

#191 A Flower Girl for May, frozen leg, socket head. Apricot satin. $85.00.

#191 A Flower Girl for May, frozen leg. Net hat. Inset lace panel. $60.00.

#191 A Flower Girl for May, frozen leg. Felt hat. Pale blue organdy dress. $65.00.

#191 A Flower Girl for May, frozen leg. Daisy organdy dress. Florist ribbon. $55.00.

#191 A Flower Girl for May, frozen leg. Yellow taffeta print. Plastic arms. Florist ribbon. $55.00.

#192 Rosebud Girl to Love Me Through the June Days, jointed leg, socket head. Dotted Swiss. Also with solid pink satin bodice. Various trim and placement of roses. $125.00.

#192 Rosebud Girl to Love Me Through the June Days, jointed leg, socket head. Solid satin bodice. Pink organdy floral overskirt. Rose in hair and on dress. Also found on frozen leg, socket head. $125.00.

#192 Rosebud Girl to Love Me Through the June Days, frozen leg, socket head. Taffeta bodice and white taffeta rose print underskirt, also a pink smaller rosebud print underskirt. Rose at waist. $100.00.

#192 Rosebud Girl to Love Me Through the June Days, frozen leg, socket head. Sateen pink floral. Also white print, variegated ribbon trim on frozen leg. $100.00.

#192 Rosebud Girl to Love Me Through the June Days, frozen leg. Flocked overskirt, pink taffeta underskirt. $65.00.

#192 Rosebud Girl to Love Me Through the June Days, frozen leg. Floral flocked overskirt. Peach taffeta floral print underskirt. Also with flocked dotted overskirt. Rose in hair. $65.00.

Left. #192 Rosebud Girl to Love Me Through the June Days, frozen leg. Net skirt with wide lace trim. Also with matching lace hat and pink and blue trim on bodice. $65.00.

Right. #192 Rosebud Girl to Love Me Through the June Days, frozen leg. Variation in bodice and hat. $65.00.

#192 Rosebud Girl to Love Me Through the June Days, frozen leg. Pink taffeta with sheer nylon print overskirt. Plastic arms. Florist ribbon. $45.00.

#192 Rosebud Girl to Love Me Through the June Days, frozen leg. Rose print skirt. Plastic arms. Florist ribbon. $45.00.

All July dolls have a red, white, and blue color scheme.

#193 Very Independent Lady for July, jointed leg, socket head. Three-inch red taffeta ruffled bottom of skirt. $125.00.

#193 Very Independent Lady for July, frozen leg, socket head. White taffeta with polka dots. $100.00.

#193 Very Independent Lady for July, frozen leg, socket head. Red and white striped bodice. Also on frozen leg mold. $100.00.

#193 Very Independent Lady for July, frozen leg. Stand-up blue felt hair. Red taffeta with red and white insert; soutache braid trim. $65.00.

#193 Very Independent Lady for July, frozen leg. Variation of fabrics. $65.00.

#193 Very Independent Lady for July, frozen leg. $65.00.

#193 Very Independent Lady for July, frozen leg. Florist ribbon. $45.00.

#193 Very Independent Lady for July, frozen leg. Florist ribbon. $45.00.

#194 A Girl for August When It's Warm, jointed leg, socket head. Embroidered taffeta. Center panel gathered. Found in various combinations of blue, pink, and white. $150.00.

#194 A Girl for August When It's Warm, jointed leg, socket head. Blue organdy with pink insert. $125.00.

#194 *A Girl for August When It's Warm,* jointed leg, socket head. Variation with sheer floral print. $125.00.

#194 *A Girl for August When It's Warm,* frozen leg, socket head. Dotted Swiss overskirt. $100.00.

#194 *A Girl for August When It's Warm,* frozen leg, socket head. Variation in taffeta with pink chiffon flocked overskirt. $100.00.

#194 *A Girl for August When It's Warm,* frozen leg, socket head. Wide lace on skirt. $100.00.

#194 *A Girl for August When It's Warm,* frozen leg, socket head. Variation in yellow. $100.00.

#194 *A Girl for August When It's Warm,* frozen leg, socket head. Ruffled blue polka dot chiffon overskirt. $100.00.

#194 A Girl for August When It's Warm, frozen leg. Flocked chiffon over vibrant floral. $65.00.

#194 A Girl for August When It's Warm, frozen leg. Peach with variation in pink chiffon and peach cotton. $65.00.

#194 A Girl for August When It's Warm, frozen leg. White eyelet skirt, black bodice. $65.00.

#194 A Girl for August When It's Warm, frozen leg. Pink eyelet and felt hat, black soutache trim. $65.00.

#194 A Girl for August When It's Warm, frozen leg. Various aqua dresses with variety of hats and trim, some with plastic arms. Florist ribbon. $45.00.

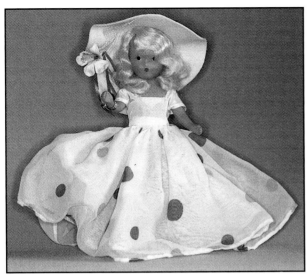

#194 A Girl for August When It's Warm, frozen leg. Various colors, polka dot dress. Florist ribbon. $45.00.

#195 September's Girl Is Like a Storm, jointed leg, socket head. Coral and fuchsia taffeta. Variation in purple and fuchsia. $125.00.

#195 September's Girl Is Like a Storm, frozen leg, socket head. $100.00.

#195 September's Girl Is Like a Storm, frozen leg, socket head. $100.00.

Left. #195 September's Girl Is Like a Storm, frozen leg, socket head. Tatting trim on skirt and over the shoulder. $125.00.

Right. #195 September's Girl Is Like a Storm, frozen leg, socket head. Close-up. Tatting shawl over right shoulder, matching trim on skirt.

#195 September's Girl Is Like a Storm, frozen leg. Two-panels of fuchsia taffeta sewn at waist. $65.00.

#195 September's Girl Is Like a Storm, frozen leg. Fuchsia satin with black lace and hat. Florist ribbon. $45.00.

Left. #195 September's Girl Is Like a Storm, frozen leg. Fuchsia and green plaid taffeta. Florist ribbon. $45.00.

Right. #195 September's Girl Is Like a Storm, frozen leg. Plaid taffeta. Green felt hat. Florist ribbon. $45.00.

#195 September's Girl Is Like a Storm, frozen leg. Green and black plaid. Florist ribbon. $45.00.

#196 A Sweet October Maiden Rather Shy, jointed leg, socket head. Burgundy and peach taffeta. $125.00.

#196 A Sweet October Maiden Rather Shy, frozen leg, socket head. Burgundy taffeta, floral taffeta front panel. $100.00.

#196 A Sweet October Maiden Rather Shy, frozen leg, socket head. Black and white checked dress with either a black or red front panel. $100.00.

#196 A Sweet October Maiden Rather Shy, frozen leg. $65.00.

#196 A Sweet October Maiden Rather Shy, frozen leg. Variation in yellow and green. $65.00.

#196 A Sweet October Maiden Rather Shy, frozen leg. Dunce-style hat of black felt. Also in gray taffeta with black and yellow trim. $65.00.

#196 A Sweet October Maiden Rather Shy, frozen leg. Burgundy taffeta. Also with lime green ribbon. $65.00.

#196 A Sweet October Maiden Rather Shy, frozen leg. Satin bodice, chiffon overskirt, variation has wide black lace on front panel. Florist ribbon. $65.00.

#197 A November Lass to Cheer, jointed leg, socket head. Pink floral flocked overskirt. $125.00.

#197 A November Lass to Cheer, jointed leg, socket head. Variation in print overskirt. $125.00.

#197 A November Lass to Cheer, jointed leg, socket head. Plain organdy overskirt. $125.00.

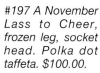

#197 A November Lass to Cheer, frozen leg, socket head. Polka dot taffeta. $100.00.

#197 A November Lass to Cheer, frozen leg, socket head. Aqua taffeta. $100.00.

#197 A November Lass to Cheer, frozen leg, socket head. Yellow taffeta and floral print. $100.00.

#197 A November Lass to Cheer, frozen leg, socket head. Floral taffeta. Royal blue. $100.00.

#197 A November Lass to Cheer, frozen leg, socket head. Variation with chiffon overskirt. $100.00.

#197 A November Lass to Cheer, frozen leg. Green or peach bodice and ruche trim. $65.00.

#197 A November Lass to Cheer, frozen leg. $65.00.

Left. #197 A November Lass to Cheer, frozen leg. Florist ribbon. $45.00.

Far left. #197 A November Lass to Cheer, frozen leg. Florist ribbon. $45.00.

#197 A November Lass to Cheer, frozen leg. Blue, green, or red taffeta. Plastic arms. Florist ribbon. $45.00.

#198 For December Just a Dear, jointed leg, socket head. Sunflower dot flocked fabric. $125.00.

#198 For December Just a Dear, jointed leg, socket head. "Cover Girl" sketch at the bottom of the filigree frame on the front of 1941 through 1947 pamphlets. Also used on the dust cover of Marjorie Miller's first-edition book on Nancy Ann Storybook Dolls. $150.00.

#198 For December Just a Dear, frozen leg, socket head. Flower cluster flocked overskirt. $100.00.

#198 For December Just a Dear, frozen leg, socket head. Wide ruffle, red taffeta underskirt. $100.00.

#198 For December Just a Dear, frozen leg socket head. Variation, same fabric as page 284 bottom, right. $100.00.

#198 For December Just a Dear, frozen leg, socket head. Variation, large floral shadow print. $100.00.

#198 For December Just a Dear, frozen leg, socket head. Embroidered front panel. $100.00.

#198 For December Just a Dear, frozen leg. Satin bodice. Variation with solid green ribbon. $65.00.

285

#198 For December Just a Dear, frozen leg. $65.00.

#198 For December Just a Dear, frozen leg. Net overskirt. Also with loop trim. Florist ribbon. $45.00.

#198 For December Just a Dear, frozen leg. Chiffon over-skirt. Florist ribbon. $45.00.

#198 For December Just a Dear, frozen leg. Variation. Florist ribbon. $45.00.

#198 For December Just a Dear, frozen leg. Rhinestone neck-lace not verified. Florist ribbon. $45.00.

#198 For December Just a Dear, frozen leg. Red and white plaid. $45.00.

#198 For December Just a Dear, frozen leg. Flocked skirt. Plastic arms. $45.00.

#198 For December Just a Dear, frozen leg. Red satin. Plastic arms. $45.00.

#198 For December Just a Dear, frozen leg. Red taffeta and netting. Plastic arms. $45.00.

• • • In Powder and Crinoline Series • • •
#250 – #261

Nancy Ann Abbott, in all probability, derived the series In Powder and Crinoline from a book of the same name, a collection of fairy tales by Sir Arthur Quiller-Couch in 1913. Kay Nielson, a brilliant illustrator, instilled in the hearts of the readers haunting images of these fairy tale characters. This enchanting book was again published in 1988 under the title of *The Twelve Dancing Princesses.*

This series consists of a prince, a princess, and ten ladies in waiting. The series is on a 7" bisque doll that is used only for this series, first with jointed legs, then a frozen leg mold.

These molds have the regular Storybook Doll USA mold mark, although on most dolls, the mold mark is very faint or not visible at all. The twelve-doll series was introduced in 1942 and only was listed for approximately two years. Only the prince and princess continued on into the plastic sleep-eye era, but the ladies in waiting were discontinued at that time. Most In Powder and Crinoline costumes have separate cotton half slips, but a few have taffeta half-slips, as noted. Many have lace-edged organdy pantalets. Most costumes in this series are fastened with the Nancy Ann ribbon closure.

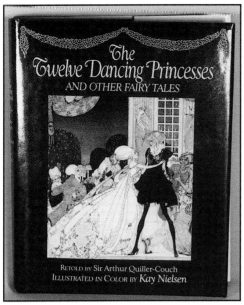

In Powder and Crinoline, a reproduction of the 1913 collection of fairy tales by Sir Arthur Quiller-Couch.

Jointed leg Prince and Princess pair.

Frozen leg Prince and Princess pair.

#250 Princess Minon Minette, jointed leg. Separate taffeta half-slip, lace edged pantaletes. Peach dress, chiffon overskirt. 2½" lace trim edged in blue ribbon. Paper crown has pink net attached. $200.00. (An unsubstantiated version is in large red flocked print overskirt.

Left. #250 Princess Minon Minette, frozen leg. Variation. Also found on jointed leg. $165.00.

Right. #250 Princess Minon Minette, frozen leg. Variation. Blue chiffon overskirt, pink ribbon trim. $165.00.

1944 Ciro perfume ad using Princess Minon Minette and Prince Souci.

1947 Ciro perfume ad using Princess Minon Minette

Left to right.

#251 Prince Souci, jointed leg. JT. Pink trousers, white shirt, lace ascot, separate coat trimmed with rickrack and spider lace, sleeves edged in ribbon and net. Three-pointed felt hat, aqua feather. $200.00.

#251 Prince Souci, jointed leg. JT. Variation. Blue print taffeta coat, no pink ribbon at waist, white feather. $200.00.

#251 Prince Souci, frozen leg. Pink print taffeta long-sleeve shirt, lace ascot, aqua taffeta trousers, Black cape with purple lining, three-pointed hat, pink feather. Also with a larger pink floral print. Also with larger print pink taffeta shirt. $175.00.

#252 – #261 are Ladies in Waiting.

#252 Felicia. JT. $135.00.

#252 Felicia, frozen leg. Variation, blue. $125.00.

#253 Charmaine. JT. $135.00.

#253 Charmaine, frozen leg. Cream floral. $125.00.

291

#253 Charmaine, frozen leg. Yellow floral. $125.00.

#254 Delphine. JT. Separate pink taffeta half-slip, daisy on skirt and hat. Variation on frozen leg with bow on skirt. $135.00.

#255 Regina. JT. Pink taffeta print dress, coat of pink bow print taffeta, edged in tulle and pink cord ties. $150.00.

#255 Regina. JT. Floral taffeta underskirt, overskirt flocked, edged with same floral print taffeta. $135.00.

#255 Regina, frozen leg. Separate organdy half-slip. Flocked taffeta dress, 2½ inch lace at hem. $125.00.

#256 Theresa. JT. Red taffeta underskirt, overskirt of organdy. $135.00. Also frozen leg. $125.00.

#256 Theresa, frozen leg. White shadow print satin underskirt and satin overskirt. $125.00.

#257 Antoinette. JT. Royal blue dress with attached underskirt of pink nylon with 2½" gathered lace trim, attached white flowers. White feather in hair. $135.00.

#257 Antoinette, frozen leg. Variation magenta or royal blue taffeta, change in underskirt lace, and no lace trim on bodice or flowers. $125.00.

#258 Eugenia Marie, frozen leg. Variation in trim. $125.00.

#258 Eugenia Marie. JT. Yellow organdy with embroidered tulle. Flowers in hair in on skirt. Separate pink taffeta half-slip. $135.00.

#259 Daralene. JT. Large flocked flowered overskirt, lavender dress. $135.00.

#259 Daralene. JT. Lavender floral dress with pink nylon overskirt. $135.00.

#259 Daralene. JT. $135.00. Frozen leg. Pink or lavender floral dress with lavender nylon overskirt. $125.00.

#260 Eulalie. JT. Pale blue floral taffeta, peach taffeta ruche trim. $135.00.

#260 Eulalie, frozen leg. Pink daisy print taffeta, bright pink taffeta rouching. $125.00.

#261 Diaphanie. JT. Pink flocked organdy over pink taffeta underskirt. $135.00.

#261 Diaphanie. JT. Variation, different flocked print. $125.00.

••• Operetta Series •••
#301 – #312

The doll used for this series is the same six-inch frozen leg mold used for the Dolls of the Months series. This remarkable series, representing Operettas, was offered first in the bisque mold, and then continued into the plastic era with characters on both the painted-eye and sleep-eye molds. During the plastic era, several new Operettas were added and some were dropped from this list of twelve. Since this book covers only bisque dolls, the dolls below are the first of this series, bisque dolls with plastic arms. Most have safety pin closures, but some have the transitional small gold snap, as the company moved into converting to this type closure.

#301 Orange Blossom. $125.00.

#302 Maytime. $125.00.

#303 Pink Lady. $125.00.

#304 Blossom Time. $125.00.

#305 Countess Maritza. $125.00.

#306 Irene. $125.00.

#307 Naughty Marietta. $125.00.

#308 My Maryland. $125.00.

#309 Red Mill. $125.00.

#310 Rio Rita. $125.00.

#311 Floradora. $125.00.

#312 Bloomer Girl. $125.00.

#305 Fortune Teller. As the company changed to the painted-eye plastic mold, they also introduced several new Operettas, and discontinued others. #305 Fortune Teller is one of the following season's new Operettas that replaced #305 Countess Maritza. It is interesting that this doll is still on a bisque mold with plastic arms and the new gold snap, since this costume is mainly found on the new painted-eye plastic mold. As this transition to new characters on the painted-eye plastic mold was gearing up, doll molds overlapped, illustrating how the company, always thrifty, used up the existing bisque doll stock first; before introducing the paint-eye plastic doll mold. $125.00.

• • • All-time Hit Parade Series • • •
#401 – #412

Mainly a plastic doll series named after songs, the All-time Hit Parade Series each year consisted of 12 dolls with elaborate costumes, similar to the Operetta series. We only mention this series here because at the end of 1947, as the company used up the old frozen-leg bisque stock, this new series temporarily used the same 6" size frozen leg bisque mold used for the Dolls of the Month and the Operetta series. By the time the company introduced this new series at the New York Toy Fair in 1948, it was now on a painted-eye plastic mold. Consequently, the only Hit Parade dolls that have been found on the bisque frozen leg mold are the two examples illustrated here. In the following years, this series continued on the sleep-eye plastic mold with several new characters being added and others dropped over the next several years.

#405 Moonlight and Roses. Gold snap closure. $125.00.

#412 Easter Parade. Gold snap closure. $125.00.

#412 In My Easter Bonnet. $125.00 each.

#412 In My Easter Bonnet comes in a box with no number and a label reading "A Storybook Doll In My Easter Bonnet."

• • • Five Little Sisters • • •

Because the company was unable legally to sell dolls using the name Dionne Quintuplets, the five little girl quintuplets born in Canada so popular at the time, we presume that they marketed their own version of these famous quintuplets under the generic name Five Little Sisters. Since the Dionne Quintuplets had brown eyes, the company painted brown eyes on their dolls. The Five Little Sisters were sold from approximately 1937 through 1939. Because very few of these Five Little Sisters have been found, we can only assume that each dress and playsuit was originally offered in five different color combinations. The Five Little Sisters series was discontinued by 1940 and eventually replaced by Margie Ann series #500 and #510.

MIJ. These five dolls are from the Salesman Sample Set. No name or numbers are on this set of dolls. The dresses are styled alike, organdy with an attached collar. The hem of dress, collar, and matching panties are picot-edged. Left to right: Doll #1, blue with blue ribbon; Doll #2, white with pink ribbon; Doll #3, yellow with yellow ribbon; Doll #4, white with blue ribbon; Doll #5, pink with pink ribbon.

Close-up of center three dolls, one with wig removed. The five dolls are each on a Made in Japan 1146 mold. They have brown eyes with black pupils. When early wool wig is removed, one can see the topknot on mold. Price: Complete set in early marble design box, not enough examples to price. Each doll separately $1,200.00+.

#500 *Five Little Sisters. MIJ. Now given a stock #500. Pink cotton corded dress with blue rickrack trim, matching panties. Doll has picot-edged matching bonnet, with blue ribbon in hair. JA sticker. White boots. Sunburst box with gold label "#500 Five Little Sisters."*

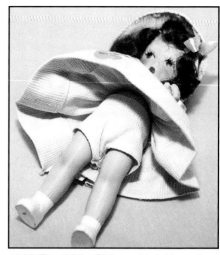

#500 *Five Little Sisters. Matching short pink cotton corded panties.*

#500 *Five Little Sisters. JA. Similar cotton corded dress, but yellow. No longer picot-edged bonnet, but machine stitched. Short white panties.*

#500 *Five Little Sisters. JA. Variation in white-corded dress.*

Left. #500 *Five Little Sisters. Left is CM Mold wearing green cotton print dress, pink rickrack trim. Right is JA same print fabric, but in blue. SBD sticker.*

Right. #500 *Five Little Sisters. MS/MB. Pink cotton dress and matching bonnet, blue rickrack. Regular white lace-trimmed panties. Silver dot box with silver label "#500 Five Little Sisters."*

Left to right.

#510 Five Little Sisters in Playsuits. MIJ. Blue cotton corded playsuit with stitching at hem of pants and hat to give picot effect. Trim on bodice. NADD sticker. Also found in light green.

#510 Five Little Sisters in Playsuits. MIJ. Variation in apricot, white boots.

#510 Five Little Sisters in Playsuits. Variation in green.

#510 Five Little Sisters in Playsuits. Variation in pink.

#510 Five Little Sisters in Playsuits. JA. White cotton corded hat and playsuit with green rickrack trim. White boots. Sunburst box with gold label.

#510 Five Little Sisters in Playsuits. MS/MB. Blue and yellow polished cotton print playsuit and hat. White boots.

Salesman Sample Sets

The following two boxes were purchased from an employee of the company, and believed to be salesman sample boxes. They contain the Five Little Sisters and assorted Storybook characters.

Five Little Sisters. The five dolls are marked "Made in Japan 1146." All have the very dark early wool wigs placed over unpainted hair. The mold has a topknot with holes for a ribbon. The wigs have no tape inside, unlike the later mohair wigs, and are just sewn with light thread. They have straight arms and black painted slipper shoes. The cheeks and knees have red blush. The eyelashes are painted a very dark brown with five heavy strokes to match the brown painted eyes. The rare marble design box is approximately 18" long, 7" wide, and 2½" deep, with a paper scalloped doily around the inside edge of the box. The five dolls are held in place with a pink ribbon around each neck and around one leg. Left to right: The organdy dresses are blue with blue ribbon, white with pink ribbon, yellow with yellow ribbon, white with blue ribbon, and pink with pink ribbon. The dresses have cut sleeve openings. There are no typical hems as each dress has a picot ruffle around the collar and skirt. The ribbon around the waist is used to close the dress. Each doll has short white pants with the front dart, and a matching ribbon in her hair. This is the only example known of boxed set, so not enough examples to price.

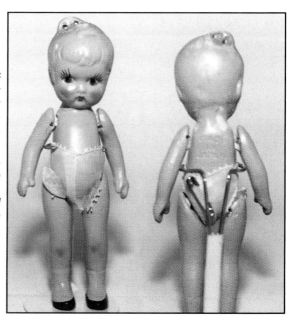

Left. One of the dolls in the Five Little Sisters set, wearing yellow organdy dress, NADD gold sticker, with wig removed.

Right. Five Little Sisters. Made in Japan mold, front and back, with picot-edged panties matching each girl's dress.

Storybook Characters Salesman Sample Set. The rare marble design box measures 8" x 24", and has a paper scalloped doily around the inside edge of the box. The six dolls are held in place with a pink ribbon around each neck and around one leg. All dolls are marked "Made in Japan 1146" and have the early wool wigs, topknot underneath wig and straight arms. Under each doll is the character name and handwritten numbers. On back of the box is written "#7 to #12 $4.80 per doz." Price: This is the only example known of boxed set, so not enough examples to price.

Left to right.

#7 Little Boy Blue, Come Blow Your Horn. Three-piece outfit. White cotton shirt with picot edge at sleeves and front opening. Medium blue corded cotton trousers with two small buttons sewn on front. Separate picot-edged collar with blue ribbon tie stitched to underneath shirt. NAAD sticker.

#7 Little Boy Blue, Come Blow Your Horn. Back view of Little Boy Blue showing collar.

#8 Little Red Riding Hood Said to the Wolf. White organdy dress with two red thread picot-edged rows of trim on skirt. Red satin cape also with picot-edged trim. Short white panties.

Left. #9 School Days, School Days. Center part early wool wig pulled to each side with dark blue ribbon. Dark blue cotton dress with red and white stars sewn to skirt. White attached organdy collar with red thread edge pinned in back. Blue ribbon sewn on front of collar. NAAD sticker, white panties.

Center. #10 Little Miss Muffet, Sat on a Tuffet. No bodice, pale yellow corded cotton skirt, picot edge at waistline. Yellow ribbon on skirt goes under arms and ties in back. Pantalets with yellow trim. White organdy dustcap with yellow thread picot edges, yellow ribbon bow on right side of head.

Right. #11 Mistress Mary, Quite Contrary, How Does Your Garden Grow? Calf-length skirt of white striped cotton and tiny blue flowers in design. No bodice, picot-edged gathered at waistline, pinned in back. Same apron as Miss Muffet with blue ribbon. Blue trim sewn on cotton skirt, white organdy sun-bonnet with picot edge. Two ribbon bows on each side of wig. Long organdy pantalets.

#12 All Dressed for a Party. Front and back view, showing circle hat and collar on dress. Short apricot chiffon overskirt with bodice, over gathered apricot taffeta underskirt. Picot edges all around everything with light blue thread. Upper chiffon skirt gathered at waistline. Satin bud trim. Attached apricot gathered underskirt. Picot-edged panties. Circle cut apricot chiffon hat with repeat of satin bud trim under side edge of wig. NADD sticker.

Boxed Gift Sets
#300 – #900

#300 Judy Ann in Story Book with Three Sets of Clothes (Judy Ann in Fairyland). This charming set, first sold on a Judy Ann mold doll, was probably offered as early as 1939. The name of the set actually applies to the character Judy Ann, not the mold marked Judy Ann. Although first sold on a Judy Ann mold, this set continued to be offered on a MS/MB mold in 1940 and on a MS mold in 1941. A photograph in the Advertising Section of this book shows this set in original box, offered for sale by FAO Schwarz Toy Company. $2,000.00.

The nursery rhyme illustrations used on the inside left of each box differ and are from either Ruth E. Newton's or Beatrice Mallet's Mother Goose books, circa 1939 – 1943. Costumes in set are To Market, Little Red Riding Hood, Alice in Wonderland, and Miss Muffet, doll in center.

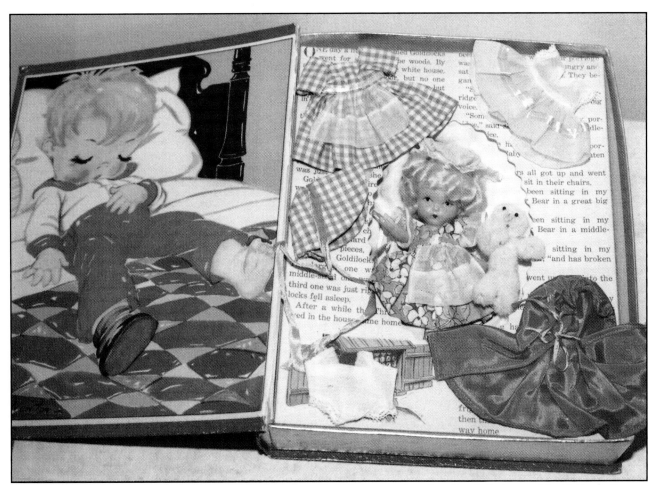

#300 Judy Ann in Story Book with Three Sets of Clothes. JA. This is an early set on the Judy Ann mold with the doll wearing Miss Muffet outfit in the center. The nursery rhyme Diddle Diddle Dumpling, My Son John illustration by Ruth E. Newton is on the left.

An example of the outside packaging used for the boxed set shown below. It came with an outer box cover with small label reading "Judy Ann in Story Book #300." Inside this box is a red box shaped like a book with the cover reading "JUDY ANN IN FAIRY-LAND." Edge of book reads "JUDY ANN IN FAIRYLAND by Nancy Ann."

#300 Judy Ann in Story Book with Three Sets of Clothes. In the center in a scalloped oval cutout is a doll wearing Miss Muffet costume and three more costumes attached to the cardboard. The top costume is To Market and at the bottom are Alice in Wonderland and Little Red Riding Hood costumes. On the left is a nursery rhyme illustration of Ding Dong Bell by Ruth E. Newton and on the right is a printed story of Goldilocks. Set in original box, $2,000.00.

#300 Judy Ann in Story Book with Three Sets of Clothes. Variation. Another nursery rhyme illustration by Ruth E. Newton on left, but same costumes, just arranged differently. Set in original box, $2,000.00.

#300 Judy Ann in Story Book with Three Sets of Clothes. Variation. Set with Beatrice Mallet's illustration of Little Betty Blue, except To Market in pink instead of blue and ribbon on Miss Muffet is yellow instead of black. Price for set in original box $2,000.00+.

#300 Judy Ann in Story Book with Three Sets of Clothes. MS/MB. Miss Muffet in the center. The nursery rhyme The Queen of Hearts illustration by Beatrice Mallet is on the left. $2,000.00+.

#400 Geraldine Ann from Movieland. MS/MB. Since Nancy Ann Abbott worked in Hollywood both in films and as a designer, it seemed appropriate that she would design a doll representing the movie scene, for what little girl didn't dream of being a movie star. However, we would love to know why she picked the name Geraldine Ann for this doll, as this is the only time she used it. This set was advertised only in the 1940 factory pamphlet. It came in dark blue box with silver dots 18" wide, 17¾" tall, and 3" deep. The lid reads "Geraldine Ann from Movieland by Nancy Ann" in silver. The box contains eight costumes. Two Cinderella dresses (her pink princess dress, and her poor Cinderella dress, dark green cotton with patches and a broom as an accessory), the #70 Tennis outfit with visor, the #63 Ballerina pink tutu, a rare flowered taffeta robe with large ruffle around the hem found only in this set, a white taffeta dress with lace sleeves and tiny narrow hem with a rose attached at waist, #81 Margie Ann in Party Dress, a pink floral print, and #72 Riding outfit. $5,000.00+.

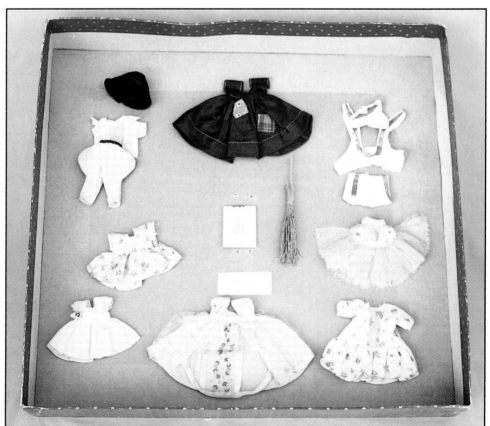

#400 Geraldine Ann from Movieland. Cast-iron movie equipment. Boom microphone, camera, director's chair, original script, and Klieg light. Doll added for effect.

#400 Geraldine Ann from Movieland. A paper Cinderella movie script with a silver label "Geraldine Ann in person."

#400 Geraldine Ann from Movieland. Close up of rare poor Cinderella dress with fabric patches.

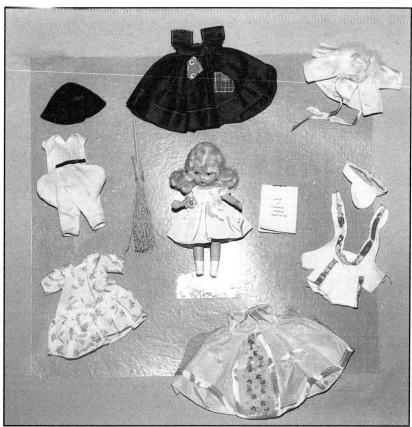

#400 Geraldine Ann from Movieland. Set basically the same, but has pink boudoir jacket with marabou collar on top right, but minus tutu and short pink taffeta dress that is in previous set. Missing movie props. If complete, $5,000.00+.

#400 Geraldine Ann from Movieland. A group of clothes believed to be from #400 set. This set has a straw hat included. Poor Cinderella dress is minus fabric patches and missing movie props.

#600 Large Storybook Set. Box cover for this set, dark blue with silver dots marked "Story Book Dolls — Nancy Ann."

#600 Large Storybook Set. M/S doll in center cutout costumed as Bo Peep. The box has a nursery rhyme print background. A photograph in the advertising section of this book shows this set offered for sale by FAO Schwarz Toy Company. Clockwise: Little Red Riding Hood with unusual red organdy dress; School Days hat; Miss Muffet dress; Curly Locks dress; Alice in Wonderland dress; Mistress Mary dress; East Side, West Side with derby hat; Mary Had a Little Lamb dress; To Market dress with purse. $3,000.00+.

#600 Large Storybook Set. Variation of set (box not original).

#700 Around the World. Large red box with silver dots Around the World gift set. Set contains seven Around the World Series costumes each with the country's flag, laid on a Rand McNally world map, circle with a cutout for Nancy Ann Storybook Doll in center wearing Colonial Dame costume. There is a photograph in the advertisement section of the book showing a Dennison's advertisement for this set. $5,000.00+.

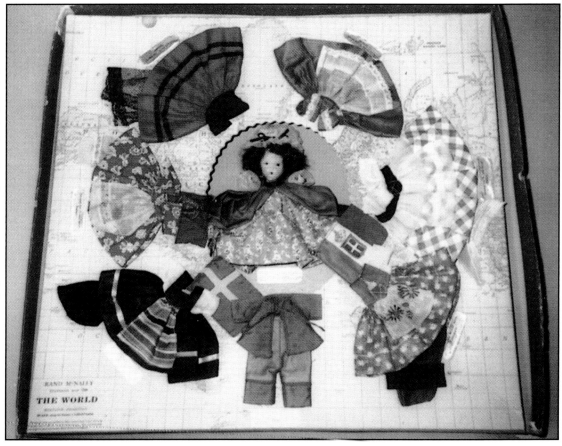

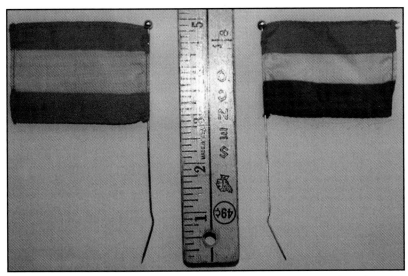

#700 Around the World. Example of flags, stitched with one row of red thread.

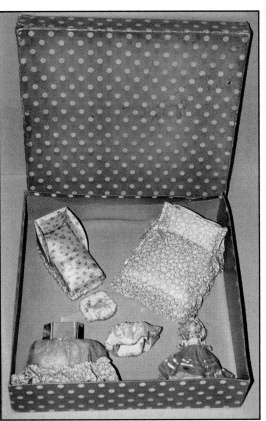

Right. #900 Boudoir Box. Large-size blue box with silver dots. Box has no label. Set was offered in the 1940 and 1941 factory pamphlets.

Below. #900 Boudoir Box. Boudoir Set includes a chaise lounge with pillow, dressing table, mirror, stool, and bed with pillow and doll. Not enough examples to price. In original box, $1,000.00.

#900 Boudoir Box. Variation. Boudoir set in pink. In original box, $1,000.00.

FURNITURE SERIES

STYLE No.

1000	Slipper Chair
1001	Wing Chair
1002	Love Seat
1003	Day Bed
1004	Settee
1005	Armchair
1006	Sofa
1007	Chaise Lounge
1008	Bed
1009	Dressing Table Mirror and Stool

—Individually packed in beautiful gift boxes.

The Furniture Series was listed in the 1940 and 1941 factory brochures, although we still find furniture in three style boxes, which would indicate they were still available in 1942 in the later white box.

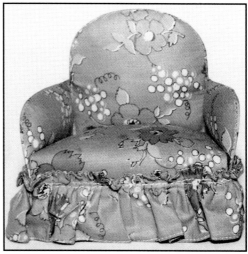

#1000 Slipper Chair. $200.00.

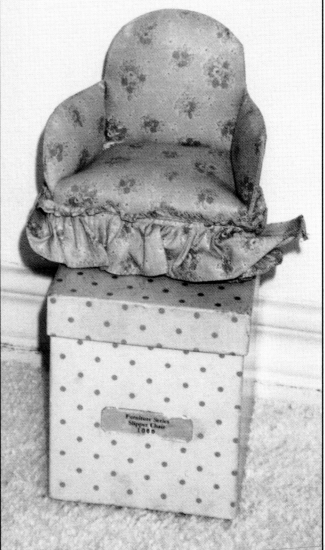

#1000 Slipper Chair. $200.00.

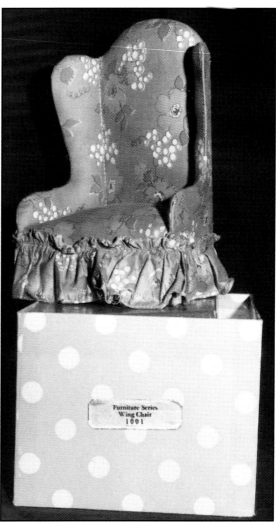

#1001 Wing Chair. $200.00.

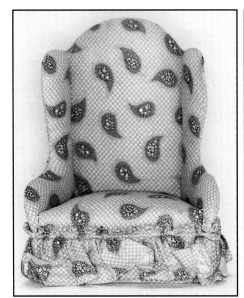

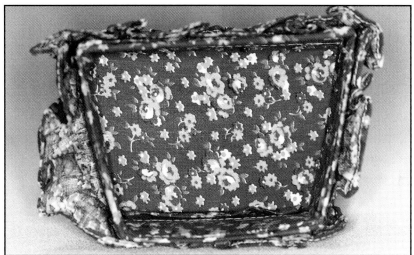

#1001 Wing Chair. Bottom view shows typical construction of furniture. $200.00.

#1001 Wing Chair. $200.00.

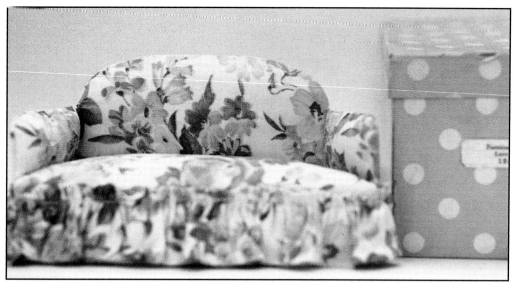

#1002 Love Seat. $300.00.

#1002 Love Seat shown with matching slipper chair. Love Seat, $300.00.

#1003 Day Bed. $350.00.

#1003 Day Bed. $350.00.

#1003 Day Bed. $350.00.

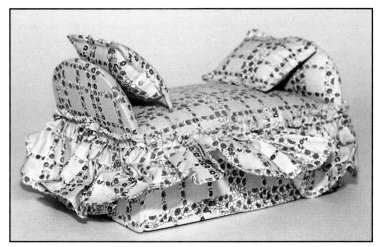

#1003 Day Bed. $350.00.

#1003 Day Bed. $350.00.

#1004 Settee. $300.00.

#1004 Settee. $300.00.

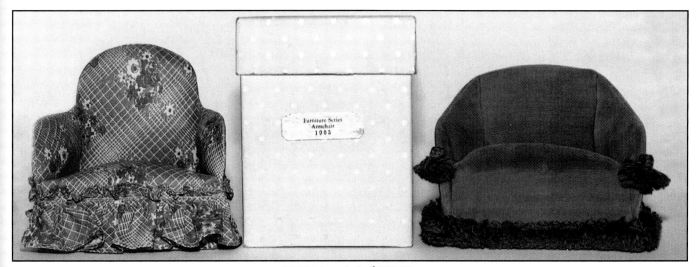

#1005 Armchair. $300.00.

#1006 Sofa. 300.00.

#1006 Sofa. $300.00.

#1007 Chaise Lounge. $300.00.

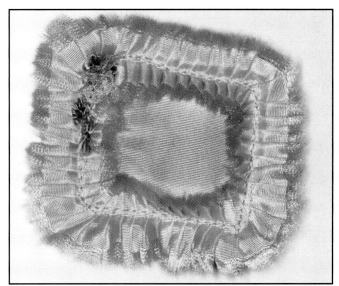

Close-up of pillow from #1007 Chaise Lounge.

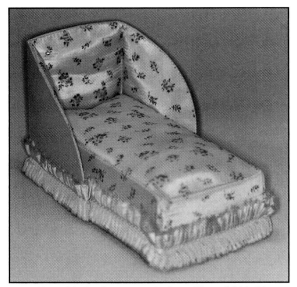

#1007 Chaise Lounge missing pillow. $300.00.

#1007 Chaise Lounge missing pillow. $300.00.

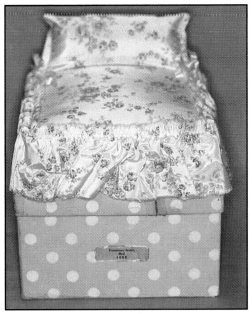

#1008 Bed. $250.00.

#1008 Bed. $250.00.

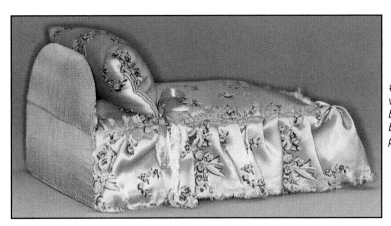

#1008 Bed. Side view, back of head-board in plain pink, bed and pillow in print. $250.00.

#1008 Bed. $250.00.

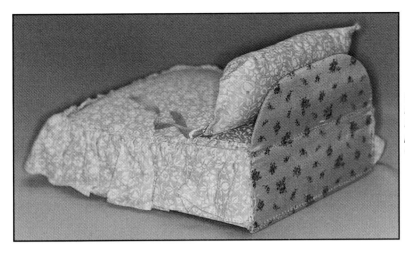

#1008 Bed. Side view, back rosebud print, bed pink and white print. Also in blue combination. $250.00.

#1009 Dressing Table, Mirror, and Stool. $300.00.

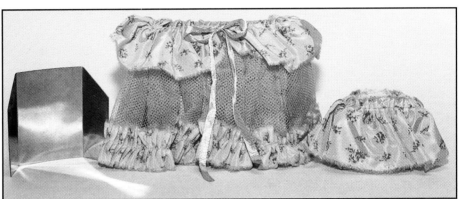

#1009 Dressing Table, Mirror, and Stool. $300.00.

#1009 Dressing Table, Mirror, and Stool. $300.00.

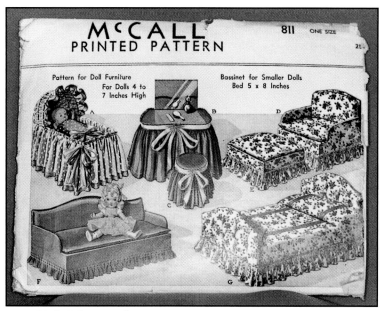

#811 McCall Pattern. $200.00. A McCall pattern to make Nancy Ann Storybook furniture.

● ● ● Costumes on Pinch Face Molds ● ● ●

Since no reference has been found in factory pamphlets to differentiate the pinch face mold costumes from the frozen leg costumes, we have no verification of just how many characters the company dressed using this pinch face mold. Shown are some examples of the costumes on this mold. The small round brass snap is used as a closure for the majority of costumes, but a few can be found fastened with the safety pin. Characters using the pinch face mold are from the Bridal, Dolls of the Day, Seasons, Fairytale, Storybook, and Nursery Rhyme Series.

#85 Bridesmaids. Variation, yellow and peach. $45.00.

#27 Eva. $45.00.

#85 Bridesmaid. Variation, flocked dot net overskirt. $45.00.

#86 Bride. $45.00.

#110 Little Miss. $45.00.

#161 Jennie Set the Table. $45.00.

#169 Goose Girl. $45.00.

#170 Rain, Rain, Go Away. $45.00.

#173 Star Light, Star Bright. $45.00.

#181 Tuesday's Child. $45.00.

#182 Wednesday's Child. $45.00.

#185 Saturday's Child. $45.00.

#186 Sunday's Child. $45.00.

#158 Sugar and Spice. $45.00.

•••Magic Light Dolls•••

Iris Halsey, with Patent 2.267.094 in hand, purchased Nancy Ann Storybook Book dolls and painted designs on their costumes with luminous paint. She sold these luminous painted dolls that glow in the dark through the company Magic Light Products, N.Y. If you have one of these painted dolls, chances are they still glow in the dark. Price: boxed with Magic Light label, add $50.00 above regular price of doll without paint. Doll with luminous paint on costume, but without box add $25.00 to regular price of doll without paint.

Margie Ann, with red label on box, luminous daisies painted on dress.

Mammy, luminous painted squares.

Variation Margie Ann, with blue label on box.

Margie Ann in Playsuit, luminous painted eyes and tulips on playsuit.

Mary Had a Little Lamb, luminous painted flowers on organdy overskirt and on dress.

Southern Belle, luminous painted dots.

Queen of Hearts, luminous painted heart on bodice and flowers on skirt.

⦁⦁⦁ Unidentified Dolls ⦁⦁⦁

The following Nancy Ann Storybook Dolls have not been positively identified as to which character they represent. Although we have theories on many of the dolls below as to their character identity, we have decided not to comment until found with either a wrist tag or box for positive identification.

Japan mold. Left: With brown sarong wrap. Right: Dress underneath the brown sarong wrap.

Left. MIJ. Early wool wig with topknot. One hand has hole in it.

Right. MIJ. Topknot. Silver slippers.

Below left. Japan. Similar to above, but in pink and also shorter dress.

Below center. MS. Glitter along the bottom of net skirt. Gathered net hat with flowers.

Below right. Jointed leg. Pink two-layer organdy dress. Hemstitching on collar. Rosette at waist. NADD sticker.

Left. Japan. Early wool wig. Dress in shadow print in pink or in yellow, matching hat with hem-stitching, beading on skirt and bodice, and trim on pantalets.

Right. CM. Silver slippers, separate slip.

MS/MB. Straw hat.

Japan. Mohair wig. Early straw bonnet, NADD sticker.

JA. Short organdy print dress, white boots.

PT. Unusual spiderweb lace at bottom of hem.

Long taffeta with blue organdy and also tulle slip.

America. Silver slippers, blue and pink wide net ruffles on skirt.

Frozen leg.

Frozen leg.

MS/MB.

PT. Spiderweb trim on hat and dress.

MS/MB.

MIJ 1146. Yellow netting dress, unusual silver Mary Jane type shoes.

•••Packaging and Marketing•••

The correct factory box, sticker/tag, and pamphlet are necessary for a doll to be considered mint-in-box. The following are illustrations of the various boxes, pamphlets, and identification methods the company used when packaging each doll for sale.

Foil Stickers

The company first used round gold foil paper stickers applied to the doll dresses to identify the company. In 1941 the company eliminated these stickers and introduced a gold foil paper wrist tag with the company's name on one side and the name and stock number of the doll on the other side. The early wrist tags are made of a little heavier gold foil paper than the later wrist tags. These wrist tags continued to be used for the balance of the company's production. The value of the doll is increased if the doll has its original sticker or wrist tag.

Box Designs and Labels

As the company struggled to identify itself to the public during the first few years, the pattern of the paper used to cover the cardboard Nancy Ann Storybook Doll boxes changed. After briefly using the marble and sunburst design box, the company introduced the polka dot design for their boxes in 1939, and it became the company's identifying logo. A clever marketing decision, the easily recognized polka dot design boxes quickly identified Nancy Ann Storybook Dolls from all the imitators that soon appeared on the doll market.

Above left. NADD sticker only. Reads "NANCY ANN DRESSED DOLLS," circa 1936 – 1937. $100.00+.

Above right. JA sticker only. Reads "JUDY ANN," circa 1938. $100.00.

Right. SBD sticker only. Reads "STORYBOOK DOLLS," circa 1938 – 1940. $50.00.

Gold foil identification wrist tag. $15.00.

A variety of early patterned boxes including the company's trademark polka dot design.

The first box design used by the Nancy Ann Story-book Company is rarely found. It is a marble design in pink or blue used in 1936, the first year of the company. It has a gold label with the character's name in center and the stock number of the doll in lower left corner. Dolls used with this marble box were imported Japan molds, usually marked "Made in Japan 1146." Box only $200.00+.

Doll molds sold in the sunburst box are as follows:
Various Japan molds ....1936 – 1937
America mold 1938
Judy Ann mold 1938
Story Book USA, Crude Mark mold 1938

The second box, a sunburst design, was introduced at the end of 1936. The dolls were packaged in an array of colored boxes such as pink, yellow, red, and an icy blue-green. The gold foil label with stock number is in lower left corner. Box only $150.00+.

A second type of label made of silver foil, wider than the early gold one, with corners cut at angles and with a raised molded edging, was introduced during 1938. $150.00+.

Colored box design, small silver dots. By 1939 as the sunburst boxes stock was used up, the new small dot box was introduced as the new design for the boxes. These boxes also came in a multitude of colors. Doll molds found in this box are Judy Ann, Crude Mark, molded sock-molded bang molds, and some molded sock dolls. Silver label: A few silver labels were still used at the end of the sunburst-box era, but most are on the colored box with silver dots. The stock number was first on the lower left, but later labels have the stock number in the center. Box only $125.00.

White box design, large polka dots. As the company entered its most prolific period, the now highly recognizable white box with colored polka dots was introduced. Glossy white paper with large red, blue, pink, or silver dots came into use in 1941. This white box with various colored polka dots was used through 1947, the remainder of the era of the bisque jointed leg mold and the frozen leg mold dolls. Box only $25.00 to $45.00.

Colored box design, large white dots. This box seems to only be used in 1940. Doll molds found in this box are molded sock and regular jointed leg Storybook molds. Silver label. Box only $80.00.

At the end of the bisque period, most dolls with the plastic arms came in a white box with the silver label that had a smaller name and a large stock number. Box only $25.00.

White box, large dots, script in between dots. Although the plastic Storybook Doll era is not included in this book, be aware that the plastic Nancy Ann Storybook doll molds were slowly being introduced in 1947 and along with that came another box design change. The words "Nancy Ann Storybook Dolls" in cursive were added between the polka dots. This box was used for both the painted eye and sleep eye plastic dolls. The white box with polka dots and the cursive company name was also used for other dolls by the company, such as Muffie, Debbie, Miss Nancy Ann, Little Miss Nancy Ann, Sue Sue, and even the beautiful 18" Style Show Doll. Box only $20.00.

Other later boxes, also with script such as this box with a white oval label, and other designs with plastic or cellophane lids are also from the plastic Nancy Ann Storybook era. $15.00.

As early as the marble box design, a cardboard brace continued to be used to hold the doll firmly in place, heavy cardboard at first, and more flimsy cardboard as the years passed.

Pairs: When dolls were sold as pairs, such as this Hansel and Gretel, a cardboard brace was designed to hold both dolls, each with their own neck brace indentation. Box for pairs only $200.00.

Factory Pamphlets

Even though Nancy Ann Abbott launched her Nancy Ann Dressed Dolls business in 1936, we have not found any official printed inventory or catalogs of the dolls she dressed until 1940. However, starting in 1940, each Nancy Ann Storybook Doll came with a one-page factory pamphlet packed in the box along with the doll. Folded in half, each 7½ inch x 5⅞ inch black and white factory pamphlet lists the dolls available at that time. Most pamphlets have the words "wholesale only" although a few do not, but the actual information inside is identical, as by now the company only sold wholesale. The pamphlet was obviously intended to persuade wholesalers to place orders. However, the pamphlet had a two-fold use. As a marketing tool, it also helped wee collectors inventory the dolls they already owned and probably was a gentle teaser meant to persuade each child to anticipate which doll from the list she hoped to add to her doll collection on her next trip to the store.

Unfortunately, none of the pamphlets were ever dated, leaving us collectors frustrated when we attempt to date the dolls by this method. If one does not find a character listed in these 1940 – 1947 pamphlets, the doll probably was sold prior to 1940 or after 1947. The doll molds used by the Nancy Ann Dressed Doll Company prior to the initial 1940 pamphlet were five-inch bisque molded sock/molded bangs dolls, either imported from Japan or made by their own pottery plant in California. These dolls came in the marble box, the sunburst box, or colored boxes with small silver dots. More than a few characters were dropped from inventory between 1936 and 1940, never appearing on any factory pamphlet, such as #6 Little Girl, #12 All Dressed for a Party, #15 Jack Tar, #17 Snow White & #18 Rose Red, #24 Tommy Tucker, #41 Poland, #62 Clown, and #83 Nurse & Baby. Some of these pre-1940 characters are illustrated in our chapter on Early Character Numbers. When trying to date dolls from these pamphlets, please remember that with each yearly change, the factory first used up previous molds, fabrics, and characters still in stock, so there will always be overlaps.

1940 Pamphlet
Molded socks storybook mold, colored box with large polka dots

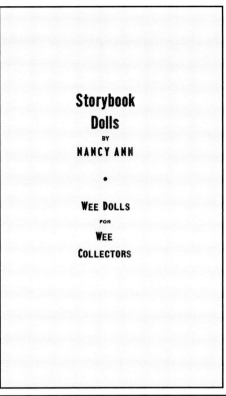

STORY BOOK SERIES	FAMILY SERIES	FLOWER GIRL SERIES	FURNITURE SERIES
STYLE NO.	STYLE No.	STYLE NO.	STYLE No.
112 A Dillar-a-Dollar, A Ten O'Clock Scholar	80 Margie Ann	1 Rose	1000 Slipper Chair
113 Roses Are Red, Violets Are Blue	81 Margie Ann in Party Dress	2 Marguerite	1001 Wing Chair
114 Over the Hills to Grandma's House	82 Margie Ann in Coat and Hat	3 Daisy	1002 Love Seat
115 Little Boy Blue	83 Mammy and Baby	4 Black-eyed Susan	1003 Day Bed
116 Little Red Riding Hood	84 Twin Sisters	5 Lily	1004 Settee
117 School Days	85 Brother & Sister	6 Violet	1005 Armchair
118 Little Miss Muffet	86 Bride		1006 Sofa
119 Mistress Mary	87 Bridesmaid	**AROUND THE WORLD**	1007 Chaise Lounge
120 To Market	87A Flower Girl	**SERIES**	1008 Bed
	88 Bridegroom	25 French	1009 Dressing Table
121 He Loves Me, He Loves Me Not	89 Mammy	26 Swiss	Mirror and Stool
122 Daffy-Down-Dilly Has Come to Town	500 Margie Ann in School Dress	27 Dutch	—Individually packed in
123 One-Two, Button My Shoe	510 Margie Ann in Play Suit	28 Italian	beautiful gift boxes.
124 Lucy Locket Lost Her Pocket	2000 Audrey Ann	29 Belgian	
125 Alice in Wonderland		30 Spanish	
126 Pussy Cat, Pussy Cat	**HUSH-A-BYE BABY SERIES**	31 Portuguese	
127 Richman Poorman	200 Short Dress	33 Chinese	
128 Goldilocks and the Baby Bear	201 Short Dress and Bonnet	34 Irish	
129 East Side, West Side	202 Short Dress and Jacket	35 Russian	
	210 Long Dress	36 Hungarian	
152 Mary Had a Little Lamb	211 Long Dress and Bonnet	37 Swedish	
153 Little Bo Peep	212 Long Dress and Jacket	38 Scotch	Your local store can
154 Curly Locks		39 Mexican	supply additional dolls
155 Cinderella	**LITTLE MISS PATTYCAKE SERIES**	40 Norwegian	for your collection.
156 Beauty (from Beauty and the Beast)	230 Organdy Dress	**AMERICAN GIRL SERIES**	
157 Queen of Hearts	231 Old Fashioned Dress and Bonnet	55 Quaker Maid	
158 Sugar and Spice and Everything Nice	232 Organdy Dress and Crochet Set	56 Colonial Dame	
159 Ring Around a Rosy, Pocket Full of Posy	233 Organdy Dress and Rosebud Robe	57 Southern Belle	
160 Pretty Maid, Where Have You Been?	234 "Dress Up" Coat and Bonnet	58 Western Miss	
	235 Dotted Swiss Coat and Bonnet		All dolls 5" high
175 Jack and Jill	277 Pillow with Extra Clothes	**MASQUERADE SERIES**	Individually packed in
176 Topsy and Eva	278 Basket with Extra Clothes	60 Gypsy	beautiful gift boxes.
177 Hansel and Grethel	279 Baby in Rosebud Bassinette	61 Pirate	
	285 Baby in Hatbox with Layette	62 Cowboy	
180 Monday's Child Is Fair of Face		63 Ballet Dancer	
181 Tuesday's Child Is Full of Grace	300 Judy Ann in Story Book with	**SPORTS SERIES**	
182 Wednesday's Child Is Full of Woe	3 sets of clothes	70 Tennis	
183 Thursday's Child Has Far to Go	400 Geraldine Ann from Movieland	71 Sailing	
184 Friday's Child Is Loving and Giving	600 Story Book Box	72 Riding	
185 Saturday's Child Must Work for a Living	700 Around the World Box	73 Skiing	NANCY ANN
186 The Child That Was Born on the	900 Boudoir Box	**SEASONS SERIES**	DRESSED DOLLS, INC.
Sabbath Day Is Bonny and Blythe		90 Spring	SAN FRANCISCO, CALIF.
and Good and Gay		91 Summer	
		92 Autumn	
		93 Winter	

Cover reads "Storybook Dolls by Nancy Ann" and below that "Wee Dolls for Wee Collectors." Unlike the subsequent pamphlets, it has no artwork on the cover and rarely shows up. Inside: This is the only pamphlet where we find the Masquerade and the Sports Series and the rare slightly larger doll, #2000 Audrey Ann from the Family Series. It also is the only pamphlet that lists #33 Chinese, #34 Italian, #35 Russian from the Around the World Series, #127 Richman, Poorman and #129 East Side, West Side from the Storybook Series. Price for pamphlet $25.00.

1941 Pamphlet (early)

Early pudgy tummy Storybook mold with short arm; socket head, jointed leg month mold; white box with colored polka dots.

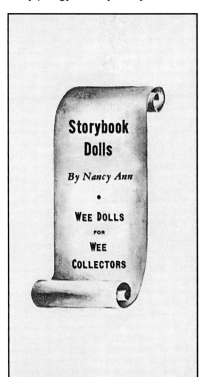

FLOWER GIRL SERIES		STORYBOOK SERIES		STORYBOOK SERIES		FURNITURE SERIES	
STYLE No.	DESCRIPTION	STYLE No.	DESCRIPTION	STYLE No.	DESCRIPTION	STYLE No.	DESCRIPTION
1	Rose	109	Little Betty Blue	180	Monday's Child Is Fair of Face	1000	Slipper Chair
2	Marguerite	110	Little Miss, Sweet Miss	181	Tuesday's Child Is Full of Grace	1001	Wing Chair
3	Daisy	111	Here Am I Little Joan	182	Wednesday's Child Is Full of Woe	1002	Love Seat
4	Black-eyed Susan	112	A Dillar-a-Dollar, a Ten O'Clock Scholar	183	Thursday's Child Has Far to Go	1003	Day Bed
5	Lily	113	Roses Are Red, Violets Are Blue	184	Friday's Child Is Loving and Giving	1004	Settee
6	Violet	114	Over the Hills to Grandma's House	185	Saturday's Child Must Work for a Living	1005	Armchair
AROUND THE WORLD SERIES		115	Little Boy Blue	186	The Child That Was Born on the Sabbath Day Is Bonny and Blythe and Good and Gay	1006	Sofa
		116	Little Red Riding Hood			1007	Chaise Lounge
25	French	117	School Days			1008	Bed
26	Swiss	118	Little Miss Muffet	187	A January Merry Maid for New Year	1009	Dressing Table, Mirror and Stool
27	Dutch	119	Mistress Mary	188	A February Fairy Girl for Ice and Snow		
29	Belgian	120	To Market	189	A Breezy Girl and Arch to Worship Me Through March		
30	Spanish						
31	Portuguese	121	He Loves Me, He Loves Me Not	190	A Shower Girl for April		
34	Irish	122	Daffy-Down-Dilly Has Come to Town	191	A Flower Girl for May		
36	Hungarian	123	One-Two, Button My Shoe	192	A Rosebud Girl to Love Me Through the June Days		
37	Swedish	124	Lucy Locket Lost Her Pocket				
38	Scotch	125	Alice in Wonderland	193	A Very Independent Lady for July		
39	Mexican	126	Pussy Cat, Pussy Cat	194	A Girl for August When It's Warm		
40	Norwegian	127	One, Two, Three, Four	195	September's Girl Is Like a Storm		
		128	Goldilocks and the Baby Bear	196	A Sweet October Maiden Rather Shy		
AMERICAN GIRL SERIES		129	Annie at the Garden Gate	197	A November Lass to Cheer		
		130	Dainty Dolly Pink and Blue	198	For December Just a Dear Oh, I Want a Girl for Each Month of the Year		
55	Quaker Maid	131	Elsie Marley Grown so Fine				
56	Colonial Dame	132	When She Was Good She Was Very, Very Good				
57	Southern Belle			**HUSH-A-BYE BABY SERIES**			
58	Western Miss			200	Short Dress and Bonnet		Your local store can supply additional dolls for your collection.
FAMILY SERIES		152	Mary Had a Little Lamb	201	Short Dress and Cape		
		153	Little Bo Peep	202	Short Dress and Jacket		
78	Margie Ann in Play Suit	154	Curly Locks	210	Long Dress and Cape		
79	Margie Ann in School Dress	155	Cinderella	211	Long Dress and Bonnet		•
80	Margie Ann	156	Beauty (from Beauty and the Beast)	212	Long Dress and Jacket		
81	Margie Ann in Party Dress	157	Queen of Hearts				All dolls 3½" to 7" high
82	Margie Ann in Coat and Hat	158	Sugar and Spice and Everything Nice	**LITTLE MISS PATTYCAKE SERIES**			Individually packed in beautiful gift boxes.
83	Mammy and Baby	159	Ring Around a Rosy, Pocket Full of Posy	230	Short Dress and Bonnet		
84	Twin Sisters	160	Pretty Maid, Where Have You Been?	231	Long Dress and Bonnet		•
85	Brother and Sister	161	Polly Put the Kettle On	232	Short Dress and Crochet Set		
86	Bride	162	Princess Rosanie	233	Long Dress and Crochet Set		NANCY ANN
87	Bridesmaid	163	Little Miss Donnet, She Wore a Big Bonnet	234	"Dress Up" Coat and Bonnet		DRESSED DOLLS, INC.
88	Bridegroom			235	Christening Coat and Bonnet		SAN FRANCISCO
89	Flower Girl	175	Jack and Jill	279	Baby in Basinette		
SEASONS SERIES		176	Topsy and Eva	285	Baby in Hatbox with Layette		
		177	Hansel and Grethel	300	Judy Ann in Story Book with 3 Sets of Clothes		
90	Spring	178	Gerda and Kay	900	Boudoir Box		
91	Summer	179	The Babes in the Wood				
92	Autumn						
93	Winter						

Additions and Deletions to the Early 1941 Pamphlet

Deleted		**Added or Changed**	
#28	Italian		
#33	Chinese		
#35	Russian		
#1 – #6	Flower Girl Series		
#60 – #63	Masquerade Series		
#70 – #73	Sports Series		
#87A	Flower Girl	#89	Flower Girl
#89	Mammy	#83	Mammy and Baby
#500	Margie Ann — School Dress	#79	Margie Ann — School Dress
#510	Margie Ann in Playsuit	#78	Margie Ann in Play Suit
#178	Gerda and Kay		
#179	Babes in the Woods		
#109	Little Betty Blue		
#110	Little Miss		
#111	Here Am I Little Joan		
#127	Richman, Poorman	#127	One, Two, Three, Four
#129	East Side, West Side	#129	Annie at the Garden Gate
#130	Dainty Dolly Pink and Blue		
#131	Elsie Marley Grown So Fine		
#132	When She Was Good		
#161	Polly Put the Kettle on		
#162	Princess Rosanie		
#163	Little Miss Donnet		
#187 – #198	Months Series		
#200	Short Dress	#200	Short Dress and Cape
#210	Long Dress	#210	Long Dress and Cape
#277	Pillow with extra clothes		
#278	Basket with extra clothes		
#400	Geraldine Ann from Movieland		
#600	Story Book Box		
#700	Around the World Box		
#2000	Audrey Ann		

Above left and right. Cover: Early 1941 pamphlet has a scroll design and was used briefly; it also is a difficult pamphlet to find. The back of the cover is blank. Inside: A most notable addition is the introduction of the twelve months of the year on the new six-inch socket-head mold with jointed legs. The Around the World #28 Italian, #33 Chinese, and #35 Russian are now discontinued along with #2000 Audrey Ann. Also dropped from the list are the endearing Masquerade and Sports Series. It is interesting that in 1940 the company sold #89 Mammy, alone. In this 1941 pamphlet, the company renumbered the doll as #83 Mammy and Baby. How poignant that some of the wonderful special sets, such as #277, #278 and #400, #600 and #700, all listed in the 1940 pamphlet were now discontinued. All boxes are now white with large polka dots and this design will remain in use until the plastic era of the company. Price $25.00.

1941 Pamphlet (late)

Pudgy tummy mold; socket head, jointed leg month mold; white box with colored polka dots.

FLOWER GIRL SERIES		STORYBOOK SERIES		STORYBOOK SERIES		FURNITURE SERIES	
STYLE No.	DESCRIPTION	STYLE No.	DESCRIPTION	STYLE No.	DESCRIPTION	STYLE No.	DESCRIPTION
1	Rose	109	Little Betty Blue	180	Monday's Child Is Fair of Face	1000	Slipper Chair
2	Marguerite	110	Little Miss, Sweet Miss	181	Tuesday's Child Is Full of Grace	1001	Wing Chair
3	Daisy	111	Here Am I Little Joan	182	Wednesday's Child Is Full of Woe	1002	Love Seat
4	Black-eyed Susan	112	A Dillar-a-Dollar, a Ten O'Clock Scholar	183	Thursday's Child Has Far to Go	1003	Day Bed
5	Lily	113	Roses Are Red, Violets Are Blue	184	Friday's Child Is Loving and Giving	1004	Settee
6	Violet	114	Over the Hills to Grandma's House	185	Saturday's Child Must Work for a Living	1005	Armchair
		115	Little Boy Blue	186	The Child That Was Born on the Sabbath Day Is Bonny and Blythe and Good and Gay	1006	Sofa
AROUND THE WORLD SERIES		116	Little Red Riding Hood			1007	Chaise Lounge
25	French	117	School Days			1008	Bed
26	Swiss	118	Little Miss Muffet	187	A January Merry Maid for New Year	1009	Dressing Table, Mirror and Stool
27	Dutch	119	Mistress Mary	188	A February Fairy Girl for Ice and Snow		
29	Belgian	120	To Market	189	A Breezy Girl and Arch to Worship Me Through March		
30	Spanish			190	A Shower Girl for April		
31	Portuguese	121	He Loves Me, He Loves Me Not	191	A Flower Girl for May		
34	Irish	122	Daffy-Down-Dilly Has Come to Town	192	A Rosebud Girl to Love Me Through the June Days		
36	Hungarian	123	One-Two, Button My Shoe	193	A Very Independent Lady for July		
37	Swedish	124	Lucy Locket Lost Her Pocket	194	A Girl for August When It's Warm		
38	Scotch	125	Alice in Wonderland	195	September's Girl Is Like a Storm		
39	Mexican	126	Pussy Cat, Pussy Cat	196	A Sweet October Maiden Rather Shy		
40	Norwegian	127	One, Two, Three, Four	197	A November Lass to Cheer		
		128	Goldilocks and the Baby Bear	198	For December Just a Dear		
AMERICAN GIRL SERIES		129	Annie at the Garden Gate		Oh, I Want a Girl for Each Month of the Year		
55	Quaker Maid	130	Dainty Dolly Pink and Blue				
56	Colonial Dame	131	Elsie Marley Grown so Fine	**HUSH-A-BYE BABY SERIES**		**WHOLESALE ONLY**	
57	Southern Belle	132	When She Was Good She Was Very, Very Good	200	Short Dress and Cape		
58	Western Miss			201	Short Dress and Bonnet	Your local store can supply additional dolls for your collection.	
		152	Mary Had a Little Lamb	202	Short Dress and Jacket		
FAMILY SERIES		153	Little Bo Peep	210	Long Dress and Cape		
78	Margie Ann in Play Suit	154	Curly Locks	211	Long Dress and Bonnet	All dolls 3½'' to 7'' high Individually packed in beautiful gift boxes.	
79	Margie Ann in School Dress	155	Cinderella	212	Long Dress and Jacket		
80	Margie Ann	156	Beauty (from Beauty and the Beast)				
81	Margie Ann in Party Dress	157	Queen of Hearts	**LITTLE MISS PATTYCAKE SERIES**			
82	Margie Ann in Coat and Hat	158	Sugar and Spice and Everything Nice	230	Short Dress and Bonnet		
83	Mammy and Baby	159	Ring Around a Rosy, Pocket Full of Posy	231	Long Dress and Bonnet	**NANCY ANN DRESSED DOLLS, INC. SAN FRANCISCO**	
84	Twin Sisters	160	Pretty Maid, Where Have You Been?	232	Short Dress and Crochet Set		
85	Brother and Sister	161	Polly Put the Kettle On	233	Long Dress and Crochet Set		
86	Bride	162	Princess Rosanie	234	"Dress Up" Coat and Bonnet		
87	Bridesmaid	163	Little Miss Donnet, She Wore a Big Bonnet	235	Christening Coat and Bonnet		
88	Bridegroom			279	Baby in Basinette		
89	Flower Girl	175	Jack and Jill	285	Baby in Hatbox with Layette		
		176	Topsy and Eva		Judy Ann in Story Book with 3 Sets of Clothes		
SEASONS SERIES		177	Hansel and Grethel		Boudoir Box		
90	Spring	178	Gerda and Kay				
91	Summer	179	The Babes in the Wood				
92	Autumn						
93	Winter						

Cover: A new front cover with a pen sketch of a picture frame and the December doll at the bottom of the frame. This same cover design was used through 1944. Inside: The inventory list is identical to the earlier 1941 pamphlet. Price $20.00.

1942 Pamphlet

Pudgy tummy mold transition to jointed leg mold; socket head, jointed leg month mold; In Powder and Crinoline mold; white box with colored polka dots

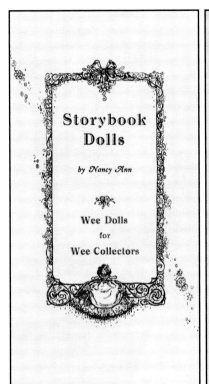

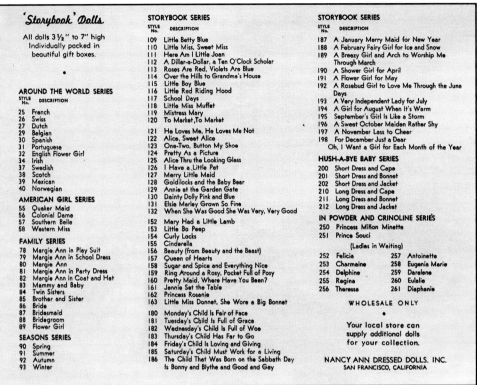

Cover: Remains the same. The back of the cover is blank. Inside: Worthy of note is the addition of #32 English Flower Girl in the Around the World Series. Another change, the beguiling character, #126 Pussy Cat, Pussy Cat, a sweet-costumed doll that came with a pipe-cleaner cat is renamed #126 I Have a Little Pet. Consequently all #126 I Have a Little Pet dolls can now have a variety of animals, instead of just a cat. An important new series, In Powder and Crinoline on a new 7" mold is introduced. Sadly, the few pairs that were in the inventory have now been dropped along with the Furniture Series and the Little Miss Patty Cake Series. $15.00.

Additions and Deletions to the 1942 Pamphlet

Deleted		Added or Changed	
#1 – 6	Flower Series		
#36	Hungarian	#32	English Flower Girl
#122	Daffy Down Dilly	#122	Alice Sweet Alice
#124	Lucy Locket	#124	Pretty as a Picture
#125	Alice in Wonderland	#125	Alice thru' the Looking Glass
#126	Pussy Cat, Pussy Cat	#126	I Have a Little Pet
#127	One, Two, Three, Four	#127	Merrie Little Maid
#161	Polly Put the Kettle on	#161	Jennie Set the Table
#175	Jack and Jill		
#176	Topsy and Eva		
#177	Hansel and Grethel		
#178	Gerda and Kay		
#179	Babes in the Wood		
#230 – #234	Little Miss Pattycake	#250-#261	In Powder and Crinoline
#1000 – #1009	Furniture		

1943 Pamphlet

Frozen leg Storybook mold; socket head, frozen leg month mold; In Powder and Crinoline mold; white box with colored polka dots.

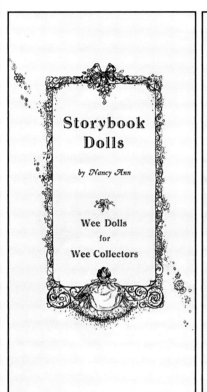

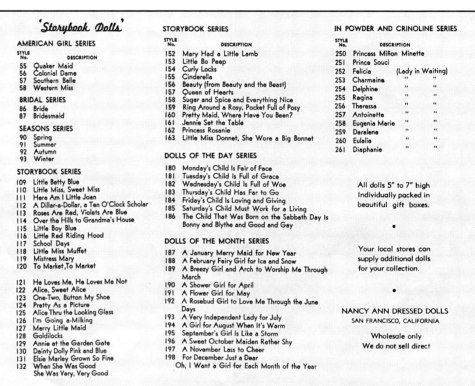

'Storybook Dolls'

AMERICAN GIRL SERIES

STYLE No.	DESCRIPTION
55	Quaker Maid
56	Colonial Dame
57	Southern Belle
58	Western Miss

BRIDAL SERIES

86	Bride
87	Bridesmaid

SEASONS SERIES

90	Spring
91	Summer
92	Autumn
93	Winter

STORYBOOK SERIES

109	Little Betty Blue
110	Little Miss, Sweet Miss
111	Here Am I Little Joan
112	A Dillar-a-Dollar, a Ten O'Clock Scholar
113	Roses Are Red, Violets Are Blue
114	Over the Hills to Grandma's House
115	Little Boy Blue
116	Little Red Riding Hood
117	School Days
118	Little Miss Muffet
119	Mistress Mary
120	To Market, To Market
121	He Loves Me, He Loves Me Not
122	Alice, Sweet Alice
123	One-Two, Button My Shoe
124	Pretty As a Picture
125	Alice Thru the Looking Glass
126	I'm Going a-Milking
127	Merry Little Maid
128	Goldilocks
129	Annie at the Garden Gate
130	Dainty Dolly Pink and Blue
131	Elsie Marley Grown So Fine
132	When She Was Good She Was Very, Very Good

STORYBOOK SERIES

STYLE No.	DESCRIPTION
152	Mary Had a Little Lamb
153	Little Bo Peep
154	Curly Locks
155	Cinderella
156	Beauty (from Beauty and the Beast)
157	Queen of Hearts
158	Sugar and Spice and Everything Nice
159	Ring Around a Rosy, Pocket Full of Posy
160	Pretty Maid, Where Have You Been?
161	Jennie Set the Table
162	Princess Rosanie
163	Little Miss Donnet, She Wore a Big Bonnet

DOLLS OF THE DAY SERIES

180	Monday's Child Is Fair of Face
181	Tuesday's Child Is Full of Grace
182	Wednesday's Child Is Full of Woe
183	Thursday's Child Has Far to Go
184	Friday's Child Is Loving and Giving
185	Saturday's Child Must Work for a Living
186	The Child That Was Born on the Sabbath Day Is Bonny and Blythe and Good and Gay

DOLLS OF THE MONTH SERIES

187	A January Merry Maid for New Year
188	A February Fairy Girl for Ice and Snow
189	A Breezy Girl and Arch to Worship Me Through March
190	A Shower Girl for April
191	A Flower Girl for May
192	A Rosebud Girl to Love Me Through the June Days
193	A Very Independent Lady for July
194	A Girl for August When It's Warm
195	September's Girl Is Like a Storm
196	A Sweet October Maiden Rather Shy
197	A November Lass to Cheer
198	For December Just a Dear
	Oh, I Want a Girl for Each Month of the Year

IN POWDER AND CRINOLINE SERIES

STYLE No.	DESCRIPTION		
250	Princess Mifion Minette		
251	Prince Souci		
252	Felicia	(Lady in Waiting)	
253	Charmaine	"	"
254	Delphine	"	"
255	Regina	"	"
256	Theressa	"	"
257	Antoinette	"	"
258	Eugenia Marie	"	"
259	Daralene	"	"
260	Eulalia	"	"
261	Diaphanie	"	"

All dolls 5" to 7" high Individually packed in beautiful gift boxes.

•

Your local stores can supply additional dolls for your collection.

•

NANCY ANN DRESSED DOLLS
SAN FRANCISCO, CALIFORNIA

Wholesale only
We do not sell direct

Storybook Dolls

by Nancy Ann

Wee Dolls
for
Wee Collectors

Additions and Deletions to the 1943 Pamphlet

Deleted		Added or Changed	
#25 – #40	Around the World Series		
#84	Twin Sisters		
#85	Brother and Sister		
#78 – #82	Margie Ann Series		
#89	Flower Girl		
#126	I Have a Little Pet	#126	I'm Going a Milking
#128	Goldilocks and Baby Bear	#128	Goldilocks
#200 – #212	Hush-A-Bye Baby		

Above left and right. Cover: Remains the same. The back of the cover is blank. Inside: With the introduction of the new frozen leg storybook mold, all the 5½ inch dolls now through 1947 will be frozen leg. Noteworthy is #128 Goldilocks, no longer with a bear. The entire Around the World Series and the Hush-a-Bye Baby Series is eliminated. The Family Series is renamed Bridal Series and only #86 Bride and #87 Groom remain. Price $10.00.

1944 Pamphlet

Frozen leg Storybook mold; socket head, frozen leg month mold; In Powder and Crinoline mold; white box with colored polka dots.

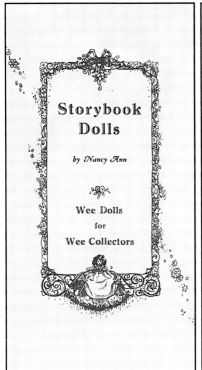

'Storybook Dolls'

AMERICAN GIRL SERIES

STYLE NO.	DESCRIPTION
55	Quaker Maid
56	Colonial Dame
57	Southern Belle
58	Western Miss

BRIDAL SERIES

86	Bride
87	Bridesmaid

SEASONS SERIES

90	Spring
91	Summer
92	Autumn
93	Winter

STORYBOOK SERIES

109	Little Betty Blue
110	Little Miss, Sweet Miss
111	Here Am I Little Joan
112	A Dillar-a-Dollar, a Ten O'Clock Scholar
113	Roses Are Red, Violets Are Blue
114	Over the Hills to Grandma's House
115	Little Boy Blue
116	Little Red Riding Hood
117	School Days
118	Little Miss Muffet
119	Mistress Mary
120	To Market, To Market
121	He Loves Me, He Loves Me Not
122	Alice, Sweet Alice
123	One-Two, Button My Shoe
124	Pretty As a Picture
125	Alice Thru the Looking Glass
126	I'm Going a-Milking
127	Merry Little Maid
128	Goldilocks
129	Annie at the Garden Gate
130	Dainty Dolly Pink and Blue
131	Elsie Marley Grown So Fine
132	When She Was Good She Was Very, Very Good

STORYBOOK SERIES

STYLE NO.	DESCRIPTION
*133	Little Polly Flinders
*134	Lucy Locket
*135	Jack
*136	Jill
*137	Topsy
*138	Eva
*139	Hansel
*140	Gretel
*141	Gerda
*142	Kay
*143	Snow Queen
*144	Polly Put the Kettle On
*145	Mother Goose
*146	Old Mother Hubbard
152	Mary Had a Little Lamb
153	Little Bo Peep
154	Curly Locks
155	Cinderella
156	Beauty (from Beauty and the Beast)
157	Queen of Hearts
158	Sugar and Spice and Everything Nice
159	Ring Around a Rosy, Pocket Full of Posy
160	Pretty Maid, Where Have You Been?
161	Jennie Set the Table
162	Princess Rosanie
163	Little Miss Donnet, She Wore a Big Bonnet

DOLLS OF THE DAY SERIES

180	Monday's Child Is Fair of Face
181	Tuesday's Child Is Full of Grace
182	Wednesday's Child Is Full of Woe
183	Thursday's Child Has Far to Go
184	Friday's Child Is Loving and Giving
185	Saturday's Child Must Work for a Living
186	The Child That Was Born on the Sabbath Day Is Bonny and Blythe and Good and Gay

Your local stores can supply additional dolls for your collection

DOLLS OF THE MONTH SERIES

STYLE NO.	DESCRIPTION
187	A January Merry Maid for New Year
188	A February Fairy Girl for Ice and Snow
189	A Breezy Girl and Arch to Worship Me Through March
190	A Shower Girl for April
191	A Flower Girl for May
192	A Rosebud Girl to Love Me Through the June Days
193	A Very Independent Lady for July
194	A Girl for August When It's Warm
195	September's Girl Is Like a Storm
196	A Sweet October Maiden Rather Shy
197	A November Lass to Cheer
198	For December Just a Dear Oh, I Want a Girl for Each Month of the Year

IN POWDER AND CRINOLINE SERIES

STYLE NO.	DESCRIPTION	
*250	Princess Miñon Minette	
*251	Prince Souci	
*252	Felicia	(Lady in Waiting)
*253	Charmaine	" " "
*254	Delphine	" " "
*255	Regina	" " "
*256	Theressa	" " "
*257	Antoinette	" " "
*258	Eugenia Marie	" " "
*259	Daralene	" " "
*260	Eulalie	" "
*261	Diaphanie	

*Temporarily out of stock

Wholesale only
We do not sell direct

NANCY ANN DRESSED DOLLS
SAN FRANCISCO, CALIFORNIA

Cover text:

Storybook
Dolls

by Nancy Ann

Wee Dolls
for
Wee Collectors

Above left and right. Cover: Remains the same. Back cover is blank. Inside: A curious addition to this pamphlet is the Storybook Series #133 through #146. Why were these characters added, yet in the same pamphlet all appear with asterisks indicating that they were immediately "temporarily out of stock"? #133 Little Polly Flinders, #145 Mother Goose, and #146 Old Mother Hubbard still remain a complete mystery. Did they ever exist? World War II was winding down and possibly the company anticipated the introduction of these new characters, but for reasons unknown, they were not marketed, as far as we know. This pamphlet also indicates that a decision was made to sell Topsy/Eva, Hansel/Gretel, and Gerda/Kay separately. The spelling of Grethel is now changed to Gretel. These characters previously had been sold as pairs and had already been dropped from the line. This may have been a financial decision, rationalizing that individual dolls would sell more easily than higher-priced pairs. However, these six dolls were listed as "temporarily out of stock" and were never produced on a frozen leg mold. This pamphlet also shows the In Powder and Crinoline Series as being "temporarily out of stock." Price $5.00.

Additions to the 1944 Pamphlet

*#133 Little Polly Flinders
*#134 Lucky Locket
*#135 Jack
*#136 Jill
*#137 Topsy
*#138 Eva
*#139 Hansel
*#140 Grethel
*#141 Gerda
*#142 Kay
*#143 Snow Queen
*#144 Polly Put the Kettle on
*#145 Mother Goose
*#146 Old Mother Hubbard

*Temporarily out of stock

1945 Pamphlet (early)

Frozen leg Storybook mold; socket head, frozen leg month mold; In Powder and Crinoline mold; white box with colored polka dots.

Storybook Doll Cabinet

Front cover: The design of the pamphlet has changed. Nancy Ann Abbott's photograph is now in the center of the picture frame, instead of the sketch of December doll. Back cover: Storybook Doll Cabinet with Little Boy Blue; One, Two Button My Shoes; and Dillar-a-Dollar boy. This pamphlet was used in 1945 and 1946. Inside: Most of the Storybook Series #131 through #146 and the In Powder and Crinoline Series are "temporarily out of stock." However, now available are the Snow Queen and Polly Put the Kettle on, each with new numbers. Price $5.00.

'Storybook Dolls'

AMERICAN GIRL SERIES

STYLE NO.	DESCRIPTION
55	Quaker Maid
56	Colonial Dame
57	Southern Belle
58	Western Miss

BRIDAL SERIES

86	Bride
87	Bridesmaid

SEASONS SERIES

90	Spring
91	Summer
92	Autumn
93	Winter

STORYBOOK SERIES

109	Little Betty Blue
110	Little Miss, Sweet Miss
111	Here Am I Little Joan
112	A Dillar-a-Dollar, a Ten o'Clock Scholar
113	Roses Are Red, Violets Are Blue
114	Over the Hills to Grandma's House
115	Lucy Locket
116	Little Red Riding Hood
117	School Days
118	Little Miss Muffet
119	Mistress Mary
120	To Market, To Market
121	He Loves Me, He Loves Me Not
122	Alice, Sweet Alice
123	One-Two, Button My Shoe
124	Pretty As a Picture
125	Alice Thru the Looking Glass
126	I'm Going a-Milking
127	Merry Little Maid
128	Goldilocks
129	Annie at the Garden Gate
130	Dainty Dolly Pink and Blue
131	Elsie Marley Grown So Fine
132	When She Was Good She Was Very, Very Good

STORYBOOK SERIES

STYLE NO.	DESCRIPTION
*133	Little Polly Flinders
*134	Old Mother Hubbard
*135	Jack
*136	Jill
*137	Topsy
*138	Eva
*139	Hansel
*140	Gretel
*141	Gerda
*142	Kay
*143	Mother Goose
152	Mary Had a Little Lamb
153	Little Bo Peep
154	Curly Locks
155	Cinderella
156	Beauty (from Beauty and the Beast)
157	Queen of Hearts
158	Sugar and Spice and Everything Nice
159	Ring Around a Rosy, Pocket Full of Posy
160	Pretty Maid, Where Have You Been?
161	Jennie Set the Table
162	Princess Rosanie
163	Little Miss Donnet, She Wore a Big Bonnet
168	Silks and Satins
169	Goose Girl
170	Rain, Rain Go Away
171	Daffy-Down-Dilly
172	The Snow Queen
173	Polly Put the Kettle On
174	Flossie Came from Dublin Town
175	There Was a Maiden Bright and Gay
176	Nellie Bird, Nellie Bird
177	See-Saw Marjorie Daw
178	Give Me a Lassie as Sweet as She's Fair
179	Daisy Belle, Daisy Belle

*

We do not sell direct

*

our local stores can supply additional dolls for your collection

DOLLS OF THE DAY SERIES

STYLE NO.	DESCRIPTION
180	Monday's Child Is Fair of Face
181	Tuesday's Child Is Full of Grace
182	Wednesday's Child Is Full of Woe
183	Thursday's Child Has Far to Go
184	Friday's Child Is Loving and Giving
185	Saturday's Child Must Work for a Living
186	The Child That Was Born on the Sabbath Day Is Bonny and Blythe and Good and Gay

DOLLS OF THE MONTH SERIES

187	A January Merry Maid for New Year
188	A February Fairy Girl for Ice and Snow
189	A Breezy Girl and Arch to Worship Me Through March
190	A Shower Girl for April
191	A Flower Girl for May
192	A Rosebud Girl to Love Me Through the June Days
193	A Very Independent Lady for July
194	A Girl for August When It's Warm
195	September's Girl Is Like a Storm
196	A Sweet October Maiden Rather Shy
197	A November Lass to Cheer
198	For December Just a Dear Oh, I Want a Girl for Each Month of the Year

IN POWDER AND CRINOLINE SERIES

STYLE NO.	DESCRIPTION	
*250	Princess Miñon Minette	
*251	Prince Souci	
*252	Felicia	(Lady in Waiting)
*253	Charmaine	" "
*254	Delphine	" "
*255	Regina	" "
*256	Theressa	" "
*257	Antoinette	" "
*258	Eugenia Marie	" "
*259	Daralene	" "
*260	Eulalie	" "
*261	Diaphanie	" "

Temporarily out of stock

NCY ANN DRESSED DOLLS
AN FRANCISCO, CALIFORNIA

Additions and Deletions to the Early 1945 Pamphlet

Deleted

#115	Little Boy Blue
#143	Snow Queen
#168	Silk and Satin
#169	Goose Girl
#170	Rain, Rain Go Away
#171	Daffy-Down Dilly
#172	Snow Queen
#173	Polly Put the Kettle on
#174	Flossie
#175	Maiden Bright and Gay
#176	Nellie Bird, Nellie Bird
#177	See-Saw Marjorie Daw
#178	Give Me a Lassie
#179	Daisy Belle

Added or Changed

#115	Lucy Locket
#143	Mother Goose

*Temporarily out of stock.

1945 Pamphlet (late)

Frozen leg Storybook mold; socket head, frozen leg month mold; In Powder and Crinoline mold; white box with colored polka dots.

Storybook Doll Cabinet

Storybook Dolls

Nancy Ann

Wee Dolls
for
Wee Collectors

'Storybook Dolls'

AMERICAN GIRL SERIES

STYLE NO.	DESCRIPTION
55	Quaker Maid
56	Colonial Dame
57	Southern Belle
58	Western Miss

BRIDAL SERIES

86	Bride
87	Bridesmaid

SEASONS SERIES

90	Spring
91	Summer
92	Autumn
93	Winter

STORYBOOK SERIES
Fairytale—Mother Goose—Fairyland Dolls and Nursery Rhyme

109	Little Betty Blue
110	Little Miss, Sweet Miss
111	Here Am I Little Joan
112	A Dillar-a-Dollar, a Ten o'Clock Scholar
113	Roses Are Red, Violets Are Blue
114	Over the Hills to Grandma's House
115	Lucy Locket
116	Little Red Riding Hood
117	School Days
118	Little Miss Muffet
119	Mistress Mary
120	To Market, To Market
121	He Loves Me, He Loves Me Not
122	Alice, Sweet Alice
123	One-Two, Button My Shoe
124	Pretty As a Picture
125	Alice Thru the Looking Glass
126	I'm Going a-Milking
127	Merry Little Maid
128	Goldilocks
129	Annie at the Garden Gate
130	Dainty Dolly Pink and Blue
131	Elsie Marley Grown So Fine
132	When She Was Good She Was Very, Very Good

STORYBOOK SERIES
Fairytale—Mother Goose—Fairyland Dolls and Nursery Rhyme

STYLE NO.	DESCRIPTION
*133	Little Polly Flinders
*134	Old Mother Hubbard
*135	Jack
*136	Jill
*137	Topsy
*138	Eva
*139	Hansel
*140	Gretel
*141	Gerda
*142	Kay
*143	Mother Goose
152	Mary Had a Little Lamb
153	Little Bo-Peep
154	Curly Locks
155	Cinderella
156	Beauty (from Beauty and the Beast)
157	Queen of Hearts
158	Sugar and Spice and Everything Nice
159	Ring Around a Rosy, Pocket Full of Posy
160	Pretty Maid, Where Have You Been?
161	Jennie Set the Table
162	Princess Rosanie
163	Little Miss Donnet, She Wore a Big Bonnet
168	Silks and Satins
169	Goose Girl
170	Rain, Rain Go Away
171	Daffy-Down-Dilly
172	The Snow Queen
173	Polly Put the Kettle On
174	Flossie Came from Dublin Town
175	There Was a Maiden Bright and Gay
176	Nellie Bird, Nellie Bird
177	See-Saw Marjorie Daw
178	Give Me a Lassie as Sweet as She's Fair
179	Daisy Belle, Daisy Belle

UNDRESSED SERIES

1	Hush-A-Bye Baby, 3½ inches
2	Rock-A-Bye Baby, 4½ inches

We do not sell direct

Your local stores can supply additional dolls for your collection

DOLLS OF THE DAY SERIES
Birthday Dolls

STYLE NO.	DESCRIPTION
180	Monday's Child Is Fair of Face
181	Tuesday's Child Is Full of Grace
182	Wednesday's Child Is Full of Woe
183	Thursday's Child Has Far to Go
184	Friday's Child Is Loving and Giving
185	Saturday's Child Must Work for a Living
186	The Child That Was Born on the Sabbath Day Is Bonny and Blythe and Good and Gay

DOLLS OF THE MONTH SERIES

187	A January Merry Maid for New Year
188	A February Fairy Girl for Ice and Snow
189	A Breezy Girl and Arch to Worship Me Through March
190	A Shower Girl for April
191	A Flower Girl for May
192	A Rosebud Girl to Love Me Through the June Days
193	A Very Independent Lady for July
194	A Girl for August When It's Warm
195	September's Girl Is Like a Storm
196	A Sweet October Maiden Rather Shy
197	A November Lass to Cheer
198	For December Just a Dear Oh, I Want a Girl for Each Month of the Year

IN POWDER AND CRINOLINE SERIES

*250	Princess Miñon Minette		
*251	Prince Souci		
*252	Felicia	(Lady in Waiting)	
*253	Charmaine	"	"
*254	Delphine	"	"
*255	Regina	"	"
*256	Theressa	"	"
*257	Antoinette	"	"
*258	Eugenia Marie	"	"
*259	Daralene	"	"
*260	Eulalie	"	"
*261	Diaphanie	"	"

*Temporarily out of stock

NANCY ANN DRESSED DOLLS
SAN FRANCISCO, CALIFORNIA

Front and back cover: Remain the same. Inside: The pamphlet is identical except that the Undressed Series of babies are back, only this time, the two size babies are sold undressed. We find that the "PAT.APP.FOR" line on the mold is begins to replace the "11" mark. Under the Dolls of the Day Series the company has added the words "Birthdays Dolls." Price $5.00.

343

1946 Pamphlet

Frozen leg Storybook mold; frozen leg Month mold; In Powder and Crinoline mold; possibly teen jointed and pinch face; white box with colored polka dots.

STORYBOOK DOLL CABINET No. 500
Fitted for Sliding Glass Fronts

NANCY ANN STORYBOOK DOLLS, INC.
SAN FRANCISCO 9, CALIFORNIA

Storybook Dolls
Reg. U.S. Pat. Off.

Wee Dolls
for
Wee Collectors

Additions and Deletions to the 1946 Pamphlet

Deleted
#55-#58 American Girl Series
#174 Flossie
*#141 Gerda
*#142 Kay
#143 Mother Goose

Added or Changed
#174 Florie
*#141 Gerda and Kay
*#142 Boy Blue

*Temporarily out of stock.

Back cover: Although the front cover remains the same, the back cover has a new cabinet design and the dolls in the cabinet have changed to the 1946 production. The "STORYBOOK DOLL CABINET NO. 500, Fitted for Sliding Glass Fronts" appears above this year's cabinet design. Inside: The company name, Nancy Ann Dressed Dolls, San Francisco, California, no longer appears in the pamphlet, as the company changed its name to Nancy Ann Storybook Dolls, Inc. on December 26, 1945. The long list of Storybook Series characters has now been divided into four groups, Fairytale Series, Mother Goose Series, Fairyland Series, and Nursery Rhyme Series. The pamphlet indicates that the company has added the "Reg. U.S. Pat. Off." under their "Storybook Dolls" heading and under the category "Mother Goose Series." The pamphlet also indicates that most of the characters have been registered at the U.S. Patent Office. Dolls can be found marked with "PAT.APP.FOR" mold. It is estimated, also, that the teen jointed leg "PAT.APP.FOR" along with the pinch face mold were introduced somewhere in 1946 – 1947. Under the Dolls of the Day Series, the company has added a trademark next to Birthdays Dolls. Obviously

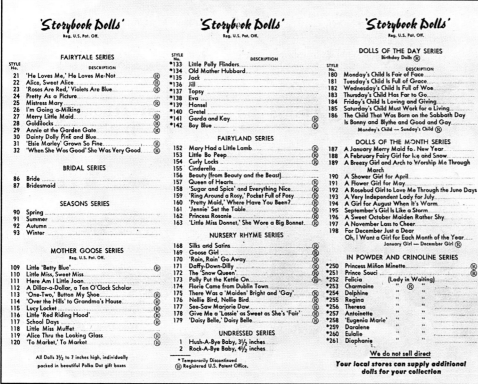

'Storybook Dolls'
Reg. U.S. Pat. Off.

FAIRYTALE SERIES

STYLE No.	DESCRIPTION	
21	'He Loves Me,' He Loves Me-Not	®
22	Alice, Sweet Alice	®
23	'Roses Are Red,' Violets Are Blue	®
24	Pretty As a Picture	
25	Mistress Mary	
26	I'm Going a-Milking	®
27	Merry Little Maid	®
28	Goldilocks	®
29	Annie at the Garden Gate	®
30	Dainty Dolly Pink and Blue	
31	'Elsie Marley' Grown So Fine	®
32	'When She Was Good' She Was Very Good	®

BRIDAL SERIES

| 86 | Bride | |
| 87 | Bridesmaid | |

SEASONS SERIES

90	Spring	
91	Summer	
92	Autumn	
93	Winter	

MOTHER GOOSE SERIES
Reg. U.S. Pat. Off.

109	Little 'Betty Blue'	
110	Little Miss, Sweet Miss	
111	Here Am I Little Joan	
112	A Dillar-a-Dollar, a Ten O'Clock Scholar	
113	'One-Two,' Button My Shoe	®
114	'Over the Hills' to Grandma's House	®
115	Lucy Locket	
116	Little 'Red Riding Hood'	®
117	School Days	®
118	Little Miss Muffet	
119	Alice Thru the Looking Glass	®
120	'To Market,' To Market	®

All Dolls 3½ to 7 inches high, individually packed in beautiful Polka Dot gift boxes

'Storybook Dolls'
Reg. U.S. Pat. Off.

STYLE No.	DESCRIPTION	
*133	Little Polly Flinders	
*134	Old Mother Hubbard	
*135	Jack	
*136	Jill	
*137	Topsy	
*138	Eva	
*139	Hansel	
*140	Gretel	
*141	Gerda and Kay	®
*142	Boy Blue	®

FAIRYLAND SERIES

152	Mary Had a Little Lamb	®
153	Little Bo Peep	®
154	Curly Locks	
155	Cinderella	®
156	Beauty (from Beauty and the Beast)	
157	Queen of Hearts	®
158	'Sugar and Spice' and Everything Nice	®
159	'Ring Around a Rosy,' Pocket Full of Posy	®
160	'Pretty Maid,' Where Have You Been?	®
161	'Jennie' Set the Table	®
162	Princess Rosanie	
163	'Little Miss Donnet,' She Wore a Big Bonnet	®

NURSERY RHYME SERIES

168	Silks and Satins	®
169	Goose Girl	®
170	'Rain, Rain' Go Away	
171	Daffy-Down-Dilly	
172	The 'Snow Queen'	
173	Polly Put the Kettle On	®
174	Florie Came from Dublin Town	
175	There Was a 'Maiden' Bright and 'Gay'	®
176	Nellie Bird, Nellie Bird	
177	See-Saw Marjorie Daw	®
178	Give Me a 'Lassie' as Sweet as She's 'Fair'	®
179	'Daisy Belle,' Daisy Belle	®

UNDRESSED SERIES

| 1 | Hush-A-Bye Baby, 3½ inches | |
| 2 | Rock-A-Bye Baby, 4½ inches | |

* Temporarily Discontinued
® Registered U.S. Patent Office.

'Storybook Dolls'
Reg. U.S. Pat. Off.

DOLLS OF THE DAY SERIES
Birthday Dolls ®

STYLE No.	DESCRIPTION	
180	Monday's Child Is Fair of Face	
181	Tuesday's Child Is Full of Grace	
182	Wednesday's Child Is Full of Woe	
183	Thursday's Child Has Far to Go	
184	Friday's Child Is Loving and Giving	
185	Saturday's Child Must Work for a Living	
186	The Child That Was Born on the Sabbath Day Is Bonny and Blythe and Good and Gay	

Monday's Child — Sunday's Child ®

DOLLS OF THE MONTH SERIES

187	A January Merry Maid fo. New Year	
188	A February Fairy Girl for Ice and Snow	
189	A Breezy Girl and Arch to Worship Me Through March	
190	A Shower Girl for April	
191	A Flower Girl for May	
192	A Rosebud Girl to Love Me Through the June Days	
193	A Very Independent Lady for July	
194	A Girl for August When It's Warm	
195	September's Girl Is Like a Storm	
196	A Sweet October Maiden Rather Shy	
197	A November Lass to Cheer	
198	For December Just a Dear Oh, I Want a Girl for Each Month of the Year	

January Girl — December Girl ®

IN POWDER AND CRINOLINE SERIES

*250	Princess Miñon Minette	®
*251	Prince Souci	®
*252	Felicia (Lady in Waiting)	"
*253	Charmaine	® "
*254	Delphine	"
*255	Regina	"
*256	Theresa	"
*257	Antoinette	"
*258	'Eugenia Marie'	"
*259	Daralene	"
*260	Eulalie	"
*261	Diaphanie	"

We do not sell direct

Your local stores can supply additional dolls for your collection

the company is now protecting themselves against lawsuits and the many copy-cat doll companies imitating Nancy Ann's creations that had entered the doll market. Interesting that the characters #141 Gerda and Kay are now listed as a pair again, yet Hansel and Gretel are still listed separately. However, both were never produced as #133 through #142 characters are "temporarily discontinued," according to the pamphlet, which is a change from the wording "temporarily out of stock." Price $5.00.

1947 Pamphlet (early)

Frozen leg Storybook mold; frozen leg month/operetta mold; teen jointed and pinch face mold; white box with colored polka dots.

Additions and Deletions to the Early 1947 Pamphlet

Deleted
*#133 through #142

Added or Changed
Babies
#210 Little Miss Pattycake
#212 Little Miss Lullabye
Operetta Series
#301 Orange Blossom
#302 Maytime
#303 Pink Lady
#304 Blossom Time
#305 Countess Maritza
#306 Irene
#307 Naughty Marietta
#308 My Maryland
#309 Red Mill
#310 Floradora
#311 Bloomer Girl
#500 Wall Cabinet
#500 Standing Cabinet
#1000 Metal Doll Stands

*Temporarily out of stock.

Cover: Nancy Ann Abbott appears in a new photograph with a more chic upswept hairstyle, but in the same picture frame. The back of the pamphlet is the same as in 1946 (early). Inside: Two dressed babies were added. Plastic arms are now being used. The company continued with its process of registering characters with the U.S. Patent Office, as not only Mother Goose Series, but also Fairyland Series and Fairytale Series are now registered. The new Nancy Ann mold change probably occurred about now. The decision was made to drop the In Powder and Crinoline Series. However, the Operetta Series took its place as a more elaborately dressed doll series. The company finally dropped that mysterious #133 through #142 group. This is the first time we see the Storybook cabinets and doll stands actually advertised. Price $5.00.

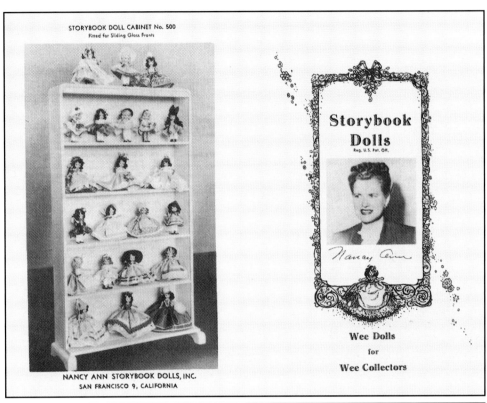

STORYBOOK DOLL CABINET No. 500
Fitted for Sliding Glass Fronts

NANCY ANN STORYBOOK DOLLS, INC.
SAN FRANCISCO 9, CALIFORNIA

Storybook Dolls
Reg. U.S. Pat. Off.

Wee Dolls
for
Wee Collectors

'Storybook Dolls'
Reg. U.S. Pat. Off.

FAIRYTALE SERIES
Reg. U.S. Pat. Off.

STYLE No.	DESCRIPTION	
21	'He Loves Me,' He Loves Me Not	®
22	Alice, Sweet Alice	®
23	'Roses Are Red,' Violets Are Blue	®
24	Pretty As a Picture	
25	Mistress Mary	
26	I'm Going a-Milking	
27	Merry Little Maid	
28	Goldilocks	®
29	Annie at the Garden Gate	®
30	Dainty Dolly Pink and Blue	
31	'Elsie Marley' Grown So Fine	®
32	'When She Was Good' She Was Very Good	

BRIDAL SERIES

86	Bride	
87	Bridesmaid	

SEASONS SERIES

90	Spring	
91	Summer	
92	Autumn	
93	Winter	

MOTHER GOOSE SERIES
Reg. U.S. Pat. Off.

109	Little 'Betty Blue'	®
110	Little Miss, Sweet Miss	
111	Here Am I Little Joan	
112	A Dillar-a-Dollar, a Ten O'Clock Scholar	
113	'One-Two,' Button My Shoe	
114	'Over the Hills' to Grandma's House	®
115	Lucy Locket	®
116	Little 'Red Riding Hood'	®
117	School Days	
118	Little Miss Muffet	
119	Alice Thru the Looking Glass	®
120	'To Market,' To Market	

All Dolls 3½ to 7 inches high, individually packed in beautiful Polka Dot gift boxes

'Storybook Dolls'
Reg. U.S. Pat. Off.

FAIRYLAND SERIES
Reg. U.S. Pat. Off.

152	Mary Had a Little Lamb	
153	Little Bo Peep	®
154	Curly Locks	
155	Cinderella	
156	Beauty (from Beauty and the Beast)	
157	Queen of Hearts	
158	'Sugar and Spice' and Everything Nice	®
159	'Ring Around a Rosy,' Pocket Full of Posy	
160	'Pretty Maid,' Where Have You Been?	
161	'Jennie' Set the Table	
162	Princess Rosanie	
163	'Little Miss Donnet,' She Wore a Big Bonnet	®

NURSERY RHYME SERIES

168	Silks and Satins	
169	Goose Girl	®
170	'Rain, Rain' Go Away	®
171	Daffy-Down-Dilly	®
172	The 'Snow Queen'	®
173	Polly Put the Kettle On	®
174	Florie Came from Dublin Town	
175	There Was a 'Maiden' Bright and 'Gay'	®
176	Nellie Bird, Nellie Bird	
177	See-Saw Marjorie Daw	®
178	Give Me a 'Lassie' as Sweet as She's 'Fair'	®
179	'Daisy Belle,' Daisy Belle	®

DOLLS OF THE DAY SERIES
Birthday Dolls

180	Monday's Child Is Fair of Face	
181	Tuesday's Child Is Full of Grace	
182	Wednesday's Child Is Full of Woe	
183	Thursday's Child Has Far to Go	
184	Friday's Child Is Loving and Giving	
185	Saturday's Child Must Work for a Living	
186	The Child That Was Born on the Sabbath Day Is Bonny and Blythe and Good and Gay	
	Monday's Child — Sunday's Child	®
210	Little Miss Pattycake	
212	Little Miss Lullabye	

Registered U.S. Patent Office.

'Storybook Dolls'
Reg. U.S. Pat. Off.

DOLLS OF THE MONTH SERIES

STYLE No.	DESCRIPTION
187	A January Merry Maid for New Year
188	A February Fairy Girl for Ice and Snow
189	A Breezy Girl and Arch to Worship Me Through March
190	A Shower Girl for April
191	A Flower Girl for May
192	A Rosebud Girl to Love Me Through the June Days
193	A Very Independent Lady for July
194	A Girl for August When It's Warm
195	September's Girl Is Like a Storm
196	A Sweet October Maiden Rather Shy.
197	A November Lass to Cheer
198	For December Just a Dear
	Oh, I Want a Girl for Each Month of the Year
	January Girl — December Girl ®

OPERETTA SERIES

301	Orange Blossom
302	Maytime
303	Pink Lady
304	Blossom Time
305	Countess Maritza
306	Irene
307	Naughty Marietta
308	My Maryland
309	Red Mill
310	Rio Rita
311	Floradora
312	Bloomer Girl

UNDRESSED SERIES

1	Hush-A-Bye Baby, 3½ inches
2	Rock-A-Bye Baby, 4½ inches
500	Wall Cabinet
500	Standing Cabinet
1000	Metal Doll Stands

We do not sell direct
Your local stores can supply additional dolls for your collection

1947 – 1948 Pamphlet

Frozen leg Storybook mold; frozen leg month/Operetta/All-time Hit Parade mold; introduction to painted eye plastic mold, white box with colored polka dots.

Cover: Remains the same, but the doll cabinet on the back has been omitted. Inside: This pamphlet probably was used at the end of 1947, or even in early 1948, as some of the new dolls added have only been found in plastic, yet others added are still frozen leg bisque molds or teen molds. It is a transition time for the company as they switched from bisque to painted eye hard plastic molds. The Bridal Series has expanded to add a full wedding party. The All-time Hit Parade Series was introduced. #174 seems to have changed back from Florie to Flossie again. Only #210 remains under the newly named Dressed Baby Series and the undressed babies have been discontinued. Price $5.00.

Additions and Deletions to the 1947 – 1948 Pamphlet

Deleted	Added or Changed
#84 Ring Bearer	
#85 Flower Girl	
#87 Bridesmaid	
#26 I'm Going a-Milking	#26 Topsy
#27 Merry Little Maid	#27 Eva
#29 Annie at the Garden Gate	#29 Merry Little Maid
#173 Polly Put the Kettle on	#173 Star Light, Star Bright
#174 Florie	#174 Flossie
#212 Little Miss Pattycake	
#305 Countess Maritza	#305 New Moon
#306 Irene	#306 Fortune Teller
	#401 – #412 All-time Hit Parade Series
Undressed Series	
Storybook Cabinets	

Post 1947 – 1948 black and white factory pamphlets were changed to color and contained all-plastic dolls, not covered in this book. Some of these all-plastic dolls include the Operetta Series, the Hit Parade Series, the Garden Series, Commencement Series, Religious Series, and the Big and the Little Sister Series. These dolls came in the white box with large polka dots and the script "Nancy Ann Storybook Dolls" between the dots.

Please note that although Nancy Ann Storybook baby dolls are also listed in these pamphlets, the babies are not illustrated in this book, but will be in our next book, now in progress.

Inserts

Periodically, the company would insert colorful cardboard designs clearly to promote sales. These inserts fit over the doll inside the various-sized boxes, so when one lifts the box lid, the doll is seen through the cutout shape of the insert. Most of these inserts are from the bisque era. A few were found out of their box, so we are not sure of their date, and a few are definitely from the plastic era of the company.

Mosaic design. $25.00.

Easter. $20.00.

Easter. $20.00.

Easter. $10.00.

Easter. $25.00.

347

Easter. $10.00.

Easter. $15.00.

Easter. $10.00.

Easter. $15.00.

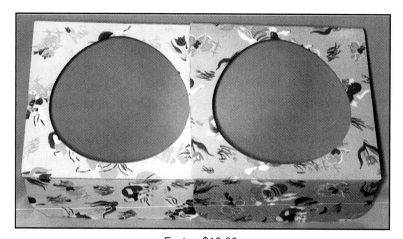

Easter. $10.00.

Easter. $10.00.

Easter. $10.00.

Easter. Plastic era. $10.00.

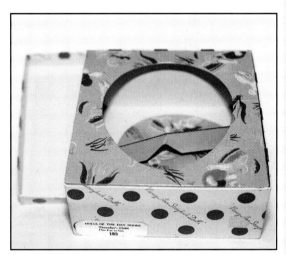

Easter. Plastic era. $10.00.

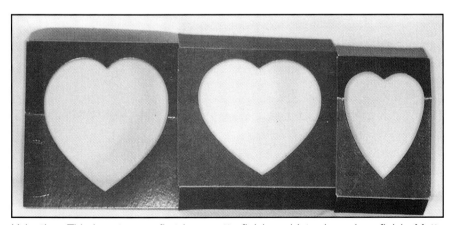

Valentine. This insert came first in a matte finish and later in a gloss finish. Matte $10.00. Glossy $5.00.

Christmas. $10.00.

Birthday. Plastic era. $10.00.

Birthday. Plastic era. $10.00.

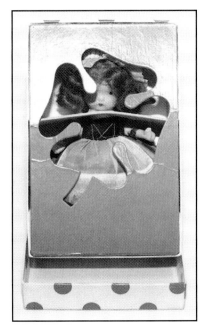

Irish Shamrock. Used in Around the World #34 Irish box. $25.00.

Special Factory Requests

Special requests often would come from department stores for unique packaging or dolls dressed in certain costumes that, reportedly, the Nancy Ann Storybook Company accommodated. No record of these was kept.

Two examples of this frozen leg doll dressed in a nurse costume have been found. One was found with a Sears Department Store sales sticker still on the dress. This frozen leg Nurse was never listed in factory pamphlets, so it must have been a special request from Sears Department Store. $75.00.

Easter Egg containing a bisque jointed leg #126.

I Have a Little Pet doll is believed to be original special packaging. This example was purchased from the original owner. Although never listed in a factory pamphlet, or found in a Nancy Ann Storybook factory box, several other Nancy Ann Storybook bisque and plastic Nancy Ann Storybook Dolls have been found in Easter eggs over the years. So whether the dolls were placed in the eggs by the factory, stores, or individuals remains uncertain, but they appear authentic.

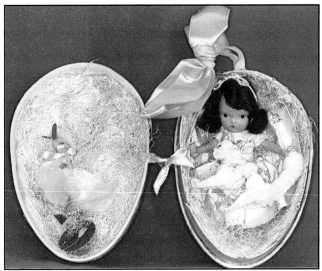

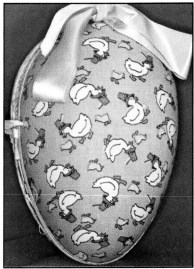

Advertisements

A major part of the success of the company was due to marketing. Examples of marketing photographs direct from the company and other advertisements are always a helpful source for identifying and dating dolls.

The following are the 1936 – 1947 addresses for the Nancy Ann Storybook Company in San Francisco, California.

- Sutter Street Book Shop
- Nancy Ann Abbott's Apartment
- Small Shop on Howard Street
- 275 Ninth Street
- Post and Franklin
- 1262 Post Street
- 1298 Post Street

F.A.O. Schwarz advertisement illustrating the Nancy Ann Storybook Doll Company's large Storybook Doll Set for $7.50. 1939.

Dennison Department Store Ad New York illustrating Around the World Box and Judy Ann in Fairyland Box, Pussy Cat, Pussy Cat, Little Bo Peep, Alice in Wonderland, and Cinderella, and two of the babies from the Hush-a-Bye Baby series. Circa 1940.

Titche-Goettinger Company ad, Dallas, Texas. Circa 1942.

Location unknown, but probably at company factory. Circa 1945 – 1946.

85¢
Mistress Mary, Quite Contrary, flowery print and poke bonnet.

$1.00
One-Two-Button-My-Shoe in red and black, specks of buttons.

$1.50
The Child That Was Born on the Sabbath Day wears white.

$1.25
Cinderella looks like any princess in sparkly peach rayon taffeta.

$1.25
Little Bo-Peep in fluffy pink, a shepherdess' hat and a crook.

2 for $1.50
Margie Ann and Millie Jane are honest-to-goodness twins dressed in little pastel dresses with hair ribbons to match. They're very blonde.

85¢
Little Red Riding Hood in a white dress, red cape and hood.

$1.50
The Bride in bouffant white with a trailing, fluffy veil.

$1.25
Winter Girl is all bundled up in a red jacket, and red panties!

Wichita, Kansas, Beacon newspaper ad 1942. Interesting ad illustrating Margie Ann and Millie Jane, two Margie Ann dolls priced at two for $1.50.

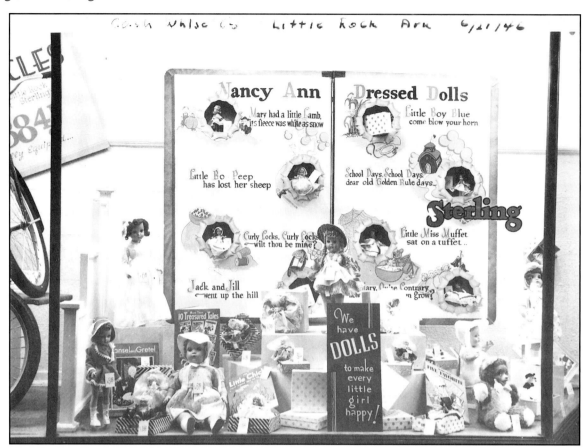

Little Rock, Arkansas, store window display from 1946. Charming display of large storybook with Nancy Ann Dressed Dolls in cutout windows.

A young Elizabeth Taylor with her doll collection, showing Nancy Ann Storybook Dolls on the shelves on the left side of photograph.

The Camera Eye *dated January 16, 1946. Nancy Ann Storybook bride and groom on wedding cake for Esther Williams's and Ben Gage's wedding.*

AMERICAN GIRL SERIES... $1.35 each

Order No. D-55—Quaker Maid ★ D-56—Colonial Dame ★ D-57—Southern Belle D-58—Western Miss

SEASONS SERIES ... $1.35 each

Order No. D-90—Spring ★ D-91—Summer ★ D-92—Autumn D-93—Winter

DOLLS OF THE DAY SERIES... $1.50 each

Order No. D-180—Monday's Child is Fair of Face
" " D-181—Tuesday's Child is Full of Grace
" " D-182—Wednesday's Child is Full of Woe

D-183—Thursday's Child Has Far to Go
D-184—Friday's Child is Loving and Giving
D-185—Saturday's Child Must Work for a Living
D-186—The Child That Was Born on the Sabbath
Day is Bonny and Blythe and Good and Gay

A good resource for identifying the company's line of frozen leg dolls. Unfortunately these Christmas motif photographs are not dated, but all appear to be from the era before the use of florist ribbon.

DOLLS OF THE MONTH SERIES ... $2.00 each

Top row left to right

Order No. D-187—A January Merry Maid for New Year
" " D-188—A February Fairy Girl for Ice and Snow
" " D-189—A Breezy Girl and Arch to Worship Me Through March

D-190—A Shower Girl for April
D-191—A Flower Girl for May
D-192—A Rosebud Girl to Love Me Through the June D[...]

Bottom row left to right

Order No. D-193—A Very Independent Lady for July
" " D-194—A Girl for August When It's Warm
" " D-195—September's Girl Is Like a Storm

D-196—A Sweet October Maiden Rather Shy
D-197—A November Lass to Cheer
D-198—For December Just a Dear

Undressed Babies

Order No. D-1—Hush-A-Bye
Baby, 3½"..50c
" " D-2—Rock-A-Bye
Baby, 4½"..75c

Bride and Bridesmaid

Order No. D-86—Bride $1.50
" " D-87—Bridesmaid ... 1.35

A good resource for identifying the company's line of frozen leg dolls. Unfortunately these Christmas motif photographs are not dated, but all appear to be from the era before the use of florist ribbon.

STORYBOOK SERIES . . . $1.35 each

Top row left to right

Order No. D-152—Mary Had a Little Lamb   D-155—Cinderella
"   "   D-153—Little Bo Peep   D-156—Beauty (from Beauty and the Beast)
"   "   D-154—Curly Locks   D-157—Queen of Hearts

Bottom row left to right   Order No. D-158—Sugar and Spice and Everything Nice   D-161—Jennie Set the Table
"   "   D-159—Ring Around a Rosy, Pocket Full of Posy   D-162—Princess Rosanie
"   "   D-160—Pretty Maid, Where Have You Been?   D-163—Little Miss Donnet, She Wore a Big Bonnet

STORYBOOK SERIES . . . $1.50 each

Top row left to right

Order No. D-168—Silks and Satins   D-171—Daffy-Down-Dilly
"   "   D-169—Goose Girl   D-172—The Snow Queen
"   "   D-170—Rain, Rain Go Away   D-173—Polly Put the Kettle On

Bottom row left to right
Order No. D-174—Flossie Came from Dublin Town   D-177—See-Saw Marjorie Daw
"   "   D-175—There Was a Maiden Bright and Gay   D-178—Give Me a Lassie as Sweet as She's Fair
"   "   D-176—Nellie Bird, Nellie Bird   D-179—Daisy Belle, Daisy Belle

This is a good resource for identifying the company's line of frozen leg dolls. Unfortunately these Christmas motif photographs are not dated, but all appear to be from the era before the use of florist ribbon. Please note, there are errors in the identification of the two rows of dolls at the bottom of this photograph. The descriptions for the bottom two rows need to be reversed.

360

Photograph from a Kodak Camera instruction book titled "How to Make a Good Movie." The date of the book is unknown. However, the child in photograph is holding a Nancy Ann Storybook Doll.

The White House Department Store, San Francisco, California. Notice the Nancy Ann Storybook cabinet is advertised for $17.50.

Photograph is reversed and later used in magazine for Kodak.

•••Doll Cabinets and Doll Stands•••

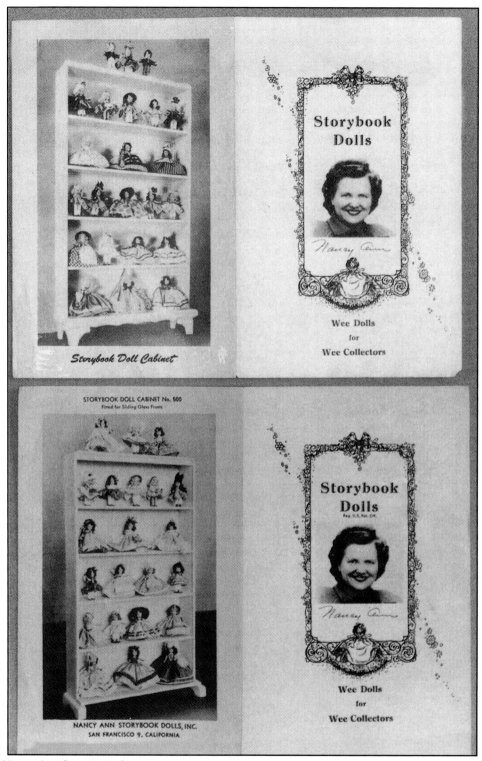

Nancy Ann Storybook Company authorized vendors to make wooden display cabinets, which were designed, especially for wee collectors to display their dolls. Illustrations of two different five-tier standing cabinets are on the back of the 1945 through 1946 factory pamphlets. However, only the 1947 pamphlet inside actually lists the #500 wall cabinet and #500 standing cabinet for sale. Several manufacturers were used over the years so measurements, construction, stenciling designs, and trim vary and only a sampling of the various styles is illustrated here. The cabinets were of simple construction and painted white on the outside and most were blue inside. Front glass shelves slide in tracks to open, some in both directions, some from alternate sides; one style has glass cut in two doll opens in the center.

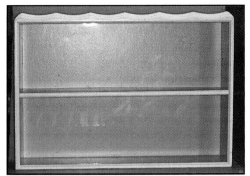

Two-shelf wall cabinet. Circa 1944. 24" wide x 17¼" high x 5" deep. $300.00. Also came in a three-shelf wall cabinet and a five-shelf standing cabinet. $200.00.

Three-shelf wall cabinet. Circa 1945 – 1947. Also came in a five-shelf standing cabinet. Approximate measurements 25" high x 24½" wide and 5½" deep. The five-shelf cabinet sold for $17.50 and three-shelf cabinet for $9.95. $200.00.

Five-shelf standing cabinet. Circa 1948 – 1952 the plastic era. Approximate measurements are 41 to 43" high x 24½" wide x 5½" deep. $200.00. There is also a four-shelf cabinet with a scallop molding on top that was made in later plastic era. The shelves in the four-shelf cabinet were made to accommodate both the Story-book dolls and the 8" Muffie doll.

Example of a label glued to back of cabinet. Early cabinets will have the Nancy Ann Dressed Dolls name on the label. Later cabinets will have the Nancy Ann Story Book Dolls, Inc. name on the label. The labels vary as different manufacturers added their own name and address.

DESIGNED & MANUFACTURED
EXCLUSIVELY FOR
NANCY ANN STORY BOOK DOLLS, INC.
by PRECISION PRODUCTS CO., INC.
COLMA, CALIFORNIA
Glass Size 7-13/16" x 24-▪▪▪"

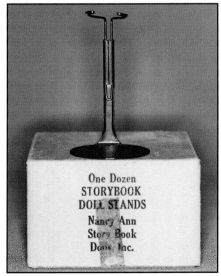

#1000 Adjustable metal doll stands. Some metal stands are marked on bottom "Nancy Ann Dressed Dolls, Inc. San Francisco, Cal." $15.00. Later metal stands are marked on the top. $10.00.

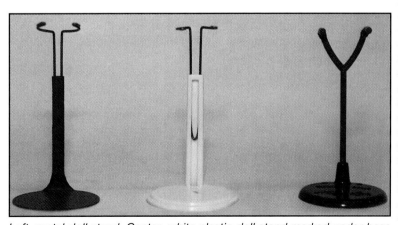

Left, metal doll stand. Center, white plastic doll stand marked under base "Nancy Ann Storybook Dolls, Inc. San Francisco, Cal." Right, brown plastic doll stand has "Storybook Dolls by Nancy Ann" on top of base. Plastic doll stands $5.00.

• • • Bibliography • • •

California Manufacturers Directory
Library of Congress
San Francisco News, 1940
San Francisco Call Bulletin, 1942
San Francisco Examiner, 1946 and 1969
San Francisco Chronicle, 1948, 1950, 1964, 1965
Marjorie A. Miller, *Nancy Ann Storybook Dolls,* 1980, Hobby House Press
Clearinghouse Newsletter
United States Patent Office Records, 1940 – 1958
The American Girl, June 1946
Glamour Magazine, December 1943
Celebrity Doll Journal, May 1979

• • • Index • • •

Numerical Listing of Items

The factory number appears first, followed by the character/item name and the page number.

For additional information on all the bisque dolls made by Nancy Ann Storybook Company, please refer to the Pamphlet Section of this book.

Alphabetical Listing of Items

The character/item name appears first, followed by the factory number and the page number.

*For complete list of all the bisque dolls by the Nancy Ann Storybook Company, please refer to the Pamphlet Section in this book.